Arra...
A History

Arran
A History

Thorbjørn Campbell

ORIGIN

This edition published in 2023 by
Origin, an imprint of Birlinn Limited
West Newington House
10 Newington Road
Edinburgh
EH9 1QS

www.birlinn.co.uk

First published in 2013 by Birlinn Limited

ISBN 978 1 83983 013 6

British Library Cataloguing-in-Publication Data
A catalogue record for this book is available from the British Library

Typeset by Hewer Text UK Ltd, Edinburgh
Printed and bound by Clays Ltd, Elcograf, S.p.A.

I.M.
Gladys Srivastava

Contents

List of Illustrations

Introduction

I first became conscious of Arran as a wee boy, paddling on the Ayr foreshore with the then (late 30s) obligatory bucket and spade. The island's sharp profile remained in my mind, but my impressions were easily confused at that stage and I mixed Arran up with Ireland, and later, during the war, with 'Canadia' – where the Canadians came from. (I was staggered, quite recently, to discover the same confusion in the mind of a grown woman, also a long-term resident of Ayr; this, in the age of mass popular tourism in Scotland, is one of the reasons why I thought I'd better write this book – for the better information of my fellow citizens.)

There is a long-standing Ayr joke to the effect that if you can see Arran it has either just been raining or is about to rain, and if you can't see Arran, it *is* raining. Certainly both Arran and its satellite Holy Island often disappear entirely under heavy cloud – which made me think of the legends of vanishing or floating islands, like the sacred island of Delos, alleged to be secured to the floor of the Aegean sea only by a golden chain. At night, too, when I took a lonely stroll along the Promenade, a light would glow out from Pladda or Holy Island, or there was a strip of red sunset under the western clouds, almost like a grin from south to north, belonging to some colossal devil which had Goatfell as a fang, the rest of the countenance masked. I would shiver and hurry home.

So much for childish imagination. Yet, a supernatural aura certainly seems to linger on Arran: I fancy you can feel it when you stand alone on the bleak plain of Machrie in the frowning presence of the giant megalithic ruins. They are uncanny in their silence, but you seem to hear faint voices and outcries in the chill wind. Machrie is a rather a terrible place, and I believe that its name, *Sliabh nan Carraigean*, can bear a 'spookier' interpretation than its normal English version, 'Moor of the Stones'. See p. 30.

To go by the great numbers of standing stones, stone circles, rock carvings ('cup-and-ring') and chambered tombs on Arran, it has almost certainly been a sacred island, a place of concentrated holiness in which the presence of the gods is almost palpable. People would fall to their knees and worship in adoration and fear.

The same people that erected the stone temples of Machrie 4,000 years ago also grew corn and herded cattle, lit fires, built houses, lived, gave birth and died – and ignorantly farmed the soil to exhaustion, destroyed the once-luxuriant forests, and covered Arran in sterilizing peat in which nothing would grow. It was probably the bloodthirsty Vikings, three to four thousand years after the Megalithic times, who revived Arran as an agricultural entity, with improved methods of soil management and cultivation. Another eight hundred years elapsed before the Agricultural Revolution arrived, heralded by the indefatigable reformer John Burrel, whose preoccupation with efficiency and productivity blinded him to the human costs of reorganizing the traditional systems of landholding. The new broom led to the traumas of Clearances, emigration and pauperization of great numbers of the countryfolk of Arran. Yet, although the efforts of Burrel and his followers succeeded in raising agriculture from the condition of mere subsistence-farming to that of relatively profitable industry, the importance of agriculture itself began to dwindle, and Arran today earns more from tourism than it does from farming.

Besides the tortured historical course of the island's agriculture, Arran politics has always followed a painful path of repeated transformations, with linguistic and cultural shifts, quarrels of ownership and nationality, and devastation after devastation by the armed men of different factions.

I do not claim that this book is a work of profound scholarship or original research (despite the number of references listed in its pages). For instance, I have not plumbed the depths of the Hamilton family archives, and many secrets therein await unlocking. I have, however, trawled many existing authorities and learned journals, and have kept in mind a primary objective, to facilitate public access to sources no longer in print or contained in journals with a circulation confined to scholars. In particular I have depended heavily upon the works of two past 'biographers' of Arran, William Mackenzie and Robert McLellan, neither now in print. The fruits of their work, together with that of others, should be preserved and renewed for the twenty first century.

I owe much to my great predecessor, William Mackenzie, author of the second volume of *The Book of Arran* (1914). Since his time conditions in Arran have changed radically, probably beyond his wildest imagination. The two major wars of the twentieth century have fatally undermined the basis of civilization in Arran as everywhere else. Apparently solid foundations have been knocked away and the whole cultural structure is in imminent danger of collapse. Language, folk-songs and folk-stories have vanished 'like snow off a dyke'. The ancient Arran dialect of Gaelic was last heard about 1950, and the custom of story-telling – bed-time stories and old wives' tales – has withered irretrievably. Belief in the supernatural has simply disappeared. Folk-song has given way to the barbaric yawp of the pop-song.

The more precious, then, are the survivals, or the recorded echoes, of genuine folk culture. It was perhaps pure chance, a stroke of great good fortune, that led Mackenzie to make a collection of the folk-songs and folk-stories that he still found current in the original Gaelic dialect, spoken by old people, in the Edwardian twilight before the Great War. He published them as the two final chapters of his *Book of Arran* together with translations, having had them checked over for dialect-linguistic authenticity by competent scholars. These pieces are of inestimable value to both philology and history. However, the two volumes of *The Book of Arran* themselves are rare and expensive finds, long out of print – even the 1982 reprint. The best tribute that I could make to Mackenzie is to make these folkloric survivals available once again to a wider public. A fair number of them now appear in two appendices at the end of this volume. For permission to reproduce I must thank the Arran Society of Glasgow and their Honorary Secretary, Miss Nan Murchie*,

---

*The permission of the Arran Society of Glasgow is granted 'in so far as they have the right to grant same'; although certain papers have been found, neither I nor the Society have any really clear idea as to the owner, if any, of the copyright of the second volume of *The Book of Arran*.

and, for reviewing Mackenzie's Gaelic (I have none), Dr R.D. Whitla of Lamlash.

I must also thank Edinburgh University Press and Messrs Edwards and Ralston for permission to reproduce in this work the clear and succinct tabular guide to the current systems of carbon-fourteen dating and notation appearing on p. 7 of their invaluable *Scotland After the Ice Age*. Similarly my gratitude must be expressed to the Society of Antiquaries of Scotland for permission to reproduce one of Dr Alison Haggerty's diagrams of the timber monument in her article 'Machrie Moor, Arran: recent excavations at two stone circles' (*PSAS* vol. 121 51–94).

In addition, with especial warmth, I must thank the Isle of Arran Heritage Museum in Rosaburn near Brodick Castle, and its devoted staff of volunteers – in particular Mr Stuart Gough, the Archivist, Mrs Grace Small, the President, Mr Tom McLeod, the Secretary, and Mrs Jean Glen, the author of *Brodick 1897–1997: a Century of Golf*, a book which gives an accurate picture not only of golfing during that century but of its social and historical context. To these four people I have had constant recourse for advice and assistance over a two-year period – as well as for physical research facilities within the Museum itself. Mr and Mrs Peter Bowers of the Lagg Hotel, Kilmory, deserve special mention for invaluable background information and in particular for drawing my attention to the affecting nineteenth-century poem 'The Cairgen Weans', originally inscribed in an early Visitors' Book belonging to the hotel (see pp. 184–5 of the present book); Mrs Bowers's mother, Mrs Margaret Maciver, formerly of the Torrylinn Creamery, helped very much with information on the milk industry and its present state on Arran.

Thanks also to Mr Kenneth Thorburn, Property Manager, NTS Brodick Castle; Miss Isla Robertson, NTS Edinburgh; Mr Andy Walker, Scottish Forestry Commission, Arran; Mr Paul Gavin, Analytical Services Division (Science and Analysis Group) of the Scottish Executive Environment and Rural Affairs Department (SEERAD); Mr Tommy Loudon and Ms Liz McKinnel, Ayrshire and Arran Farming and Wildlife Advisory Group; Mr Ian Fraser; the West Highland Free Press; the staffs of Ayr Carnegie Library, of the Ayrshire Archives Centre, of North Ayrshire Library Headquarters, Ardrossan, of Glasgow University Library, and of the Ayrshire and Arran Tourist Board (Brodick Pier Office). I should acknowledge my use of the free 'Canmore' database of Historic Scotland. Finally, I should record my profound gratitude to Mr Hugh Andrew and Mr Andrew Simmons of Birlinn for advice, patience and understanding; to Mrs Kate Blackadder, copy-editor and to my sister, Mrs Aase Irvine, for her usual unstinted support and help.

Chronology and Currency

Chronology

A word about the dating system or systems employed in the first part of this book, in the sections devoted to prehistoric times. The familiar way of dating the 'prehistoric' was to use the birth of Christ as a marker: events and eras which occupied time before then were labelled before Christ, BC, and those which came after that occurrence were Anno Domini, AD, 'In the year of our Lord'. Rome was founded in 753 BC, and the Norman Conquest of England took place in AD 1066. However, since the discovery of radioactivity and its long-term decay over a fixed period sometimes covering hundreds of thousands of years, scientific archaeologists and others have sought to make use of it in dating, and have been successful in creating a 'carbon-fourteen' system, which seems to push historical phenomena further back in time than formerly accepted. A difficulty arises when attempting to correlate this scientific system with the historian's conventional BC/AD chronology: ^{14}C years are bewilderingly 'out of sync' with BC/AD years. A third, independent method, dendrochronology ('tree-ring dating'), had to be introduced to provide a secure basis for comparison, allowing statisticians to work out a system of calibration between ^{14}C and conventional BC/AD as a reliable guide to past chronology. This system's notation, however, can be very cumbrous; when it is necessary to date an event, many workers choose to give both methods side by side, and this can be bewildering, especially when the ^{14}C date is quoted as 'BP' ('Before the Present' – the Present being taken as AD 1950). For example: Edwards and Whittington give dates for 'the inception and extension of blanket peat' at two different locations in Scotland, widely separated in time: (1) Carn Dubh (Perthshire): '9,800–9,200 BP [9040–8320 cal BC]'; (2) Starr (Ayrshire): '2,415±25 BP [520–400 cal BC]'. However, since I have drawn my prehistoric examples from a variety of sources, and it would be impractical to reduce them to a common format, the most expedient course will, I think, be to quote directly from Edwards and Ralston's guide to the standard notation of dates and in this book to adhere as closely as possible to their system as set out in their recent publication *Scotland after the Ice Age*:*

(i) Uncalibrated radiocarbon dates will be cited in years BP.

(ii) Calibrated radiocarbon dates will be cited as years cal BC or cal AD . . . but only for dates more recent than 10,000 BP. Figures following BP dates, and labelled cal BC or cal AD as appropriate, identify the corresponding calibrated chronological ranges at one standard deviation. The term 'cal BC' will be applied to longer time-spans (e.g. millennia) where the period concerned has been primarily defined by use of calibrated radiocarbon dates.

(iii) The use of BC or AD [by themselves] in relation to a specific date will mean that this has not been derived from radiocarbon, but normally from historical sources.

(iv) The calibrated radiocarbon date derived from a raw radiocarbon determination (i.e. including the ± standard deviation associated with it) will be expressed, rounded to the nearest decade, as a one standard deviation corrected range or the extremes of corrected ranges where these are produced (e.g. 3,880±60 BP becomes, upon conversion and rounding, 2460–2200 cal BC.'

NB It should be noted that in the above instructions there is a difference in meaning between large CAPITALS and small CAPITALS.

Currency

Here and there throughout the book, monetary values have had to be mentioned, especially in connection with the major economic difficulties experienced in Arran during the fifteenth century. Sources indicate a 'pounds, shillings and pence' basis for calculating rent, along with the system of

---

*Edwards K.J. and Ralston I.B.M. eds, *Scotland after the Ice Age: Environment, Archaeology and History 8000 BC–AD 1000* (Edinburgh [2nd ed.] 2003). Cited with the permission of Edinburgh University Press.

'grassums' – contributions to rental in kind with monetary equivalents. In the twelfth century David I established a silver standard in which a pound of silver was divided into 240 pennies (12 pence to a shilling, 20 shillings to a pound). This system, originally English (Norman), suffered devaluations and massive fluctuations throughout the centuries, and in the end the most comprehensible estimates are of the number of pennies minted from an ounce of silver. In late Viking times eighteen or twenty pennies had made up an ounce of silver. In Scotland in 1440 the number of pennies to the ounce is recorded as 64, but in 1453, at the height of the Arran devastations, the number was 96 pennies to the ounce and in 1458 it had soared to 140. During this period and later, the unit of preference was the mark (or merk) Scottish, and this stood at 13 shillings and 4 pence, i.e. two-thirds of a pound or 160 pence. I have chosen to use the merk to express monetary values at this time.

It is relatively simple to express fifteenth-century merks in terms of modern values, using the price of silver on today's markets, but to deduce from this a purchasing power is a more formidable problem, and I do not pretend to have solved it. In mid-fifteenth century an Arran 'mart' – a cow or an ox – was valued at five merks, £3 6s 8d, which could perhaps be 'translated' into approximately £58 at present-day silver values. But the average value of a cow or ox last year (2006) was £1,000, and one greatly prized specimen – from a Campbeltown farm, just across the Kilbrannan Sound from Arran – went at a Carlisle sale for 2250 guineas in August 2006. How to reconcile these values requires greater financial expertise or wizardry than I am able to command, and at least indicates an astonishing improvement in beef quality in our times – and colossal currency inflation.

From the period of the Union of Parliaments(1707) onwards, the English and Scottish currencies were officially brought into line, although the Pound Scottish continued to be used as an accepted unit of exchange north of the Border at about £12 Scottish to £1 sterling until nearly the end of the eighteenth century. After that, both English and Scottish pounds are subject to the same inflationary pressures. I have not attempted to convert nineteenth-century prices into present-day equivalents, but have left them to speak for themselves.

1.   Early Times

Geology

The Firth of Clyde in south-west Scotland is big enough to be called an inland sea, bounded on the west by Argyll and the Kintyre Peninsula and on the east by the Ayrshire and Galloway mainland. In the middle of the Firth is an archipelago of islands, the most striking of which are Ailsa Craig and Arran. Arran is the largest, more than four hundred square kilometres in area.

The first thing that you notice about Arran when viewing it from the Ayrshire coast is a marked contrast in silhouette: the north is spectacularly mountainous, with jagged, lofty heights; the south has a much lower profile, appearing from a distance to be almost flat. (It is in fact rolling moorland with its own ups and downs.) The contrast is superficial only in a special sense: the two halves of Arran have actually floated and collided on a kind of basalt surface from almost opposite ends of the earth, in what is known as continental drift.

In Cambrian times, nearly 600 million years ago, there was no Atlantic Ocean, and the northern section of Arran, together with most of Scotland, was a part of what is now Canada. It lay much further south than at present, and the climate was sub-tropical. England and Wales, with what was to be the southern section of Arran, were further south again, in a colder position on the globe.

Throughout the hundreds of millions of years the continents slid together and apart, and oceans opened and closed in very slow motion, with a kind of swirling movement. When the land-masses collided, as they often did, the results were spectacular distortions, folding and crushing of the earth's surface, and orogenies, episodes involving the birth of mountain ranges.

Arran's northern mountains were born during the Caledonian Orogeny, in the Silurian age about 400 million years ago, affecting Scandinavia, Scotland, Greenland and what is now eastern North America. A great stretch of water known as the Iapetus Sea closed up, bringing together Scotland and England with their respective halves of Arran.

Much later, about 65 million years ago (in the 'Tertiary' era), the North Atlantic opened up and the Alps were formed during the Hercynian Orogeny, the result of a collision between Europe and Africa. This was accompanied by intense volcanic activity, which is still going on in Iceland. Both halves of Arran were left on the east of the ocean. The north of the island is the southernmost part of what is known as the Tertiary Volcanic Province, one of the five geological areas into which Scotland is divided. Other parts of the Province include several Hebridean islands and the Ardnamurchan Peninsula.[1]

The north of Arran is dominated by four clusters of spectacular granite mountains, jagged and craggy. The tallest of these is Goatfell (874 metres), which rises impressively above Brodick Castle to the north of the coastal village of Brodick itself. Above the village and below the granite slopes of the mountain is a high bank, the Thousand-foot (300 metres) Platform, which forms a girdle round the entire northern part of Arran. This platform represents the oldest rocks in the island, the 'Dalradian' schists, dating back to Cambrian times – although the section from Corrie to Brodick also contains younger rocks, two layers of Old Red Sandstone as well as other varieties. It was through the Dalradian schists that in Tertiary times a great eruption of lava burst from depth, forming a 'pluton' (a mass of solidified rock) two kilometres below the surface, where a kind of giant blister or dome formed. Through erosion and pressure from ice this blister weathered into the fantastic shapes of the peaks as we now see them.

South-west of Brodick is the site of an actual surface volcano (the 'Central Ring Complex', an oval area nearly five kilometres in diameter), which in the Tertiary period poured out lava across the southern half of Arran, covering basic Permian and Triassic sandstones.[2] This process has created the typical

12

'organ-pipe' crystalline cliffs of the Arran coastline, with headlands at Drumadoon Point, Brown Head, Clauchlands Point and elsewhere, including the mighty upward curve of Holy Island. At Drumadoon Point a small volcanic vent can be seen, tilted on one side like a ladle in a steel-works, with a faulted lava sheet spreading out in front of it. An almost identical formation is to be seen at the south-west point of the Heads of Ayr on the eastern shore of the Firth of Clyde.

Evidence of widespread eruptions, producing similar cliffs, can be seen all along the eastern rim of the present North Atlantic – in the Faroes, St Kilda, Staffa ('Fingal's Cave') and the Western Isles. In Arran, cataclysmic folding and distortion of the rocks has led to very complex stratification, e.g the inverted succession of strata at the north-eastern coast (North Newton to Corloch), where different layers of rock are arranged in mirror formation around a slate core.[3]

Much of the surface geology, indeed, consists of mudstone and sandstone of two main varieties, Ordovician and Permian, but at all points throughout the island a kaleidoscopic jumble of layers and epochs is immediately evident to the eye, from Dalradian (Cambrian) and Ordovician to Old Red Sandstone, Carboniferous, Permian, Triassic, Jurassic and Cretaceous through to Tertiary, all in close proximity to one another, with innumerable subdivisions and rarities. Hence Arran has been a geologist's paradise, a prime site for researchers and students, right from the days of the father of Scottish geology, James Hutton (1726–97). Hence too, the present notices warning against damaging rare kinds of stone by too free use of the hammer.

Geological folding relates the rocks of Arran to other formations in the mainland of Scotland, the Cowal and Aberfoyle Anticlines, and more generally to the Highland Boundary Fault.[4] This fault passes right through the centre of the granite Goatfell complex, showing the relationship of North Arran to the Scottish Highlands as opposed to the gentler landscape of the south.

One of the ways of telling the age of rocks is by the fossils of creatures embedded in the rocks and revealed by weathering as well as quarrying and mining. For example, an animal that inhabited the area now included in Arran was detected in 1975 by its fossilized spoor, indented in a stretch of sandstone about a kilometre north-west of Laggan. This was a gigantic centipede-like creature, Arthropleura, which grew up to six feet long, although this specimen seems to have been only three feet in length. It may have lived about 320 million years ago, in a coal-swamp habitat in the delta of a large river running through central Scotland. It fed on forest litter and thus was an important contributor to early soil-formation.[5]

Fossilized tracks of another kind of animal were found in 1992–93 on Levencorroch Hill, and the western shore south of the King's Cave near Drumadoon. This was the Chirotherium, literally 'Hand-Monster', so called because of a fancied resemblance between an enormous human hand and the footprint. The creature appears to have been a predecessor by some hundreds of millions of years of the dinosaurs, not a dinosaur itself. It lived in the Triassic period, and moved on four feet. It may have had a long neck and a small head. One can imagine this creature lurching and squelching through the primeval swamp, going down to drink. It would leave footmarks that dried in the sun. In the course of time these were covered with blown sand later impacted into solid rock: thus a fossil was born.

That the animal lived in a part of the world that later became Arran is of course the result of pure chance: similar tracks have been discovered as far apart as Arizona, Argentina and Europe. No fossil of the actual creature has so far been discovered anywhere, but a likely representation of it is displayed in the Arran Heritage Museum in Rosaburn, Brodick.[6]

Other fossil remains include plants and bark, creatures such as brachiopods and coral, and bivalves from the Arran coal-measures.[7]

Intense vulcanism can produce several varieties of gemstone, and precious and semi-precious stones have often been found in Arran. Among these are sapphires (of rather uncertain quality) discovered near the Rosa Burn. Quartzes include rock crystal, citrines and amethyst, and topaz, beryl, garnet and tourmaline have been found, as well as agates, chalcedony and opal.[8]

The Ice Ages

Æons after the last major volcanic outbreaks, the great Ice Ages set in. The phases of these are measured in thousands rather than millions of years, and provide an intelligible time-scale against which the history of humans in these islands can be measured. The latest intense glaciation (the 'Devensian') appears to have reached a maximum over most of Scotland and North England about 23,000 or 22,000 BC. The ice then started a long period of gradual retreat northward, punctuated by pauses and even 're-advances'. Its withdrawal left a landscape recognizably modern, including valleys gouged out and hills rounded and depressed by the great weight of ice sometimes kilometres thick. The word 'nunatak' (taken from the Inuit language) has been used to describe the topmost bits of mountains sticking up from the ice cover, as for example in the present Greenland: the peaks of Northern Arran may have been nunataks during the Ice Ages, and this may explain why they have remained jagged rather than smoothed and rounded like the southern hills.[9]

Glaciers are like slow-moving rivers of ice. There was a massive glacier flowing south from the Argyll and Loch Lomond region. Arran stood in its way, and the island was robust enough to divide the stream. Through the centuries the ice trenched deeper and deeper on either side, producing Kilbrannan Sound on the west of Arran and the Firth of Clyde on the east. In spite of being surrounded by billions of tons of ice in this manner, Arran had a distinct local glacier, which produced valleys radiating from a centre probably in the cluster of high mountains in the north.

The weight of ice split the original northern volcanic dome with three clefts running north and south. There are actually four major valleys in the northern part of the island, each with its own river system: (1) Glen Chalmadale – North Sannox, (2) Glen Rosa, (3) Glen Iorsa – Easan Biorach, and (4) Glen Catacol – Loch Tanna – Glen Scaftigill; there is one additional system in the middle part, Gleannan t' Suidhe – Glen Shurig. The river systems represent ancient glacier courses, with characteristic signs of decayed glaciation, such as moraines, drumlins, kames and eskers (all names for differently shaped heaps or ridges of broken or crushed stone[10]). The slow movement of glacier ice is also responsible for the transport of massive boulders (erratic or wandering blocks) from their original sites, such as the Clach a' Chath (popularly known as the 'Cat Stane' north of Corrie on the east coast).

As the ice receded, the volume of water in the oceans correspondingly increased, drowning many coastal locations. Gradually, however, the land which had been crushed by the weight of the ice began to rise again (in isostatic recovery), leaving raised beaches which can reach 15 to 20 metres and upwards above the present shore line. Raised shore lines can be traced round most of Arran's coasts. It is often upon raised beaches that we discover signs of early human habitation on Arran and in other locations in Britain.

OS references

Geology
Drumadoon Point NR 882 287
Brown Head NR 902 252
Clauchlands Point NS 057 237
North Newton NR 937 157
Corloch NR 993 485
Laggan (Arthropleura) NR 978 507
Levencorroch Hill (Chirotherium) NS 005 216
King's Cave NR 884 308
Drumadoon NR 891 291
Rosaburn NS 004 369
Glen Chalmadale NR 950 503

The Ice Ages
North Sannox NS 009 466
Glen Rosa NR 990 380
Glen Iorsa NR 920 383
Gleann Easan Biorach NR 948 485
Glen Catacol NR 920 470
Loch Tanna NR 919 430
Glen Scaftigill NR 905 405
Gleann an t' Suidhe NR 960 355
Glen Shurig NR 992 367
The Cat Stane (Clach a' Chath) NS 020 444
Corrie NS 026 434

2.   Human Colonization

Mesolithic times

Human beings colonized Britain before the great glaciation, but no signs of these 'Palaeolithic' – Old Stone Age – peoples have survived in Arran as far as we can tell at present. Ice made most of Britain inhospitable to non-Arctic life until about 10,000 BP, although there had been a break in the very cold conditions for about 1,500 years after 13,000 BP.

In the pioneering archaeology of Scotland and indeed Arran, modern research has brought to bear the techniques of pottery dating, soil science, palynology (pollen analysis), stratigraphy, radiocarbon dating and more, all subject to constant methodological revision. But the more that we reveal by the application of these techniques the more we discover our ignorance: we now can tell the approximate period at which humans started to colonize Britain after the ice-age, and recognize that there were two stages – Mesolithic and Neolithic – in the development of early Scottish civilization; however, just when the transition took place between the two phases remains obscure. The best we can say is that the change-over between hunter-gathering (mesolithic) and farming (neolithic) happened at different times in different places, was gradual, and may have involved the older and the newer strands running side by side in certain places.

The bare ground left by the ice around 10,000 BP was almost completely sterile, made up of silt and coarse gravelly rubbish. A few clumps of sedges of one sort or another were the only growing things in the desolation. Then, over

the next thousand years or so, mosses of different kinds formed a carpet in isolated locations, and heaths and grasses began to come in, followed by small
shrubs and low tundra plants such as juniper and whortleberry. About
9,000 BP the first trees, birches, began to spread north and group themselves
into forests. Later the hazel appeared. For the next several thousand years, new
tree species proliferated, in rather warmer conditions than now – elm, oak and
pine, ultimately forming the Caledonian Forest, of which a few remnants survive
to the present day. And, with the forests, post-glacial land animals roamed into
mainland Scotland as the conditions improved – wolves, wild horses, aurochs
(the predecessors of modern cattle), deer, beavers, wild cats, and pine martens.

Not many of the animal species reached Arran, since it became an island
early, even before Britain became isolated from Europe. Similarly, Arran's once
luxuriant growth of birch and hazel in the non-mountainous parts began later
than in mainland Britain, probably because the tree fruits were prevented from
spreading to the island by the water barrier. Pollen analysis based on soil samples from Machrie Moor shows that the hazel species (Corylus) may have
arrived in Arran about 8,665±155 ^{14}C BP, contrasting with an estimated
Corylus rise on the southern Scottish mainland of about 9,200-9,300 BP;[1]
human beings used hazelnuts as a source of nutrition, and may have brought
the fruits to the island by sea.

For human beings in primitive times the sea surrounding Britain was the
principal means of communication, since overland routes were difficult and
dangerous. People early learnt to navigate on water, and the sea became a
through-route to the north-west of Europe. Men, women and children
entrusted themselves to log canoes and light skin-covered wooden frames
('coracles'), and doggedly fought their way round the Atlantic coasts to colonize the western islands of Scotland – which were not so bleak and barren ten
thousand years ago as they are now. It is not unlikely that the islands developed
maritime communities well before pioneers ventured upon the mainland: the
direction of the prevailing currents would carry the voyagers to relatively easy
landing-spots on islands like Man and Arran.[2]

The exact period when people began to settle in Arran and the Western Isles
after the Ice Age is still uncertain. In this geographical area there are few artefacts datable to the earliest times. We have to infer a human presence from
'proxy' evidence – environmental pointers such as the state of the soil, signs of

fire, survival of pollen grains buried at various levels, and the probability of forest clearance. We may also get clues from organic debris left in great piles of 'kitchen' food rubbish in caves and at places taken to be camp sites.

At any rate, the first people to colonize Scotland after the Ice Age, whenever they did so, were Mesolithic, that is, of the Middle Stone Age. The earliest yet known place that they settled is Kinloch in the Island of Rum, where fire-charred hazelnut shells have been dated to 8,590± 95 BP (7700 – 7500 cal BC).

Mesolithic people were hunter-gatherers, nomadic in lifestyle, moving from place to place in search of food and shelter. Island-hopping in the west of Scotland meant that their food consisted largely of fish and shellfish, as well as seabirds and their eggs. On land they found nuts and berries. In order to catch mobile food both on land and sea, Mesolithic people used sharp weapons – stones 'knapped', struck against each other and broken into jagged shapes suitable for cutting, piercing and scraping.

In Old Stone Age, pre-glacial times, flints had been comparatively large and coarse in appearance, but by the dawn of the Mesolithic age, the weapons and tools were very much smaller and more elegant, called microliths. It is perhaps difficult to visualize how tiny and precise these little slivers of shaped stone are; some are less than a centimetre in length. Specimens found in Arran can be seen in the Heritage Museum at Rosaburn.

There is a difference in style between microliths of the early Mesolithic period and those of the later stage: a development in knapping technology has been tentatively identified, from broad-blade production at the beginning of the period to narrow-blade later on. Much has still to be learnt about the functions of microliths of both kinds. It is thought that several stuck into a wooden shaft would make a harpoon; they were also obviously shaped as arrow-heads, and some were used as 'burins', to scrape e.g. skins for clothing and tent-covering. They could also have been of service in clearing scrub and dense undergrowth, and even, perhaps, for felling trees.

Many sites in Arran are prolific in microliths, and some show large lithic scatters and stone waste, indicating 'knapping floors', where production of stone weapons was undertaken almost on an industrial scale. Knapping sites are found in Arran, for example at Machrie Moor.[3] The stone used varies from pitchstone (volcanic glass), flint, and chert (a flint-like stone) to agate. The pitchstone is peculiar to Arran (a-clach-neonach, 'the strange stone',[4] found at

Woodside near Brodick). It seems to have been specially prized in Mesolithic times: pitchstone microliths have been found in England and Ireland as well as mainland Scotland, and seem to indicate a very early trade network, if not a primitive kind of currency.

In Arran several occupation sites datable to Mesolithic times have been discovered on raised beaches, at Catacol,[5] Kildonan,[6] Dippin (Porta Leacach)[7] and elsewhere. A site at Auchareoch is interesting, as it is some way inland, showing that Mesolithic people did not necessarily choose to live only on the beach: it is 'on a kame terrace overlooking a former glacial dead ice basin' about four kilometres north of the coast near the cycle track between Torr Dubh Mor and Cnoc Donn. Here not only microliths but datable hazelnut shells and charcoal from firespots have been found. Radiocarbon determinations have dated these discoveries to 6100–5350± 90 cal BC.[8]

One of the characteristic signs of mesolithic occupation is the shell-mound, sometimes described as a '(kitchen-) midden', the accumulated shell-fragments of sea-creatures such as the whelks and limpets which the mesolithic maritime settlers ate. A small shell-mound has been discovered beneath the present floor-level of the King's Cave[9] and there may have been another at the Black or Monster Cave.[10] One was also discovered in 1908 in St Molaise's Cave on Holy Island.[11]

The Neolithic and Bronze Ages

In Arran we can only see the uncertain shadows of Mesolithic people – just inferred effects, proxy evidence, of human habitation. But with the dawning of the Neolithic – the New Stone Age – we begin to come in contact with less ghostly beings, who left more defined signatures on the natural environment. All over Britain and Europe in this period stone begins to be used for a variety of purposes – in the construction of dwellings for the living and chambered (communal) tombs for the dead, and, towards the end of the period, the erection of massive stone monuments arranged in mysterious, probably religious, patterns. Other materials than stone, of course, were used for these purposes, earth and timber in particular. It was also discovered that certain varieties of earth, when combined with water and hardened with fire, could be shaped into containers – the invention of pottery.

These developments show that human beings were taking a more proactive, constructive attitude to the environment, instead of simply hunting and gathering. Above all we can make out the first signs of farming, when people began to settle down in a community in one place, in order to give time for corn to ripen and for foals, calves and lambs to be born and grow up. All over northwestern Europe, agriculture and stock-breeding became more and more usual.

As with most investigations of such early periods, however, evidence for the Scottish Neolithic is uncertain and sometimes even self-contradictory. Evidence is building that Neolithic culture developed unevenly in separate regions in Scotland (e.g. Orkney and the Clyde). Some of this evidence seems to run counter to previously held ideas, for instance, that Neolithic culture in Britain would naturally spread from south to north: it has recently been shown that the monuments known as 'henges' as well as a particular kind of pottery ('Grooved Ware') have radiocarbon dates earlier in Scotland (Orkney) than in England.[12]

As mentioned above, in Mesolithic and Neolithic (and later) times the sea was the primary means of communication. Northward ocean currents ran west of the British Isles and, taking into account the primitive state of navigation in those days, western isles such as Man and Arran could have been more accessible as landfall than the mainland. Communities might have grown up in the islands which, because of their maritime skills, might have imported agricultural techniques direct from Europe earlier than communities on the mainland – or, of course, an invading race of Neolithic peoples could have brought the techniques with them. Thus, it is possible that Arran may have been among the earliest sites in Scotland in which farming started.

The development of arable farming in Neolithic times generally is thought to have been accompanied by tree felling. Pioneers may have used fire to clear areas of forest for growing crops and for grazing animals – 'slash and burn' farming. Over time this destructive technique would lead to massive soil deterioration, a growth of heathland and blanket peat. So, in Arran in Machrie Moor soil, samples and pollen analysis[13] show that extensive woodland clearance began about 5,750 BP; pollen samples show a decline in tree population corresponding to a rise in heathland pollen and charcoal. Weeds such as plantains and buttercups, which are associated with cereal crops, appear in the pollen record. At a number of similarly dated sites, including one, Cashelkeelty in Ireland, cereal pollen-grains were discovered, indicating domesticated food cultivation.[14] In Arran, in the Machrie Moor area, cereal pollen grain dated to 5,375 BP has been discovered – the earliest secure evidence of seeming Neolithic cultivation in Arran.[15]

An adjustment in era identification may be in order here, since 5,375 BP is nearly three hundred years before the traditionally accepted end of the Mesolithic (hunter-gatherer, nomadic) era around the time of the 'elm decline' in Western Europe: this was a major ecological disturbance resulting from an infestation very similar to the Dutch elm disease recently devastating the modern elm population, and seems to have begun around 5,100 BP. Thus, cereal crops in Arran may have been planted before the elm decline by people whom we would regard as Mesolithic – or the Neolithic era started earlier in Arran than elsewhere.

By means of soil-sampling and pollen analysis at various levels, we can trace the evolution of farming in Arran through several phases, from the primitive 'slash and burn' beginnings, through periods of very intensive exploitation and repeated exhaustion of land. Ultimately, Neolithic and Bronze Age farming practice led to an almost total blanketing with peat, leading to the near abandonment of the island in favour of the relatively untouched forests and soils of Ayrshire and Galloway. Going by parallel evidence from Ireland, soil deterioration and recovery may have been cyclic in Arran before the final abandonment of most agriculture in the island.

OS references

Mesolithic times; Neolithic and Bronze Ages
Machrie Moor NR 895 337 (knapping site)
Machrie Moor NR 901 329 (woodland clearance)
Machrie Moor NR 898 329 (cereal pollen grain)
Catacol NR 911 495
Kildonan NS 035 210
Porta Leacach (Dippin) NS 041 214
Auchareoch NR 995 247
Torr Dubh Mor NR 989 239
  and Cnoc Donn NR 990 252
Black or Monster Cave NR 9930 2027
St Molaise's Cave NS 0586 2972

3. The Ancient Monuments (1)

The chambered cairns

The earliest surviving monuments in Arran – structures put together by human hands and still surviving above ground – are the chambered cairns, of which there are many examples in the island. Several kinds of chambered cairn exist in Scotland, and the Arran tombs are almost exclusively of the Clyde variety: stone passages built, corbelled inward and roofed with heavy slabs, issuing directly into the open air. They were divided into compartments by transverse stone lintels, and used as communal burial places revisited and reused over a long period of time. These tombs are covered and stabilized with large, often long, mounds ('cairns') of stone and earth, narrower at one end than at the other, entrance, end. Sometimes the wider end would be built out at either side to tapering horns which would enclose a sort of stone concourse used perhaps for ceremonial purposes. The whole assemblage could be surrounded with a ring of orthostats, upright standing stones. (This does not mean that rings of standing stones were always associated with tombs: quite often they were not.)

All the chambered cairns visible in Arran have been heavily damaged. Perhaps the best preserved one is at Carn Ban in the south of the island, not far from the Mesolithic site at Auchareoch. Other well-known examples are at Torrylinn Water, Giants' Graves South and North, two at Tormore – Crochandoon and Machrie Moor – another at Monyquil (Moinechoill), Gleann an t'Suidhe, and one at Meallach's Grave, Monamore. None of these is very easy to get to. I should recommend the Torrylinn Water monument for the faint of heart and/or weak of ankles.

Although the landscape has changed radically in the last few millennia, it is still possible to gauge the relative positions and visibility of these tombs at the time of their construction. One theory is that the Arran series were built and spaced where they were in order to act like territorial markers, showing the extent of the control of each family or clan within the island. Perhaps the collective dead of the place, concentrated in a conspicuous chambered tomb, acted like supernatural sentinels over a certain geographical area – and everybody was aware of this. The tombs are arranged at fairly regular intervals around the island, and this regularity could be a pointer to the extent of Neolithic settlement in Arran, if not to the numbers involved. But no certainty can be reached in the case of these enigmatic mausoleums.

The dating of the chambered cairns is difficult, but it is accepted that they were built at an earlier period than other Neolithic monuments and that they were in use for a very long time. Only a handful of sites in Arran have been given a carbon-fourteen date, but the Monamore tomb has yielded two results: the deeper sample, at seven inches above the subsoil, has been dated to 5,110 ±110 BP (3160 ±110 cal BC). This indicates the approximate date of the foundation of the grave. The upper sample, just below the blocking layer, gives 4,190+/-110 BP (2240±110 cal BC), showing the later estimated limit of the grave's period of use, approximately 1,000 years.[1] These readings are for one location only, but it is not unlikely that similar results would be obtained for the other chambered tombs in the island, construction taking place towards the end of the early part of the Neolithic age, round about the turn of the fourth millennium cal BC.

The Monamore dates overlap with one of the major periods of pastoral agriculture i.e. when intensive cereal cultivation had slackened due to soil exhaustion, which led to an extension of heathland suitable only for browsing animals like sheep, goats and cattle. Soil studies of the only extensive plain in Arran, Machrie Moor in the south-west (including the Tormore area), show that this phase lasted from about 5,750 BP to 4,740±85 BP i.e. c.3800 BC to c.2800 BC;[2] for a space of a thousand years signs of woodland clearance and intensive agriculture imply a significant if not a dense population in the Machrie Moor area.

Domestic traces

The question of permanent dwellings made of stone or other materials in the Neolithic Age is difficult and although definite traces of stone foundations exist – at first sub-rectangular and later circular ('hut circles') – none in Arran have so far been dated earlier than the Bronze Age, in fact, none before 2000 BC. It could be that the art of building permanent homes for people did not percolate to the west of Scotland until after the close of Neolithic times. Not that the construction of sometimes massive buildings was unknown in Scotland during the period. We have the evidence of the very large timber structure whose crop-marks were discovered by air photography at Balbridie in Kincardine, dated to around 3,900–3,500 cal BC i.e. in the early Neolithic period.[3] It is likely that this was a 'long-house' with accommodation for people as well as storage space for cereals. Another long-house has recently been discovered at Callander in Perthshire, and this has been associated with finds of early Neolithic round-bottomed pottery.[4] Balbridie is, however, on the east coast of Scotland, facing Europe: sophisticated farmers could have immigrated to eastern Scotland from the near continent long before their methods could be taken up on the Atlantic side of the country.[5]

'Hut circles', the round remnants of the foundations of houses, are the monuments most frequently surviving from the Neolithic and Bronze Ages in Scotland. They are often detected nowadays by aerial photography. The appearance of such houses is associated with the emergence of small communities, the forerunners of hamlets and villages. Social organization also begins to emerge. A community leader, for instance, can sometimes be identified by the larger size of his house and its position, some way apart from the rest of the dwellings.

There are many hut circles in Arran, but it is difficult to assign a period to most of these, since the style of building survived a long time, perhaps more than three thousand years. At least, houses and settlement sites unearthed beneath the peat blanket, which started to spread as early as 1200 BC and which reached its final cover perhaps about 500 BC, may be classed as prehistoric. Similarly, field clearance mounds and fragments of prehistoric fields have often been discovered beneath peat cover in Arran, but most have not been precisely dated. Buried agricultural soil has been discovered beneath peat at e.g. Bridge Farm at the eastern edge of Machrie Moor, and this has been identified as belonging to the Bronze Age by the marks left by 'ards' (primitive ploughs) sealed under the peat.[6] The ards left traces of charred material indicating a primitive method of manuring the soil; the peat must already have started to be a worry to the farmers following the effects of prolonged leaching and exhaustion of the soil. The Bridge Farm site is adjacent to a Mesolithic knapping site prolific in pitchstone and flints.

Two settlement areas in particular, Tormore and Kilpatrick, were made the subject of archaeological investigation in successive seasons (1978 and 1979). At a particular site in the Kilpatrick area a complex field system has been identified in part as representing a possible early prehistoric phase.[7] Associated with this field system is a cairn beneath which the ground surface has been dated to 1885±55 cal BC, that is, the early Bronze Age. A habitation site at Sliddery has been assigned to the same period.[8] Sliddery appears also to have been a flint-working site.

A large number of hut-circles have been identified in the south-west of Arran at Tormore and Kilpatrick, and some of these have been excavated, revealing methods of construction such as wattle lining on the interior of walls and holes in the floor for posts supporting the roof.[9] It is currently thought that the Tormore 'round-houses' were built in the period 2000–1750 BC, roughly contemporary with the Sliddery and Kilpatrick sites. But, later than these, at Machrie Farm a basal peat sample taken from an 'area in the vicinity of well-preserved hut-circles and clearance cairns' was radiocarbon dated to about 500 cal AD, during the Iron Age.[10]

Field clearance mounds – the piles of stone removed from fields to prepare them for agriculture – are very frequent in Arran and elsewhere. And, within the last few years, several examples of burnt mounds have been unearthed in Arran – for instance, at Glaister Farm:[11] these are collections of stones which have been heated and thrown into containers of water (often wooden troughs) to boil it for cooking purposes. One such trough may have been discovered in recent years and is kept at the Arran Heritage Museum (not on display). A similar method of cooking is still currently in use among the nomadic herdsmen of Western China; it is thought that in the case of Arran, and Scotland generally, burnt mounds are associated with hunting or herding camp sites.

Burials with grave goods; votive burials

Communal burials gave way to single burials often covered with a cairn, a mound of stones and earth concealing a cist, an oblong box made of stone slabs. Cists could be long or short, the latter containing a body in a crouched position.

Accompanying these burials are often grave-goods, including stone axes, characteristic leaf-shaped arrow-heads, microliths, pottery, and, from the Bronze Age, bronze and gold weapons and ornaments. Many of these items, of course, are found in isolated locations not associated with burials, for instance bronze spearheads and flat bronze axes (e.g. in Glenrickard Forest),[12] or ornaments (e.g. a gold 'lunula' a crescent-shaped part of a necklace, discovered in Kiscadale).[13] Four gold armlets found during drain-digging at Ormidale[14] were donated to the then National Museum of Antiquities as treasure-trove in 1864. Two deliberately broken flanged bronze axes (from about 1400 BC) were discovered where they had been buried near Rubha Ban north of Pirnmill on the north-west coast of Arran. These finds, and especially the position of the Rubha Ban axes (right on the sea-coast), make one suspect that they are votive burials,[15] treasured possessions sacrificed to a god – perhaps a water divinity. Similar, though larger, hoards are to be noted in Ayrshire, at Dalduff (Kilkerran) and Lugtonridge, as well as at Duddingston near Edinburgh.[15]

In Arran at least four copper or bronze cauldrons were dug up over a century ago, three at Glen Cloy and one at Auchencairn: the cauldron was a very sacred vessel connected in the Bronze and Iron Ages with the cult and ritual of the god Daghda. Perhaps the outstanding example of the cauldron as ritual object is the great silver-plated copper vessel discovered in a peat bog at Gundestrup in Denmark in 1891, decorated with scenes that recall Buddhist and Indian (Mohenjodaro) rituals, hinting at a basic Indo-European religious continuum. It is also not impossible that the Arthurian quest for the Holy Grail, a divine silver cup or goblet, reflects Celtic ritual practice and mystery, 'remastered' to agree with accounts of the Christian crucifixion. Cauldrons are relatively frequent archaeological finds, especially in Ireland.[16]

Some of the stone axes are very elegant and highly polished (e.g. one discovered at Kirklea: a small, perfect, ground and polished stone axe, greyish, with buff inclusions;[17] see also specimens in the Arran Heritage Museum). These give the impression that they were purely ornamental in function or even a kind of currency or used in barter. It is clear that the use of stone for tools and ornaments persisted into the Bronze Age and in fact beyond.

Chief among the grave-goods, however, is pottery (mostly broken) of various styles which change and develop through the centuries. At one time it was thought that the different pottery styles – plain round-bottomed containers, food vessels, beakers, bucket-style pots, and different styles of decoration on all of these, would provide a reliable guide to the chronology of goods recovered both from tombs and from round-houses. It was, for instance, thought that the introduction of beakers signalled the arrival in these islands of an entirely new population, the so-called 'Beaker People', who would have subjugated the aborigines and prepared the way for the Bronze Age, which perhaps came in around 2200 BC. Plain, round-bottomed pots are early, discovered in association with chambered tombs. 'Grooved Ware', seemingly originating in Orkney, is associated with the beginnings of the Bronze Age.

However, while pottery may give a rough guide to 'periodization' in history, it is not a basis for secure speculation about population changes, invasions and the like. The adoption of Beaker pottery may simply have been a matter of changing fashions and ideas rather than the result of an 'invasion' of foreigners; the same may be true of the gradual introduction of metal (bronze etc) technology at the end of the third millennium BC.[18]

The 'Bronze Age', lasting roughly from then to about 1200–1000 BC, and frequently associated with images of heroes driving chariots and hurling spears at each other, may not have represented as radical a change from Neolithic times as is sometimes suggested. The discovery that metal may be worked is undoubtedly an important development in human culture, but in many respects Neolithic culture continued to be predominant. It may be said to have persisted even to the present day – especially in the use of stone in houses for the dead and the living.

At least, for the period conventionally called Bronze Age in Machrie in Arran, there seems to have been a relatively large population increase, to go by the number of house circles at Tormore, the signs of intensive agriculture and the concentration of apparently sacred megalithic symbols.

OS References

The Chambered Cairns
Carn Ban NR 9910 2620
Torrylinn Water NR 956 211
Giants' Graves South NS 0430 2463
                          North NS 0429 2467
Tormore – Crochandoon NR 9031 3106
Machrie Moor NR 9063 3224
Monyquil (Moinechoill, Gleann an t'Suidhe) NR 9407 3526
Meallach's Grave, Monamore NS 0176 2888
Machrie Moor in the south-west (including the Tormore area (NR 8908 3026–8977 3155 etc)

Domestic traces
Bridge Farm NR 926 321
Kilpatrick NR 907 263
(particular site in the) Kilpatrick area NR 9100 2640
Sliddery NR 935 242
Machrie Farm NR 9078 3385
Glaister Farm NR 928 349

Burial with grave goods; votive burials
Glenrickard Forest NS 00 34
Kiscadale NS 04 25
Ormidale NR 99 34
Rubha Ban NR 8745 4504
Pirn mill NR 873 444
Glen Cloy NS 00 35
Auchencairn NS 040 278
Kirklea NR 943 219

4.   The Ancient Monuments (2)

The great stone rings

The ancient monuments for which Arran is best known are the megalithic
stone settings including circles and single standing stones. There are many
in the Tormore–Machrie area, which, if we accept that the stone circles had
a religious significance, seems to have been particularly sacred. To this day,
there is a certain presence – of ancient supernatural power, investing the
place, enhanced by its wild, bleak loneliness, the moor's barrenness, and the
windworn stone remnants towering, or arranged in ritual patterns whose
meaning is forgotten. In Gaelic the area is called *Sliabh nan Carraigean*,
– 'The Moor of the Stones' or '. . . of the Standing Stones' (Mr Fraser).[1]
Without disputing the modern literal translation, it seems rather bland
for this ancient eerie place – why single out the stones? There are plenty
in Machrie and in Arran as a whole. Can we attribute mere topographical
'thinghood' to any ancient Gaelic placenme? A better interpretation may
be suggested by the Breton French word *Korrigan*, a likely cognate of
Carraigean: a Korrigan is an evil sprite haunting locations like the Carnac
stone alignments in Brittany. *Sliabh nan Carraigean* could mean something
like 'The Moor of the Stone-Ghosts'. (*Cf.* also p. 277 n. 13 ch 16)

In spite of the otherworldly terrors pervading the sites – and these were
probably responsible for the survival of the ruins during the Christian
period – they began to arouse the scientific and anthropological interests of
archaeologists from the nineteenth century onwards, and Machrie Moor was
subjected to a succession of excavations, some decidedly more clumsy than
others.[2] In the vicinity of the now abandoned Moss Farm (Sliabh Farm) there
are at least six stone circles partially or wholly buried in peat. One circle has

only a single stone slab still erect, 4.3 metres in height; other stones have been located by probing beneath the peat surface. Another circle consists of three upright slabs between 3.7 and 4.9 metres in height; the rest lying on or under the peat. An attempt, probably in the eighteenth century, was made to split up one of the fallen stones for millstones and two stone rounds still lie roughly on the site of the original upright. Other circles are more complete – much lower, rounded boulders arranged in penannular settings. One of these is called in Gaelic *Suidhe Coire Fhionn*, Fingal's Cauldron Seat. This is a double ring, and on the inner ring the great Celtic hero Fhionn ('Finn mac Coull') was supposed by the later Gaels to have set his cauldron to cook – while his dog Bran was tethered to one of the outer stones by means of a hole bored right through it. Near this site another kind of setting is to be seen, a typical 'four poster', four stones arranged in a square or diamond shape.

A major investigation into two of the rings, site 1 and site 11, was conducted by Dr Alison Haggerty over two seasons, in 1985 and 1986. The ring at site 11 had been completely buried under peat and its stones were located by probing. Excavation of the two rings, positioned close to each other, was very thorough, and revealed features going right back into early Neolithic times. Underneath the existing stone circles the researchers found evidence of earlier timber circles. In the case of circle 1, there were three concentric wooden rings or designs of wooden uprights, the inmost consisting of five large timbers erect, the middle ring of about fifty posts and the outermost of more than thirty-four. The wood had of course long rotted away, but the excavators were able to pinpoint the location of each timber by the holes which had been made as sockets for the upright posts. The wooden circles were later abandoned, the location was given up or returned to agricultural use during a lengthy intervening period, and ards (primitive ploughs) left marks on the ground over and surrounding the sites. The area was evidently divided into separate fields, as shown by the traces of wattle fencing found – among the earliest in the country – traversing the circles. Yet, puzzlingly, perhaps centuries later, stone circles had been laid out with at least some individual boulders positioned precisely over the post-holes of the seemingly long-obliterated timber circles. Unfortunately radiocarbon dating has been difficult in the case of the stone circles themselves[3]. Dating estimates vary widely, indicating a long period of construction and renewal – perhaps from 3000 BC to 1500 BC.

What did the circles mean?

The question of the meaning of stone circles, religious or otherwise, is vexed. It is always advisable to be cautious about interpreting the relics of a pre-literate people – like the Picts of Scotland, or the Neolithic/Bronze-Age inhabitants of Arran. It is accepted up to a point that the arrangements of stone circles and other monuments are or can be connected with the movements of the sun and moon. A well-known example is to be found in Orkney, at Maes Howe, where the internal passage of the great tomb there is aligned on the winter solstice, so that the sun at that time shines through a slot onto a small area in the opposite internal wall, producing a striking spot of light amid the gloom of the interior. Clearly, the movements of the sun and moon would arouse the mythopoeic and religious instincts of the people, quite apart from their practical importance as guides to the growing and harvesting seasons for farming. However, the alignments at Maes Howe and elsewhere are accurate only within a few degrees and anything like scientific accuracy is most unlikely. Nor is there any evidence of formal sun worship as such in Britain.

Despite scepticism, in the case of stone circles, including those in Arran, attempts have been made to prove that the position of the stones has a precisely calculated connection with star movements – but the circles themselves are imprecisely laid out, with wide variations in, say, the intervals between the stones, their relative heights and the kinds of shape represented on the ground. They are more to be described as penannular, 'near-circular' formations than true circles, although some have been built using a central point and a cord or rope to describe a circumference. The trouble with the 'star-related' theory of the position of stones is that an infinite number of star positions in the sky can be calculated from any given point on the ground, and, following from this, an infinite number of predictions or meanings of all sorts can arise from any alignment. Some researchers have gone as far as to suggest that there was a very organized theocratic society controlled by a priestly caste who calculated exact alignments on heavenly bodies marked by the exact position of each individual stone or group of stones: it is claimed that it would have been impossible for Neolithic civilization to have developed as it did unless it had been led by an élite of wise men, high priests and the like.[4]

Some arrangements like this have been mooted for the ancient Aztec civilisation of Central America, but in the case of the British Neolithic and Bronze Ages, there is not a shred of archaeological evidence confirming the existence of such a leadership caste.

The underlying implication of many 'theocratic' theories is that primitive humans weren't so primitive after all, but used many scientific methods and ideas long before modern times. If we point out the mythical basis of ancient ritual practices, our objections are often dismissed with the airy observation that myth was 'the way in which early peoples expressed their scientific under-standing' – a position only betraying ignorance of the distinction between mythic thought and scientific cognition. The central fear of the Mexican theocracy was that the setting of the sun represented its being swallowed by the powers of darkness – the Lords of Xibalba – and that it would never reappear, as it were regurgitated, at dawn unless the underworld gods were placated by holocaust human sacrifice. This fear is strictly and specifically mythic and as such can have nothing to do with the calmer, more abstract analysis and synthesis of science.

A primitive form of astrology (i.e. non-scientific star-lore) may well have been expressed in megalithic monuments; it is also quite possible that the cir-cles have multiple strands of meaning, which certainly can only be disentangled with hindsight, but do not involve assuming anachronistic preci-sion. Above all, even if the egg-shapes, pear-shapes, ellipses, and the like that some researchers profess to detect in the settings are claimed to express scien-tific understanding, '[t]here is no necessity,' as G. J. Barclay states, 'to assume that the complex geometries used by proponents of these beliefs to describe the shape of a circle ... [were] originally used to *set out* that circle.'[5] Barclay quotes with approval the phrase 'delusions of accuracy' used by researchers to describe these 'beliefs'.

In order to clarify at least one additional meaning, perhaps we should jour-ney about eighty miles south of Arran to another island in a nearly land-locked sea: the Isle of Man.

There survive on Man perhaps three stone settings describable as near-circular. However, it is not from these physical relics that we seek information:

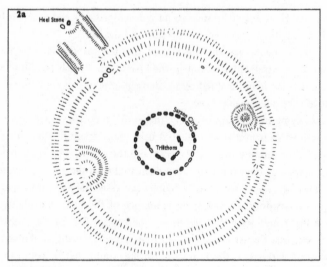

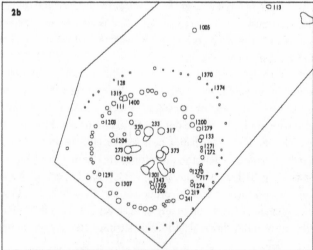

(2a) Diagrammatic representation of Stonehenge
(2b) Diagram of Dr Alison Haggerty's excavation of Phase 2 (wooden) of Circle
      1 at Machrie Moor, Arran, showing the double circle and central 'horse-
      shoe' organisation (i.e. the 'open' formation of larger timbers in the centre
      of the circles. Figures on the drawing are excavators' catalogue
      numbers. Reproduced by kind permission of the Society of Antiquaries of
      Scotland

instead we shall consider a symbol that has been associated with the Isle of Man since time immemorial; the mysterious 'Three Legs', in its modern form three actual legs running or revolving round a central point – appearing on the island's flag and postage stamps. (Man is still formally an independent nation, with its own parliament, owing allegiance directly to the monarch of the United Kingdom.)

The three legs often perform their race within a disc. When we contemplate the symbol for a little while, other examples of the same kind of design come to mind. Perhaps the most obvious of these is the notorious Swastika or Hakenkreuz annexed for their own purposes by the German National Socialists before and during the Second World War. The swastika is an ancient Aryan symbol, and it was taken over by the Nazis under the influence of their racial ideology, which aspired to connect the German people with the Aryans, allegedly the oldest and purest form of the Indo-European race. The running 'three legs' of the Isle of Man are bent at the knee in precisely the same attitude as the crooks of the 'crooked cross'; the Manx symbol is visibly a Swastika minus one leg; it also has the same background disc, though the colour of this is not the red and white decreed by Hitler. In its Manx version, it is obviously a triskele, literally a 'three-legged design', often occurring in Celtic iconography and ornaments.

Another example of a circle with an internal organization is the theta, the Greek letter ϑ, in its capital form Θ, which is clear in its relation to forms like the Swastika and the Manx symbol. In very early Greek script the letter is a round disc with a 'St Andrew's Cross' design dividing it internally into four quarters. As actual jewels, thin gold circular plates, 'sun discs' containing an elaborate cross design, are known in early Irish iconography from Beaker (pre-Christian) contexts.[6] And, although it lacks the background disc, the Christian Cross itself might be said to be reminiscent of this pervasive symbol. The Chinese Yin-Yang disc recalls the design although the internal organization in this case has curves creating two compartments, each containing a small disc.

The Sanskrit word for a symbolic circle or magic ring is *mandala*, and this word has been taken over by modern psychologists as a term for a basic, psychophysical design. The psychologist Carl Gustav Jung traced the mandala-form back into the primitive psyche of the human race, with examples taken from the ancient iconography of many peoples.[7] The educationist Sir Herbert

Read noted that this was one of the 'primordial images' of children's art, spontaneously appearing in the drawings of children from a very early age.[8]

We do not have to accept Jung's psychology or theory of race memory, or Read's educational theory, to appreciate the universal spread of the mandala-image in human minds, mythology and art. It is not unlikely that the Three Legs of Man are the echo of a culture that expressed itself physically in the form of stone or wooden mandalas. We only have to look at an aerial photograph of Stonehenge to realize that this megalithic setting looks very like a mandala, with the massive trilithons outlining a 'horseshoe' in the centre of the ring giving the central organization which most mandalas have. What is more, Dr Haggerty's drawing of the wooden stage, Phase 2, of Circle 1 at Machrie in Arran, indicates a double ring as in Stonehenge with a similar central organization in a 'horseshoe' formation; the wooden posts constituting the horseshoe were very much larger than the stakes forming the inner ring (0.5m in diameter as opposed to 0.35m).[9] (See diagrams on p. 34.) This resemblance between Stonehenge and Machrie Circle 1 is significant, despite McLellan's opinion to the contrary.[10] The double ring and central organisation can actually be seen in the Fingal's Cauldron Seat stone ring on the surface adjacent to the scene of Dr Haggerty's work, which she has of course reburied.

We can be fairly confident that ancient stone circles where they occur have a connection with the primitive mindset that produces mandala designs. There is also a very marked relationship between some mandalas and human sexual function; the miracle of sex, and in particular of motherhood, is and was as important to all civilizations, including those of the Neolithic and the Bronze Age, as the controlling movements of the sun and moon, and a lot more accessible. Worship of the sexual force is well-known, and may have been central to ancient Egyptian, Babylonian, Hittite and other religions.

The worship of Magna Mater, 'Great Mother', an earth-and-fertility-goddess of vast power in the Mediterranean region, is well-known from contemporary literary sources. This goddess may have analogues in pre-Christian Celtic religion, for instance the goddess Bridget (Christianized as 'Saint Bridget'), or even in Christian terms as the Great Mother of God, the Virgin herself, Saint Mary: both these deities have dedications in Arran in the form of church/parish names, Kilbride and Kilmory.

Precise physiological links to the shape of the Bronze Age stone rings have been indicated by Dr Anthony Perks, who as a professional gynaecologist[11] has recently offered a well-informed speculation on the matter.[12] According to Dr Perks's theory, the two-rings-plus-horseshoe design of Stonehenge and similar monuments constitutes an image of the female genital organ. If we think of this theory as valid, it would not be difficult to supplement it by bringing in the movements of the sun and the moon (respectively male and female) as apparently linked to the pattern of the stones – ritually, if not with anachronistic 'scientific' precision.

One form of monument of which there are two or three examples in Arran may be relevant here: the petroglyphs or 'cup-and-ring' stone markings to be found in Stronach Wood above Brodick. The Arran examples appear as two concentric rings with a 'tail' which could be interpreted as corresponding to the megalithic arcades leading from the upright stone rings to some worship point. It is not clear whether any such arcades exist in Arran, but they do occur in places such as Callanis, Stonehenge, and Carnac in Brittany. The Stronach Wood petroglyphs have no central organization as such but elsewhere many have a central hole or cup – perhaps, as Dr Perks says of the horseshoe formation at Stonehenge, representing 'the opening to the world, the birth canal', honouring the Earth Mother for 'giving both life and livelihood'.[13]

The well-known authority on prehistoric petroglyphs, Stan Beckinsall, has published a selection of cup-and-ring markings culled from several locations, which show circles or penannular figures with a variety of internal designs, including one like a wheel with spokes, and others closely resembling the Stronach Wood carvings. He even exhibits one design which dispenses altogether with a circular rim, appearing simply as a bare cross.[14] Some of Beckinsall's more complex examples, with two or three linked circles, could be taken as representing penetrative sexual intercourse – as indeed could the designs resembling the Stronach Wood symbols at a more elementary level. Some of the (? more sophisticated) designs employ a circular arrangement of 'dots' within the outer circle, surrounding a central dot or hole, and these dots are reminiscent of the inner circles of individual stones seen both at Stonehenge and on Machrie Moor.[15]

Another form of probably religious significance is the carved stone ball, numerous examples of which have been found in Scotland, mostly but not exclusively in the east of the country. One ball, with four carved discs on its surface, is recorded as having been found at Dippin in 1891 (present where-abouts unknown).[16] The circularity or in this case the globularity may indicate a religious function, perhaps connected with the equally mysterious ball-like objects found in Ireland and known as crotals.

One general point, however: concentrated in this relatively small island, there are so many monuments of various kinds – tombs, standing stones, stone circles and petroglyphs – that we begin to feel a pervasive religious tone about the place, almost as if Arran in the remote past were a sacred island – like Delos in Greece or the Queen Charlotte Islands off Western Canada. These monuments have been scattered throughout Arran, but the highest concentration is in the south-west, in the Plain of Machrie, facing Ireland, which itself, as a whole, may have had a heightened religious aura in Neolithic times. Then of course we remember the sage words of scholars like Jane Ellen Harrison (*Prolegomena to the Study of Greek Religion*) to the effect that in ancient pre-Christian Greece the entire spectrum of human activity was infused by supernatural awareness, that every move that a human being made was governed by *deisidaimonia*, a fear, an acute sense of being monitored by the spiritual, whether divine or demonic. This almost physical feeling of being watched from on high would suffuse geography as well, and it might be unwise to seek to identify one particular area as possessing more divine radiance than another. But nodes did develop, and particular spots came to possess peculiar sacredness.

OS references

The great stone rings
Sliabh nan Carraigean NR 908 324
Moss Farm (Sliabh Farm) NR 908 324
Fingal's Cauldron Seat (Suidhe Coire Fhionn) NR 9088 3235
site 1 NR 9120 3239
site 11 NR 9121 3241

What did the circles mean?
Kilbride NS 033 323
Kilmory NR 965 215
Stronach Wood NS 004 366
Dippin NS 04 22

5. The 'Dark Ages'

The Iron Age

The developments discussed in the last sections took place 'before the [all-covering growth of] peat' that ultimately devoured the Isle of Arran. In the words of Robinson and Dickson, referring to the two time zones between 800 BC and AD 700, Arran may have been 'effectively abandoned as being unproductive, and inroads [may have been] made into the tracts of largely untouched woodland on the mainland in preference.' They continue, 'Certainly the Machrie Moor area, which is very much marginal land today and which by this time had suffered human interference for well in excess of five thousand years under conditions of exposure and an increasingly oceanic climate, would have had few areas which were not covered in acid heath or blanket mire'.[1] The triumph of the peat, virtually sterilizing the land for arable agriculture, roughly coincides with the inception of the Iron Age, the time when man's metallurgical skills reached beyond tin and copper, bronze and gold to the new, harder metal, iron, more suited to weapons of war. While the potentialities for conflict burgeoned, human destruction of the environment embraced not only Arran but the entire Western Highlands and Islands region, which in our own time has been described as 'a wet desert'. In this barren wilderness the ancestors of the modern Scots settled and fought and struggled towards statehood.

Finds of individual relics identified with the Iron Age in Arran are rare.[2] Animal figures discovered in the King's Cave near Drumadoon are reckoned to belong to this period.[3] (See below.) The existence of a 'bloomery' (a primitive furnace for the conversion of iron ore into iron bars) adjacent to a possible Late Iron Age house was established by a rescue dig at Glen Cloy (Auchrannie). But there is no way of firmly dating these exceedingly scanty finds. Carbon-fourteen analysis of a basal peat sample near some well-preserved hut circles at Machrie Farm gives a result of about AD 500 (see chapter 3), but the radio-carbon dating technique itself is uncertain and very vague for this period.

Hillforts

However there is one class of monuments which is accepted as Iron Age *par excellence*, even though no-one can yet tell precisely when they were built or reconstructed. Hillforts and duns have powerfully and permanently remoulded the landscape itself in an unmistakably human fashion, and they are recognized as for the most part belonging to the Iron Age.

In Arran some nineteen Iron Age sites have been identified, including fourteen hillforts and duns. These are arranged strategically, either in the north, overlooking important west–east passes, or in the south, built on mainly coastal promontories.

The inland forts are built high above the valley floors – Cnoc a' Chlochair watching the present Brodick to Shiskine pass (at the east end of the 'String' Road, perhaps corresponding to the unfinished fort at Cnoc Ballygown at the Shiskine end); and Torr an t-Sean Chaisteil (North Glen Sannox) controlling the Sannox–Lochranza route. Perhaps the last-named should be taken as part of the same defensive system as the vitrified coastal fort An Cnap above Sannox,[4] and, on the west side Lochranza Fort (on Coille Mor above and south-west of Lochranza itself – not to be confused with Lochranza Castle).

In the south part of Arran, likely centres of Bronze-Age / Iron-Age population cluster round the forts built on promontories and sea-cliffs – Dun Fhionn at Clauchlands, Dippin Fort, Kildonan Fort (again, not to be confused with Kildonan Castle), Bennan Head and Drumadoon Fort ('The Doon'). Glenashdale Fort is built on a promontory some way inland, but has a good lookout eastward over Whiting Bay, as well as controlling what may have been a meeting of three routes, from the Whiting Bay region, from the south coast in the Bennan Head-Torrylinn-Sliddery area, and from the north, from the general area of the present Lamlash (Monamore). Torr a' Chaisteil, King's Cross Point and Kilpatrick are coastal defences.

Kilpatrick, which is associated with other, earlier structures, has a wide view of Drumadoon Bay from the south, across to The Doon atop its spectacular cliff. The latter, of all the earlier defensive structures on Arran, has most title to be called an oppidum, that is, a fortification which includes enough space within its walls to shelter people and cattle in an emergency, and may occasionally constitute a small or large village (cf. Traprain Law in East Lothian). Besides fortifications, there is evidence of settlement on the top and on the landward slopes of Drumadoon Cliff. A small but prominent standing stone in the conventional trapezoidal shape overlooks the Bay and the Shiskine golf-course. Also a 'souterrain' or semi-underground structure is reputed to exist somewhere on the slopes but I was unable to discover it.

Duns are circular fortifications possibly developed on the model of circular wooden dwelling-houses and built with stone for better defence under pressure of warlike times in the Iron Age. At King's Cross Point it can be seen that the roughly circular drystone wall has both inner and outer facing stones sandwiching a rubble filling. At North Glen Sannox there are apparent traces of a mural room built into the thickness of the wall. Before falling into ruin both buildings may have been tall enough to be called 'towers'. Here, and at other Arran forts or duns, we may see a stage in the process which led first to the 'galleried dun' and later to the stone-built broch (looking like a miniature cooling tower), many examples of which occur in north and east Scotland, in historical Pictish territory; this might be an added hint at an early Pictish culture in the west of Scotland too, i.e. before the area's 'Gaelicization'.

Linguistic and tribal

This epoch of Scotland's history extends into the time of literacy and Christianity, and we might expect to be at least partially enlightened by written records as well as by linguistics. But no records for Arran's Iron Age exist at all, apart for some very uncertain hints culled from mythology and classical and ecclesiastical lore. Historians find themselves in the position of reasoning from the uncertain to the unknown.

The Celts are supposed to have invaded the British Isles and Ireland in at least two 'waves', one in about 1000 BC, and the other about 600 BC. Each spoke a different variety of Celtic: the earlier wave came to Britain and spoke 'P-Celtic' or Brythonic (Brittonic), represented today by the languages of Wales, Cornwall and Britanny; Cymric and in all likelihood Pictish are extinct varieties of P-Celtic. The second wave went to Ireland and spoke 'Q-Celtic' or Goedelic (today Scottish and Irish Gaelic as well as Manx). Irish and Scottish Gaelic remained almost indistinguishable until the fifteenth century AD.

Doubts have been expressed about the chronology of these events, and even whether the invasions actually took place. But at all events, the two language systems are still extant, and preserve the P-Q difference: an example is the word for 'son': in Brythonic it is 'map', and in Goedelic it is 'maq' (Gaelic 'mac'). And, however they arrived, the Celts brought with them the Iron Age culture, as well as the specifically Druidic ('La Tène') religion.

The now-extinct variety of early Welsh called Cymric (or Cumbric) was spoken in the south-west of Scotland, and many traces of the language are still to be found in place-names in Ayrshire opposite Arran. In Arran, however, between Britain and Ireland, no trace at all of Cymric or any P-Celtic tongue is to be found in place-names or any other context. The language and culture of Arran is uniformly Gaelic, although a special Arran variety of the speech did develop, last heard about 1950. This did not evolve into a separate language like Manx, although certain similarities have been observed.

In spite of this Q-Celtic uniformity, however, a P-Celtic language may have been spoken in the region at some period: one ground for this speculation is the very first map of Britain, apparently compiled in the second century AD by an Alexandrian Greek geographer named Ptolemy. In this map, the Kintyre peninsula, adjacent to Arran, can be identified as *epidion akron* (Epidium Promontorium). This name means the Promontory of the Horse People (or Horse Lords) and employs the Brythonic (P-Celtic) letter 'p'; in old Irish writings the Kintyre peninsula is called Ard Echdi, also meaning the Promontory of the Horse People. This is to say, 'Echdi' is the equivalent of 'Epidium' : a Q-Celtic (Gaelic) sound, 'ch' (or 'q'), was substituted for the Cymric sound 'p'.[5] This could mean that a Brythonic language (?Pictish) was spoken in the area in Ptolemy's time. Of course, the two different peoples could each have had their own name for the same place, and Ptolemy had access only to one version. Nonetheless the name 'Epidium Promontorium', and other local indications, may mean that the Brythonic-speaking people possessed the lands of West Scotland including Argyll and Arran before and during the second century AD. If we accept traditional chronology, the Irish did not start to come across the North Channel to the Mull of Kintyre in significant numbers until about AD 450–500, well after Ptolemy had compiled his map.

It is generally accepted that settlers or colonists from the north-east of Ireland extended an Ulster kingdom called Dalriada (or Dal Riata) across the water to what is now the maritime Argyll and western Clyde area of south-west Scotland. These settlers were known as Scots, a designation which may even have meant 'Irish pirates'. From ancient Irish texts we know the name of the man – or his son – who is supposed to have led these Scots from Antrim: Erc or Eirc, who died around AD 500, and who had a son, Fergus Mor mac Erc. Fergus died very shortly after his father, just after arriving in Scotland, and his son in turn died in c.507, possibly after or during the subjugation of Kintyre; perhaps this rapid turnover in leaders represents determined local resistance to the Irish invaders. The son was succeeded by Fergus's two grandsons in succession: Comgall who died after a peaceful reign about 537–8, and Gabran twenty years later. After the pacification of Kintyre, it is conjectured that the grandsons would move to conquer the neighbouring lands to the east, Cowal and Arran. These four men may have established Dalriadic Irish rule and Gaelic language on a secure basis, settling certain Cenela or clans in various locations throughout the region.[6]

The Cenela adopted the names of the original chieftains, which became attached to their respective territories. The names have been modified by linguistic changes through the centuries, but some are still recognizable today, perhaps the most obvious surviving relics of Dalriada: the territory associated with the Cenel nGabhrain became Gowrie, that with the Cenel nLoairn(d) became Lorne, and that with the Cenel nComgall became Cowal (but that with the Cenel nOengusa became Islay, seemingly not derived from an Irish personal name). A territory named Airgialla is recognizably Argyll.

In this connection the name of Ailsa Craig is of some interest. This is a very tall islet, in fact a volcanic plug, towering sentinel-like 300 metres out of the southern Firth of Clyde about half way between Carrick in Ayrshire and Kintyre. The name has been connected with the personal names Æla or Aili (short for Ælfsige) or even with Ealasaid, Elizabeth.[7] However, I would suggest that the name is a doublet. On the analogy of Ail Cluaith (Dumbarton) = 'Rock of the Clyde', the word Ailsa would mean 'Rock' in Cymric – as does Craig in Gaelic. In around AD 500 'Ailsa Craig' would be a boundary marker, possibly even explicitly agreed as dividing the two linguistic spheres of influence. To the west it signalled the newly conquered and now Gaelic-speaking realms of Argyll and Arran; to the east, on the mainland, Carrick and Strathclyde, still Cymric-speaking for many centuries after 500.

It is also of interest to note that whereas the names of sites and features in Ayrshire and Galloway with a Cymric background often preserve the names of pagan deities 'disguised' (e.g. 'Ayr' < Agrona, one of the Celtic goddesses of slaughter, or 'Doon' < Devona, the patron goddess of the Damnonii tribe), Arran names appear to be severely limited to the literal and topographical. If there is any force in the suggestion that the doublet Ailsa Craig was explicitly agreed as a linguistic boundary, it may be that the invading Gaelic power brought with it a gallery of Christian enforcer saints who ruthlessly eradicated all traces of pagan nomenclature from areas like the newly 'Gaelicized' Arran just west and north of Ailsa Craig.

Another facet of the argument can be displayed by pointing to the name Arran, which is wrapped in mystery. It appears not to be the same as the name Aran, applied to the islands off the west coast of Ireland. The Welsh *aran*, ' a peaked hill', is said to be a 'very appropriate' derivation:[8] this is indeed based upon a topographical resemblance, thus acceptable in the light of the 'anti-pagan' renaming which I suggest above. But in this case, doubt remains – it somehow does not ring true. Doubt also applies to the derivation proposed by Dr Alexander Cameron of Brodick in 1889 – that the name actually means kidney because of the kidney-shape of the island (as seen from above!): 'Arran (older form Aran) is an inflection of Ara, the old name of the island, as Alban (Scotland) is an inflection of Alba, and Erenn (Ireland) is an inflection of Eriu. The genitive of Ara is Aran . . . In both form and declension, Ara, gen. Aran, agrees exactly with the word ara (kidney), gen. aran . . .'[9] Cameron's detection of the Gaelic genitive ending is accurate, but, as Mr Fraser points out, '[t]here is absolutely no reason to believe that Dark Age man looked at Arran as an entity in the shape of a kidney.'[10] One has a momentary vision of a spear-carrying Dalriadic warrior striding into a butcher's shop, his eyes sparkling with delighted recognition as he inspects the offal counter.

Should the name not rather derive from that of its conqueror or Cenel? There is, then, another possibility: among the several Irish peoples participating in the Dark-Age invasion of Scotland the name Erainn – representing 'the people of Dalriada'[11] – is mentioned several times in the Annals of Ulster, the Annals of Tigernach and other sources. The Erainn may have operated in coalition with the Dal Fiatach – or may have been identical with the Dal Riata, or have included them: they may have been identified as occupiers of Arran at some time. Apparently the possibility of 'E' changing into 'A' over the centuries in Gaelic is not outside the rules of philology: 'Erainn' could have changed into 'Arainn', the present Gaelic spelling of the name of the island; Mr Fraser cautiously allows that it could have been so.[12] Thus, the modern name 'Arran' might derive from yet another 'Cenel' or tribal grouping, along with Cowal, Gowrie and Lorne.

The substitution of 'A' for 'E' is paralleled in e.g. 'Argyll' < 'Ergathel', 'Airer Gaidel' < [c16] 'Eir-ghaodheal' . . . 'Earra-Ghaidheal'.[13] The Vikings probably called Arran 'Herray'. But admittedly this is mere speculation, reasoning *per incertum in incertiora*.

The different clans rose and fell in ascendancy over the two hundred years following AD 500 and formed, in a more or less loose confederacy, an overseas Scottish province of the Irish Dalriada. This province itself also became known as Dalriada, as a separate unit, and began to grow away from the older kingdom after a conference known as the Convention of Druim Cett held in AD 575. It finally became detached from the Irish Dal Riata in 637 after the battle of Magh Rath: the Scots lost *eorum sceptrum regni huius de manibus suis*, 'their sway over this kingdom [the Irish realm] out of their hands'.[14]

How does Arran fit in with the kaleidoscopic succession of battles and various supremacies that flit in and out of vision during this period? The answer is that nobody knows for certain. There is no mention of Arran at least by that name in the very confusing records surviving from the early period, not even in the *Senchus Fer nAlban*, 'The History of the Men of Alba [Scotland]', a tract, which seems to have been transmitted from that time, and which mentions by name places and tribes quite close to Arran: *Cenel ngabrain in so. tri xx. taige ar c[h]oic c[h]etaib cend tire ¬ crich c[h]omgaill cona insib*, 'This is the Cenel nGabhrain, five hundred and sixty houses, Kintyre and Crich Chomgaill with its islands . . .'[15] Arran would be one of those islands of Crich Comgaill apparently owing allegiance to the Cenel nGabhrain, in the *sinus maris per-maximus*, the 'very extensive arm of the sea', as Bede, the earliest real historian of those times, calls the Firth of Clyde.[16] It is speculated that the island was simply 'bolted on' to Kintyre and the early Gabhrain supremacy. This would take it within the sphere of Dal Riada. The *Senchus Fer nAlban* may have been compiled in the seventh century AD, when, as the above extract shows, the Cenel nGabhrain held sway in Cowal and Kintyre. Later, in the eighth century, the Cenel Comgaill, giving their name to Cowal, where they were the ruling kindred, supplanted the Cenel nGabhrain – but the latter must have made some recovery, since the ninth-century unifier of Picts and Scots, Kenneth mac Alpin, is reputed to have been of their royal stock.

OS references

The Iron Age
Glen Cloy (Auchrannie) NS 008 359

Hill forts
Cnoc a' Chlochair NR 9533 3578
Shiskine NR 912 299
'String' Road NR 980 360
Cnoc Ballygown NR 9202 2911
Torr an t'Sean Chaisteil (North Glen Sannox) NS 0018 4738
An Cnap NS 0172 4606
Coille Mor NR 925 508
Lochranza Castle NR 934 506
Dun Fhionn NS 047 338
Dippen Fort NS 0510 2238
Kildonan Castle NS 036 209
Kildonan Fort NS 044 219
Bennan Head NR 9975 2082
Drumadoon Fort ('The Doon') NR 8860 2925
Glenashdale (Whiting Bay) Fort NS 0308 2520
Bennan Head–Torrylinn–Sliddery area NR 990 210–930 229
Lamlash (NS 029 314)

Monamore NS 010 300
Torr a' Chaisteil NR 9217 2326
King's Cross Point NS 0560 2827
Kilpatrick NR 9065 2619

Linguistic and tribal
Ailsa Craig NX 023 994

6. Myth and Religion

King Arthur

Our next glimpse of Dark Age Arran is in the distorting mirror of semi-mythological history: the Arthurian cycle of poems and stories, supposedly originating in post-Roman Britain, when that was under threat from the Anglo-Saxons. Six hundred and fifty years after the Roman withdrawal, the Anglo-Saxons in their turn had been conquered by the Normans under Duke William. William's successors strove to legitimize themselves, and appropriated Arthurian folklore as propaganda: it showed the basic right of the Norman (Plantagenet) kings to rule as British leaders i.e. as enemies of the Anglo-Saxons, whom Arthur and his cohorts also resisted. Geoffrey of Monmouth, a partly Welsh chronicler of the twelfth century AD, was primarily responsible for preserving and embroidering the originally British Arthurian stories for these propaganda purposes, and he highlighted Celtic – Welsh, Irish and Scottish – traditions.

In fact, actual references now surviving in pre-twelfth century sources to any Arthur, let alone King Arthur, are sparse and most uncertain. But a man called 'Artur' [sic] is mentioned in the *Senchus Fer nAlban*. This 'Artur' appears to have been the son or possibly the grandson of the Aedan referred to earlier. Aedan was one of the most energetic kings of Dalriada, himself the son of Gabhrain, one of the founding tribal leaders in the kingdom. Artur may have lived in the late sixth century, when there was a more or less constant state of war between Dalriada and the mainland British kingdoms of Strathclyde and

'Pictavia', and he may have been killed in the Battle of 'Miathi' in 592. This man, whose stamping-ground undoubtedly included Arran and the surrounding area, could, just possibly, be a credible candidate for 'King Arthur'. The trouble is that his dates are said to be too late for the King Arthur of the romances; in the end we have to allow that the king must be an amalgam of several historical and non-historical figures.[1]

However, the narratives include a description of the final battle of the saga, in which King Arthur receives an apparently mortal blow, but is borne away over the water to a magic island where he will be healed of his wound. The name of that island is Avalon, literally 'The Place of Apples'. In Gaelic poetry and mythology frequent references occur to a magic place called Emhain Abhlach, 'Emhain [Place] of the Apples', and this has been reliably identified with the Isle of Arran, the residence of Manannan MacLir, the sea-god's son. Rival claims have been advanced in favour of the Isle of Man, but the balance of probability indicates Arran. And if we consider Arran as the objective of a sea-voyage by King Arthur in search of healing, we must also think of the association in Gaelic literature of Arran with a magic fountain of healing or rejuvenation – and of the magic voyage of the hero Bran, Christianized as the adventurous St Brendan, and topographically associated with the Kilbrannan Sound between Arran and Kintyre.[2]

We are not informed whether the apple tree (pyrus malus) specifically formed part of the regenerated woodland of Iron-Age Arran, but it is one of the Rosaceae family, which, though apparently not prolific, does appear in Arran's pollen record.[3] The apple is one of the magic objects of Celtic – and other – mythology, associated with rejuvenation: the character of the Isle of Arran, as a magical place of healing, could be expressed in the name Emhain Abhlach, a source or place of apples. Nowadays, according to Robert McLellan, traditional Arran cottages often have apple trees in their gardens, along with plum trees and other fruits.[4]

The soil science and palynological data mentioned earlier indicate the near-abandonment of arable agriculture in Arran due to soil exhaustion: the podzolized, boggy heather and grass moorland would still provide nutriment for grazing animals, which include deer. The seas around Arran were teeming with fish, and birds and small land animals must have provided food for birds of prey. Regeneration of woodland is also typical of land that is not used for arable purposes. Arran provided an ideal environment for hunting, as attested in literature:

Arran of the many stags, the sea reaches to its shoulder; island where companies were fed, ridge where blue spears are reddened.

Wanton deer upon its peaks, mellow blaeberries on its heaths, cold water in its streams, nuts upon its brown oaks.

Hunting-dogs there, and hounds, blackberries and sloes of the dark blackthorn, dense thorn-bushes in its woods, stags astray among its oak-groves.

Gleaning of purple lichen on its rocks, grass without blemish on its slopes, a sheltering cloak over its crags; gambolling of fawns, trout leaping.

Smooth is its lowland, fat its swine, pleasant its fields, a tale you may believe; its nuts on the tips of its hazelwood, sailing of long galleys past it.

It is delightful for them when the fine weather comes, trout under the banks of its rivers, seagulls answer each other round its white cliff; delightful at all times is Arran.[5]

This poem in its present form survives from the twelfth century, but is probably much older. Hunting, an activity originating in Mesolithic and earlier times, has been perpetuated through the ages in Europe and elsewhere as a non-essential luxury for leaders, kings and aristocrats; locations like the Isle of Arran may have been preserved as hunting 'forests' for privileged people, as the Cumbrae islands in the Clyde are known to have been.

Christianity: St Molaise and others

At some time during the period between Ptolemy's map and the era of Aedan mac Gabhrain of Dalriada, Christianity must have come to the kingdom and to Arran.

Ptolemy called Kintyre 'Epidium Promontorium' and, as we have said, this means the Promontory of the Horse People; the horse was a sacred animal in the Celtic religion throughout Europe, and representations, stone carvings, have survived in France and elsewhere of the Horse Goddess Epona riding side-saddle on her steed. The Horse Lords of Kintyre in the second century would head a tribe devoted to this particular (totemic) form of 'Druidism'. Whether their influence would extend to Arran we do not, of course, know, but we have no evidence to the contrary. What we can be sure of is that the religion of Christ eradicated Celtic 'paganism' very thoroughly.

Christianity took root in mainland Britain during the Roman occupation. Britons were Christians before the Anglo-Saxon invasion and probably converted their conquerors. Also, according to K. H. Jackson, they introduced Christianity to Ireland and were responsible for its initial organization and development in that island.[6] The most famous Irish missionary was, of course, St Columba, who first settled in an unidentified island called 'Hinba' round about 563 AD and then set up the more famous religious centre at Iona.

Irish Christianity laid stress upon the virtues of the solitary life, and it was common practice for devout holy men to seek out 'deserts' or 'wildernesses', often remote and relatively inaccessible islands, where, as hermits, they could retreat for fasting, prayer, meditation, and frequently instruction of postulants to the religious life. 'Hermitage', life as an anchorite, is to be seen almost as a rite of passage in the career of a saint. Arran, having long been abandoned for the purposes of arable agriculture, and thus presenting a rather shaggy, desolate appearance, might well fill the bill for a 'desert'. Thus it comes about that the first really reliable evidence involving or at least mentioning Dark Age Arran comes from Christian sources: some time in the late sixth or early seventh century AD a hermit called Laise or Laisren took up residence in a cave about three-quarters of the way along the cliffside path on the west coast of Holy Island. The cave is some ten metres above the level of the path, so that one has to scramble to reach it. It is formed by an overhang in the cliff, with a sharp drop at the entrance, negotiated by a crude staircase. Standing on the cave bottom one can touch most of the ceiling, which slopes right down at the back to floor level. Covering both ceiling and rear wall are a dense collection of carved crosses (probably not as early as Laise's time) and inscriptions, some of the latter runic (see Vigleikr section, chapter 8). The cave has a fairly wide mouth opening directly to the full force of the south-westerly gales and cannot have given much shelter, but we gather that discomfort was part of the treatment for early hermits. This hermit, who gained a reputation for great holiness, became sanctified and was called 'Mo' Laise; the Gaelic prefix 'Mo', meaning 'my' or 'my little', became the equivalent of 'Saint'. The name of 'Holy Island' was originally Eilean M' Laise, 'the island of Molaise', gradually transformed into 'Lamlash'. This name in turn was transferred to the recently enlarged Arran village (originally 'Kirktoun of Kilbride') facing the island across the waters of 'Lamlash Bay'. When the renaming happened, about 1790 (before the building of the village really got under way[7]), the island became 'Holy Island'.[8]

St Laise went on to become Abbot of Lethglenn in Ireland, and died in 639.[9] His ancestry included King Aedan mac Gabran, who was born in 533, and so Laise may have been a late contemporary of 'Artur', son or grandson of Aedan. He was also related to Columba.

The life eremitical did not involve complete isolation from the world: in some places colonies of hermits came together in 'coenobitic' life, living and praying as a dispersed community. On Holy Island there is some evidence that St Molaise was not the only hermit, for instance in the so-called Smugglers' Cave, where early carved crosses are also to be found.[10] Another saint, Blaise of Armenia, is traditionally associated with the tiny islet of Pladda (Insula Sancti Blasii de Pladay).[11]

Sometimes the hermit had his retreat in proximity to an early form of monastery, and it is just possible that there was such an institution on Holy Island in Laise's time, about two kilometres north of St Molaise's cave. One of the earlier writers on Arran, Dean Donald Monro, remarks (1549) that on the 'little ile callit the yle of Molass – there was foundit by Johne, Lord of the Isles, ane monastry of friars, which is decayit'.[12] Friars do not live in monasteries, and John Lord of the Isles lived in the fourteenth century, but another reference indicates that a monastic order was founded in the twelfth century in Holy Island by Ranald, King of the Isles and Argyll. Both of these putative foundations are wildly out of the period of St Molaise (seventh century), but the stories, confused as they are, could point either to twelfth- or fourteenth-century buildings refurbishing an ancient establishment, or to the tradition of a foundation at some time in the past. Such a foundation could be represented by recently (re)discovered cliffside ruins at the north end of the island. The site has now been surveyed and photographed but not yet investigated.[13] The ruins themselves are of course not likely to date from the seventh century.

Near St Molaise's cave the remnants of the cistern for a holy spring or well are to be seen (St Molaise's Well), although the spout leading into it has long disappeared. The usual traditions of curative and miraculous powers exist, and people are reputed to have travelled long distances to be healed by the waters. In this case there is a fair chance that the association with the saint is genuine, but other examples are more doubtful. St Columba's Well (Tobar Challumchille) at Mid Thundergay, is about the only site associated with Columba in Arran, but there is no clear evidence that he ever visited the well. Sacred wells are traditionally supposed to be linked with the presence at some time of an eponymous saint, but this is often very obscure: the sacredness is more likely to have been inherited by Christianity from a Celtic predecessor, for there was a cult of miraculous wells in Celtic pagan religion.

Also near St Molaise's cave is a natural feature called St Molaise's Table, a circular flat-topped rock on the sides of which have been cut four seats. A ring-topped cross, thought to be early, is carved on the east face.[14]

There are clear indications of Iron Age religious and other use in the so-called King's Cave on the west side of Arran itself. This cave is one of the larger sandstone caverns on the coast of the island, north of Drumadoon Cliff in the south-west. In this cave, included in a fascinating jumble of carvings of various periods, are a number of carved crosses large and small, and human and animal figures. A large cross incorporates 'tree of life' features typical of Early Christian art, and nearby a human figure raises its arms in an 'orans' (praying) attitude[15] – or, perhaps, holding a bow with both hands above its head.[16]

Among the carvings are images of interlaced snakes, and natural cracks which have been used as 'stem-lines' for Ogham inscriptions. Ogham is an ancient Irish system of writing ostensibly based upon the Latin alphabet but consisting of a series of strokes and notches at right angles to a (frequently vertical) straight line.[17] It is supposed to have been introduced into Ireland by the god Oghma or perhaps Oghmios, a Hercules-like figure who included in his functions that of leading souls to the abode of the dead, binding and carrying off the deceased – like the Indian God Varuna.[18] The philologist K. H. Jackson has deciphered one of the three mutilated but recognizable Oghams in the King's Cave as reading EOMEQE, which appears to include the Q-Celtic word MEQ = son, i.e. the Ogham carver would be a Goidel probably from Ireland.[19] This would be the earliest documentary evidence of a Goedelic (Gaelic) presence in Arran.

Columba himself, of course, was one of the shaping spirits of northern

Christianity, and his influence persisted both in a positive and negative sense long after his death. He came to 'Hinba' from Ireland when he was forty two years old, some say exiled to Scotland after misdeeds committed in battle. Gifted with great intellect and energy, he was a first-rate diplomat and a political fixer of genius, with personal authority stemming from royal family connections and influence. He settled in a comparatively minor province of Dalriada, the territory of the Cenel Loairn – basically, the Firth of Lorne area – and most of his monastic foundations are located within this region. At the same time he sought to extend his mission north-eastward to the principal centre of Pictland, the hill-fort now called Craig Phadraig near Inverness. Columba trekked perhaps several times through the Great Glen, on one occasion meeting and pacifying the man-eating Loch Ness Monster. A tradition states that Columba had to use an interpreter at Craig Phadraig i.e. he spoke Q-Celtic Gaelic but the Picts spoke a variety of P-Celtic Brythonic.

Reading between the lines of Adamnan, Columba's biographer, we may suspect that Bridei, the King of the Picts, successfully resisted conversion at least at first – in spite of Columba's magic proving more powerful than that of Bridei's Court Druid. In the end, however, the Picts bowed to Columba's Christianity if not to Dalriadic force of arms. A story recorded by the Venerable Bede (yet disputed by modern scholars) is that Bridei granted Iona to Columba; if true, this would be further confirmation that the whole of the west coast of Scotland had been populated and controlled by Picts before the arrival of the Dalriadans.

The association of Columba with his eponymous well at Mid Thundergay may be uncertain, but his influence, or that of the church he represented, is very evident in Arran, where the names of the ancient churches and parishes are all prefixed with the syllable 'Kil-' – Kildonan, Kilpatrick, Kilmory, Kilbride. This 'Kil-' is the Gaelic *cill*, the dative form of *ceall*, 'cell', i.e. *Kildonan* is '(at the) cell of Don(n)an'. Christianity, we gather, was not wildly popular with the Picts, and on the island of Eigg on 17 April 617 a party of them murdered a saint called Donan and his community. St Donan, a younger contemporary if not a disciple of Columba, was commemorated in Arran by the now-vanished Kildonan Chapel in the neighbourhood of the present Kildonan Farm. This chapel was recorded by Balfour in 1910, as were Kilbride Chapel at Bennan and Kilpatrick Chapel, both of which have similarly disappeared. The latter should not be confused with the site at Kilpatrick, which at one time was regarded as incorporating a 'cashel', an early Christian monastic site, but, following Barber's investigations, is now recognized as a typical late Neolithic / early Bronze Age settlement area, overlaid by an Iron Age dun. (See Domestic Traces Section, Chapter 3 and Hillforts Section, Chapter 5).

Among the mass of Europeans exposed to Christian proselytization some would cling obstinately to the older traditions, including the belief in and ritual of 'pagan' deities. The Christians countered the survival, as indicated above, by suppressing pagan names or, if this didn't work, by simply annexing the names of the local gods and making them saints attached to localities and churches. Hence the 'St Bride' (Bridget) of Kilbride descends directly from the ancient Celtic goddess Brigit. Probably the St Mary of Kilmory represents a pre-Christian Celtic deity analogous to the Magna Mater, the Great Mother of the Mediterranean region (see chapter 4, p. 36). She is the dedicatee of the present Kilmory Parish Church, built 1785; the remnants of a primitive St Mary's Chapel may yet be rediscovered in that vicinity or at Sliddery.

The name Kilmichael, marked on Blaeu's map, was applied to what was later known as St Molaise's Chapel in the Clauchan burial ground at Pien (Shiskine). The name of St Michael, respected in the Western Isles, apparently conceals the identity of the Celtic god Brian, son of Brigit, patron of the arts and letters.[20] A ruined church still stands in Pien, but this dates only from 1805, and once again the original building has disappeared. An effigy, built into the tower of the present 'St Molio's Church' at Shiskine and nearly completely effaced, is said to represent none other than St Molaise himself, but, to go by the vestments and tonsure, it is more likely to be the portrait of a thirteenth century abbot (? of Saddell in Kintyre). Another St Michael chapel is said to have stood in the present graveyard between Corrie and South Sannox; again, a stone allegedly representing St Michael is built into the north wall of the cemetery, but all signs of the chapel have been obliterated

'Kil-' churches and placenames – e.g. 'Kilmarnock' or 'Kilwinning' – are widespread over the south-west of Scotland, signifying the extent of the influence of the Irish church in the early days; they are to be distinguished from church names beginning with 'Kirk-', which indicate an Anglian or sometimes Norse influence, e.g. 'Kirkoswald' in Carrick, commemorating the martyred St Oswald, Anglian King of Bernicia.

OS references

Christianity: St Laise and others
Holy Island NS 060 300
Smuggler's Cave NS 0530 3031
Pladda (Insula Sancti Blasii de Pladay) NS 027 193)
St Columba's Well (Tobar Challumchille) NR 8807 4659
Mid Thundergay NR 881 466
St Molaise's Cave and Table NS 0587 2969
St Molaise's Well NS 0587 2968
Kildonan Chapel NS 036 213 (conjectured)
Kilbride Chapel NR 033 323
Kilpatrick Chapel NR 9032 2685
Kilpatrick NR 907 263
Kilmory Parish Church NR 9633 2185
Sliddery NR 9399 3034
Kilmichael (St Molaise's Chapel–Clachan) NR 9216 3034
Pien NR 919 304
(St Michael's) graveyard (near Corrie) NS 0146 4528

7. The Early Middle Ages and Arran

The Vikings

We have no records of any armed invasion of Arran by Dalriadic or other Irish colonists, although one probably took place. Arran avoided conquest by the Romans, probably because the attention of the Romans was engaged elsewhere, and the advent of Christianity is likely to have been peaceful. However it is very probable that contact with the next wave of foreigners was warlike: the Vikings first present themselves as murderous robbers in the west of Scotland and elsewhere.

The Scandinavian peoples seem to have taken a notion for foreign adventuring when they developed a new ship technology – the famous longships, fast, manoeuvrable and capable of distance raiding – together with improved weaponry and armour. The first sign of Viking danger came in 792 or 793, when the longships descended upon Lindisfarne – the one-time home of the Venerable Bede – on the east coast of Anglian Britain, and sacked and slaughtered with impunity. Monastic foundations were regarded by Christians as sacred and inviolable, and so were undefended; they fell easy prey to the fierce Nordic pagans, to whom they were simply display cabinets full of gold and wealth for the looting.

The north and west of Scotland were speedily conquered by the Vikings and most of the religious communities were torn asunder. Iona itself fell victim to repeated raids (the first in 802), although the monks were prudent enough to remove themselves and their possessions to the south of Ireland, probably preserving one of the great monuments of Dark Age art, the Book of Kells, written and decorated some time after the death of Columba. Some Iona monks, under an abbot called Blathmac, decided to endure the storm, but were massacred in a peculiarly brutal manner in 835.

Nearly the whole of the western seaboard of Britain was subjugated by the Scandinavians. The southern Hebrides were taken, and these included Arran. Viking control extended as far south as the Isle of Man and Dublin, and in time Viking kingdoms were set up in the north of England, at York and right down to the south-east (under the Danes, to be distinguished from 'Vikings' proper, who came out of 'viks', the fjords and creeks of western and south-western Norway).

In the course of time, even with the Vikings, thieving and murdering gradually gave way to peaceful occupations like farming and trading, and, in conquered territories, the Scandinavians began to settle and send down roots. So many colonists descended upon the north and west of Scotland that in time the indigenous Pictish way of life in Orkney, Shetland, Caithness and Sutherland was almost completely supplanted by Scandinavian language and culture. Further west, in the Innse Gall, the Outer and Inner Hebrides, a more even mix was obtained, and intermarriage between Viking and Gael produced a fierce warrior people called Gall-Ghaidhil, 'Stranger Gaels', who controlled many territories in the west of Scotland, including Galloway, whose name may be derived from the designation 'Gall-Ghaidhil'. These people brought about one of the two most significant developments in the course of Scottish history in the later first millennium: the Gall-Ghaidhil from the islands under the Viking King Ivar 'the Boneless' joined forces with Dublin Vikings under Olaf the White in attacking Strathclyde and destroying the British *caput*, the fortress *Ail Cluaith*, 'the Rock of the Clyde' (Dumbarton) in 870. Thenceforward British Strathclyde became more and more a subject kingdom, eventually just an 'appanage', a perquisite of the royal house of Alba. The British (i.e., early Welsh) influence dwindled in Scotland after 870, and the Cymric language had probably disappeared by the time of King David I in the twelfth century.

The kingdom of Alba was brought into being as a result of the second pivotal development in pre-1000 Scottish history, the union of the Scots and the Picts under Kenneth mac Alpin, which took place some time between 847 and 852, approximately twenty years before the sack of Dumbarton. This unification was, however, balanced by the loss of the Dalriadic heartland and the entire Scottish north and west to the Norsemen.

There are no certain written records of a Viking occupation of Arran from this time, yet we know that the Vikings were there, and settled to farm and trade as in other parts of the Inner Hebrides. This is clear from place names in Arran. Important place names are Norse, less important Gaelic – corresponding to an imbalance between Norwegian masters and farmers and Celtic tenants and farm-labourers. Thus in Arran we have Ormidale, 'Orm's Valley'; Chalmadale, 'Hjalmar's (or Hjalmund's) Valley', Sannox, through Gaelic Sannaig from Sand-vik, 'Sandy Bay'; and Brodick from Breida-vik, 'Broad Bay'. Gaelic and English names tell of rental paid to Viking landlords – Feorlines (feorlain), 'Farthing-land'; and Pennyland – the penny referred to being a Norse silver coin.

McLellan says, 'We can deduce little from the fact that there are several place names prefixed by "bal" or "bally", as Balnacoole, Ballygow(a)n, Ballymeanoch, and Ballygonnachie, for the word baile came to denote simply a village, standard or not.'[1] However, following the lead of W. F. H. Nicolaisen, we may understand something of the occupational and social make-up of the Arran population during and after the Viking occupation from this linguistic element: there are also many names beginning with 'Auchen' and 'Aucha' (Auchencar, Auchagallon, Auchamore, Auchencairn, etc). In Gaelic 'Auchen' (achadh) means simply a field, while 'bal' (baile) means primarily a dwelling. The Gaels who lived, say, in Balnacoole, would have a settled dwelling there, i.e. they would be the landowners, while, at Auchencar, Gaels might till the fields or herd the cattle but they would be the farm-servants of the occupying Vikings.[2]

So the Vikings changed from being marauders to landlords, farmers and traders – although island settlements might relapse into piracy now and again. Mixed farming was given a new lease of life in Arran: towards the end of the first millennium AD the poor soil of the island, previously exhausted by millennia of slash-and-burn agriculture, was revived and enriched to some extent, the weather having got noticeably better; soil science indicates that the Vikings took advantage of this improvement to engage in both arable and pastoral farming, probably with new agricultural techniques.[3]

We owe to the Vikings the first 'roughly precise' date in Arran history. In 1909 Balfour uncovered a boat-shaped Viking grave at King's Cross Point which contained various articles including calcined human bones, Viking boat rivets, and a styca, a coin of Wigmund, Archbishop of York between 837 and 854; at least we know that the Viking was buried no earlier than 837, though we cannot tell how much later the funeral took place. The year 837 and the immediately succeeding period are early days for Viking penetration. It is of interest, however, that a shield-boss and some fragments of a Viking-type sword found in a burial mound (Lamlash) in 1896 (but now lost) were fairly securely dated to the period around 750, much earlier than the first reported Viking raids at the end of the eighth century.[4]

Somerled

The history of the Western Isles becomes a little clearer and more detailed after the turn of the millennium, but it does not say much specifically about Arran. The narrative of the times, however, shows the forces that shaped Arran politically as it eventually emerges into the light of historical day.

Within the long stretch of island and coastal territories constituting the Nordic empire in Scotland different centres of independent power began to develop – the Earldom of Orkney and the Kingdom of Man in particular. Perhaps, as suggested by Mackenzie, the Manx kingdom was the stronger of the two, especially after the death of Earl Thorfinn of Orkney in 1064:[5] Man was further from Norway with richer opportunities for trade; its links with metropolitan Norway grew weak, and it exerted a strong southward attraction on the Western Isles region.[6]

Within this region itself, however, yet other nuclei of power developed. The 'Gall-Ghaidhil' in the Innse Gall grew restive not only under Norwegian but also under Manx control. At the Battle of Clontarf in 1014 Irish Celts under 'Brian Boru' (Brian mac Cennedaigh) inflicted the first crushing defeat for many years upon Norsemen. The spirits and strength of the long-subdued Dalriadic coast of Northern Ireland rose again. In Argyll, in Scotland, a new Celtic kingdom was probably established as early as the eleventh century. At length, in the second quarter of the twelfth century, a quasi-independent coastal realm was set up in Argyll (Morvern) by a certain Somhairle or Somerled (Old Norse: 'Somarliðr'), the offspring of a Viking and a Gaelic princess; he may have been born in 1113.

At the beginning of Somerled's career his family are said to have led an unsuccessful revolt against the 'Lochlannach' and the 'Fin-Gall' (both terms mean Norsemen or Vikings). The family took refuge in Northern Ireland with their relatives Cenel Colla, a clan whose remote ancestors were supposed to have included Fergus mac Erc, the founder of the Scottish Dalriada. Later, encouraged by a clan conference in Fermanagh, Somerled and his father Gillebride na h'Uaimh ('Gillebride of the Cave') reputedly returned to Morvern to reclaim their lost lands at the head of a large, enthusiastic band of young men – and promptly disappeared from view. However, about the year 1130 the Clans MacInnes and MacGilvray apparently discovered Somerled living in the wilds of Morvern, biding his time; they begged him to lead them against the Lochlannach, who had been making life miserable for them; he accepted, and succeeded in driving the Norsemen from Morvern, Lochaber and northern Argyll, recovering his family's lands. Later he conquered southern Argyll together with its islands, which would include Arran.

Somerled's career coincides with that of David mac Malcolm – King David I of Scotland, whose reign lasted twenty-nine years (1124–53). Somerled was the leader of the West Highland contingent in the King's army which marched against the Norsemen in about 1138, and it probably was David who elevated him to the rank of Thane or Regulus ('Kinglet') of Argyll.

After consolidating his rule in Argyll, the ambitious Somerled turned his attention to the Kingdom of Man. He did not love the Manx King Olaf, but decided to marry Olaf's daughter Ragnhild. The story goes that Olaf was on his way north with his war-galleys to do battle with the Skyemen when, at Ardnamurchan Point, Somerled appeared with two galleys and offered to join the expedition if Olaf would give him Ragnhild's hand. Olaf refused point blank and simply commanded Somerled's war service against the king of Skye as of right. Somerled apparently caved in and meekly joined Olaf's battle-fleet. However, during the night, a naval diver secretly swam under Olaf's flagship and in its hull bored holes which he plugged with tallow and butter. When the fleet moved in the morning, the motion washed out the plugs and the king's ship began to sink. Somerled then hailed Olaf, telling him that he would not be rescued unless Ragnhild became his bride. Olaf, seemingly up to his knees in water, consented, and Somerled sent his artificers over with wooden plugs prepared in advance. He married Ragnhild in 1140. After this, he went from strength to strength, building ships of improved design, with a stern rudder, and exercising firm control over the whole of the western seaboard of Scotland. All this took place during the reign of King David I of Scotland.

Somerled, styled Lord of Argyll, remained friendly to the king of Scotland until David I died in 1153. After the old king's death, however, another episode took place in the long-standing troubles involving Malcolm mac Heth, Mormaer (Earl) of the vast northern province of Moray, who had married Somerled's sister. In January 1154, the sons of Malcolm mac Heth rebelled against David's successor, King Malcolm IV. Somerled joined with his nephews against the King, but the rebellion was unsuccessful; and in 1156, Malcolm mac Heth and his son Donald were arrested and imprisoned in Roxburgh Castle. Somerled, however, seems to have remained at liberty and turned his attention to his own side of the country once more, although remaining for many years at odds with Malcolm IV.

In the west, King Olaf of Man had been assassinated in the year of King David's death, and his successor, Godred, became very unpopular with local chieftains through his tyrannical rule. The son of an important chief, Thorfinn son of Ottar, then offered the Kingship of the Isles to Somerled's son Dugall, and saw to it that all the chieftains swore allegiance to Dugall. This naturally incensed Godred and in 1156 there was a great sea-battle off Islay between the Manx fleet and Somerled's ships. The action was so fierce that both fleets were equally devastated, although Somerled seems to have won on points.

It is at about this time that we begin to encounter mentions of Arran by that name. The Irish annals mention a sea battle in (apparently) 1154 in which one of the opposing parties brought in fighting men from Arran: *Do-chuas o Chenel Eoghain, & o Mhuirchertach, mac Néill dar muir co ruaiclidis .i. go cendcadis longas Gall-Ghaoidel Arann, CinnTire, Manann & centair Alban archena . . . ,* 'The Cinel-Eoghain and Muircheartach, son of Niall, sent persons over the sea to hire (and who did hire) the fleets of the Gall-Gaeidhil, of Ara [Arran], of Ceann-tire [Kintyre], of Manainn [Isle of Man], and the borders of Alba in general . . .'[7] On this occasion the Arran folk were on the wrong side and were soundly beaten; *ro benadh a fhiacla a mac Scelling,* 'the teeth of Mac Scelling [the commanding general of the Gall-Ghaidail, 'the Foreigners'] were knocked out'.

Somerled and Godred came to terms with each other, agreeing that Godred should retain the Isle of Man and all the islands north of Ardnamurchan, while Somerled should have all the islands south of Ardnamurchan, including Kintyre and Arran. This arrangement did not hold, and in 1158 Somerled invaded and occupied the Isle of Man itself. King Godred fled to Norway. Two years later, in 1160, Somerled came to terms with Malcolm IV, after another rebellion in which he and other semi-independent leaders, including Fergus (the probably Gall-Ghaidhil) Prince of Galloway, had besieged Malcolm in Perth.

OS references

The Vikings
Feorlines (Farthing-land) NR 905 281–909 289
Balnacoole NR 915 306
Ballygow(a)n NR 912 291
Ballymeanoch NS 025 217
Ballygonnachie (Auchareoch) NR 995 247
Auchencar NR 892 367
Auchagallon NR 894 346
Auchamore (Mossend) NS 011 394
Auchencairn NS 042 279

Lamlash burial mound NS 0335 3189

8. Reorganizing the People

Parishes and feudalism

During the reigns of King David I and Somerled respectively, certain trans-forming factors of great importance began to appear, in the field of religion and in other respects.

Previously Christianity had been maintained by the successors of men like St Columba or St Molaise of Lamlash, with originally Irish liturgies modified by the results of the Synod of Whitby, held in 664 before the Viking incursions. In later times the Christian tradition had been upheld by the *Celi De*, the 'Culdees', a loose organization of 'servants of God', often secular or married priests who grouped themselves in various communities throughout Scotland. King David's devout mother, Margaret, Saint and Queen, who had been under the influence of the great St Stephen of Hungary, set herself to reform Scottish Christian practice after her marriage to King Malcolm III Canmore, probably round about 1071. She had taken steps to refurbish the decayed monastery at Iona. But it was left to her equally devout and energetic youngest son, David I, to make a systematic reorganization of the Scottish Church, establishing a parochial framework for the whole country, with clusters of parishes recog-nizing the central authority of an abbey (of one of several different kinds of Order), and an additional level of supervision in the shape of bishops estab-lished in cathedrals.

Of parallel and equal importance for Scotland, the feudal system was first brought in by David I and his successors, with its emphasis on hierarchies of (predominantly) military service extending downwards from the king through earls and barons and lesser landholders, each of whom had the right and the duty to erect a castle – initially wooden, on a mound or motte. The king was recognized as owning the land, and tracts of the land were conferred upon magnates such as earls or barons, vassals of the king, in return for their homage which they expressed not only formally in various elaborate ceremonies but practically, in military or knight service or in other forms of tribute. In turn, the major landholders – which included religious corporations such as abbeys – conferred smaller portions of territory upon lesser vassals in what was known as 'subinfeudation', where homage was made directly to the magnate and tribute was paid quite often in kind but sometimes in money. In the case of the religious corporations, individual parishes were in the position of vassals, and these made contributions to the upkeep of the abbeys and cathedrals. In this way a grid of mixed secular and religious institutions was imposed over the whole country, effectually subordinating and re-Christianizing the population.

During David I's reign and those of his immediate successors, Malcolm IV and William the Lion, it became customary for magnates possessing lands in Scotland under the king to make extensive provision for the maintenance of the Church in their territories. A blend of obligation and looked-for prestige induced the great feudal landowners to establish abbeys in particular, each with its own set of parishes, and in addition to donate large extents of tributary land and property directly to the abbey. To these reforms we owe the abbeys at Paisley, Kilwinning, Crossraguel, Dumfries ('Sweetheart Abbey'), Dundrennan and many others.

Inheritance and identity

Feudalism also favoured the rule of primogeniture, the succession of the eldest son, as against the ancient Celtic tradition of 'tanistry', whereby the successor to a king or leader was often chosen from a circle of relatives (brothers, uncles, cousins) within the extended family.

This was a fundamental constitutional change, not only affecting the law of inheritance but penetrating to the life of the people, their culture, even their recognition of identity: during this period, a general change in naming customs is noticeable, and many recognizable Scottish family names begin to emerge. Previously, individuals had been distinguished by patronymics, e.g. Somerled had been mac Gillebride, 'Gillebride's son', and Dugall had been mac Somerled, 'Somerled's son'. But the son of Ragnvald's son Donald was mac Donald, and succeeding generations transmitted this name from father to son as a surname irrespective of the father's given name: they became the MacDonald Lords of the Isles. Dugall's son became mac Dugall, and the MacDougall lords, together with another emergent clan, the Campbells, became rivals of the MacDonalds for the lordship of the isles.

Gradually the Scottish kings broke up the old system of landholding in areas such as David's former appanage of Strathclyde, and the Lothians. In order to implement the feudalization of Scotland, David I and his successors brought in actual feudal magnates, Norman–French associates of David from the English court, as well as second-generation settlers from Wales and the English regions, and other adventurers. Names which were Norman French or Flemish in origin and quite different from native Scottish 'mac' names – Brus (Bruce), Montgomery, Comyn (Cumming), Lockhart and others – now made their appearance in Scotland for the first time.

Transfer of allegiance

Poised as it were between tanistry and feudal succession, Somerled effectively held the Kingship of the Isles. He had three sons, Dugall ('black stranger' = Dane), Ragnvald (Reginald or Ranald), and Angus; rather than leave the whole of his realm to a tanist, he decided to make a King-Lear-like division: to Dugall, the eldest son, he left Argyll and some of the islands, to Ragnvald, the second son, he left Islay and Kintyre, and to Angus, the youngest, he left Bute. These arrangements took effect after Somerled himself was decapitated under mysterious circumstances during a renewed skirmish with King Malcolm's men on the upper Clyde in 1164. Angus and Ragnvald could not agree about who was to have Arran, and in the ensuing struggle Angus and his sons were killed. Ragnvald attained the rank of King of Kintyre and Arran and other small territories – in effect the equivalent of a Scottish earl, with an earl's rights and duties. Thus, even though still formally a member of the Norwegian empire, he decided to 'join the [Scottish earls'] club' by founding an abbey at

Saddell in Kintyre.[1] To this foundation he gave wealthy property at Shiskine in western Arran, an indication of an effective controlling interest in Arran.

Ragnvald may also have refurbished the monastic institution at the north end of Holy Island (if it had been there previously). Perhaps this was a hospice for pilgrims to St Molaise's cave rather than a full-blown monastery.

However, it was a direct representative of the new order, Alexander, the Steward of Scotland, who in 1210 gave the first sign that Arran would move decisively away from the Norse-Celtic empire of the Isles towards close integration with feudal Scotland: Alexander married a grand-daughter of the slain Angus, who was heiress to Bute and probably Arran, and thereby obtained a first foothold in Arran for the Stewart family. (The Norman colonizers also changed their naming customs: Alexander, son of Walter, was indeed FitzWalter ('Fitz-' = Fils, son) but the style (or even 'job description') supplanted the French patronymic as a family surname: Alexander the Steward became Alexander Stewart. Another example is Camerarius, 'chamberlain', which became the surname 'Chalmers'.)

The marriage of Alexander Stewart did not indicate instant feudalization for Arran, which remained nominally under Nordic control until 1266, three years after the Battle of Largs (see below). No motte or bailey has so far been discovered in Arran, unless Brodick Castle conceals underlying Norman earthworks on its knoll.[2] The earliest known parts of Brodick Castle have been dated to the cusp of the thirteenth and fourteenth centuries, i.e. during the period of the Wars of Independence, and the great time of motte-building is about a century earlier.

The Battle of Largs

Minor disputes and quarrels between the islands and various western coastal locations were eclipsed in the thirteenth century by the conflict which arose between Norway and the developing state of Alba, now to be known as Scotia or Scotland. Power had been ebbing away from Norway for a long time. The Norwegian possessions on the Northern mainland – Caithness, Sutherland, Ross – were absorbed into Scotia with relative ease, and King William the Lion had checkmated a threat by the Gall-Ghaideal descendants of Fergus of Galloway to extend their control in south-west Scotland: he had planted a castle ('opidum') at the mouth of the River Ayr in 1197, strategically between two blocks of Galloway-leaning territory (Cuninghame to the north, Carrick to the south). He later chartered a Royal Burgh in Ayr, the first in the west, with steadily increasing shrieval power over both Cuninghame and Carrick.

Norway, however, wished to restore its suzerainty over the Northern and Western Isles of Scotland, and the history of the middle years of the Scottish thirteenth century is that of the struggle between one man, King Håkon IV of Norway, and the second and third Alexanders, sovereigns of Scotland after William the Lion, about the Western Islands.

The first phase of the struggle began in 1230, when a grandson of Somerled, Uspak, who preferred King Håkon's authority to that of Alexander II, was despatched at the head of a battle-fleet to reassert Norwegian power in the Northern and Western Isles. This attempt was relatively successful: the Norwegians captured the stone castle at Rothesay and occupied Bute, as well as repeatedly raiding Kintyre – suggesting that Scottish authority was already established there.

Uspak died, and his fleet returned home in only qualified triumph. Attempts at a financial settlement, offering to buy the islands from Norway, broke down, and the situation festered until the late 1240s, when King Alexander II decided to take the islands by force. However, the King died in Oban in 1249 while marshalling his forces, and the situation remained unresolved for nearly fifteen years.

In 1263 King Håkon, by now an aged man, having restored Norwegian control in Iceland the year before, made up his mind to give the Scottish islands the same treatment. He sailed down to the west gathering a considerable fleet on the way, including ships from Man and most of the western territories; Argyll's leader, King Ewen, decided not to break his previously given oath of allegiance to the King of Scots, preferring simply to give up his kingdom.

Down they went to the Mull of Kintyre and eastward into the Firth of Clyde, where they anchored in Lamlash Bay, which happened to be – and still is – an excellent 'roadstead' for the gathering of large fleets, sheltered by Holy Island off the east coast of Arran. A fair amount of pillage and slaughter ensued, though perhaps not in Arran itself. Alexander III hastened to the castle at New Ayr ('Novar'), where he held urgent talks with Norwegian emissaries under truce. The Scots begged at least for the Clyde islands – Arran, Bute and the

Cumbraes – to be transferred to Scottish sovereignty, and held out for this, but Håkon was having none of it. He suspected the Scots of playing for time, in view of the anticipated autumn gales (it was late September).

Håkon suspended the truce, brought the fleet to the Cumbrae islands off the Ayrshire coast, and, to drive home the point, sent a raiding party up to Loch Lomond and the Lennox area to devastate the countryside. However the Scottish temporizing paid off and, on 1 October 1263, a formidable gale descended upon the Norwegian ships, some of which dragged their anchors. Several beached on the shore at Largs, among them a merchant ship full of stores for the fleet. The local Scottish defence force came down to shore to loot the cargo, and the Norwegians, including Håkon himself, descended in their turn and drove them off. The ship was nearly emptied when Scottish reinforcements arrived. The Norwegians evacuated their King immediately and for a full day (Wednesday, 3 October) they held out against what seems to have been a superior force. The weather was atrocious, and prevented a relief force from landing. At length, however, the wind slackened and the Norwegians were able to re-embark and get back to the fleet, which sailed back to Lamlash in Arran. Such was the Battle of Largs. Håkon IV died in Orkney two months later, on 16 December 1263. His failing health may have had something to do with the inconclusive nature of the battle: the old man was unwilling, it is said, to see people getting hurt.

It was not a decisive action, and neither side was fully engaged, but it was a turning point in the history of Scotland. After Largs, Norwegian suzerainty over the Western Isles of Scotland was non-existent, and was formally brought to an end by the Treaty of Perth in 1266.

Vigleikr

As we have seen, a religious community of some sort is reputed to have existed on Holy Isle, the spectacular volcanic rock opposite Lamlash. It was probably founded many centuries after the time of St Molaise (see chapter 6), and its precise nature is in some doubt, but reports of its existence come from both the twelfth and the fourteenth centuries. All traces on the ground were thought to have vanished, but recently an extent of masonry built against the cliff at the north-west end of the island has been identified as part of an old, possibly religious, building; however no further investigation has been undertaken so far.

Covering both ceiling and rear wall of the existing St Molaise's cave are a dense collection of carved crosses and inscriptions, some of the latter runic.

The crosses are not likely to date back to St Molaise's time (seventh century) but by their design appear to be no earlier than about AD 1200, i.e. during the period including the Battle of Largs. While the Norwegian fleet was at anchor in Lamlash Bay in 1263 before that battle, some Norwegians apparently landed on Holy Island and made their way to St Molaise's Cave. One or two of them carved their names in runic lettering in the cave, and they may be read (with some difficulty) to this day – for instance:

(1) *(+ n)[ik]ul[os] [*] [ahæni]+ ræist = Nikolas a Hæni reist,* 'Nikulos of Hæn carved [these runes].'

(2) *uiklæikr s*allariræisst = Vigleikr stallari reist,* 'Vigleikr the king's [horse-] marshal carved [these runes]'.

The Vigleikr who carved the second inscription was probably Vigleikr Prestsson, one of the leaders of the 1263 expedition.[3] These inscriptions provide that rarest of archaeological coincidences, evidence on the ground confirming written historical records.

9.   Arran in Bruce's Wars

Who controlled Arran after 1266?

The question of land ownership of and within Arran now arises. Since the coming of the feudal system the Norman-Scottish Stewart family and others had been hovering vulture-like over the dying Norwegian empire in the Clyde region: the Bisset (Bysset) family in particular appears to have had a shadowy connection with Arran, when the island was still formally Norwegian before Largs, and continuing up to and including the War of (Scottish) Independence.

The Bissets were both powerful and treacherous. In 1242 they were suspected of the murder of Patrick, the Earl (designate?) of Atholl, slain probably because he stood in line to inherit the extensive western possessions once held by Alan Lord of Galloway. These may have included some kind of a right to Arran or to lands within Arran. The killing itself was a mysterious affair, worthy of Agatha Christie: the house in Haddington in which it occurred was burnt down, probably in an attempt to conceal the fact that the victim had been murdered in his bed.

No-one has succeeded in unravelling the mystery completely, but suspicion fell upon two Bissets in particular, Walter and his nephew John, who was also the cousin of Patrick of Atholl. John Bisset fled, an act seeming to admit guilt. By October 1242 he had obtained a fief in Ireland in exchange for service in France to Henry III of England, thus perhaps bypassing the Scottish inheritance arrangements and at least gaining an Irish base for his operations. His uncle, Walter Bisset, exiled from Scotland, eventually turned up in England, where for five years he privily reported to King Henry III on the negotiations between Scotland and Louis XI of France.[1]

In 1248 we find Walter fortifying Dunaverty on the Mull of Kintyre, opposite Arran and also opposite the Bisset island of Rathlin off the coast of Northern Ireland. But a representative of the Galloway dynasty, Alan, illegitimate son of Thomas of Galloway, took back Dunaverty the same year, 1248, and may have captured Walter Bisset. In 1251, in England, Walter Bisset is reported dead, when and how not known, 'For he died far off in Scotland, in a certain island called Arrane'.[2]

Then, nearly fifty years later, in 1298, during the early part of the Wars of Independence, after Edward I of England had defeated William Wallace at Falkirk and had come down to Ayr on the west coast opposite Arran, Thomas Bisset, nephew of Walter, offered Edward not only his own services but those of Arran. At that stage Edward I seemed likely to be a final victor in the war, and the Bissets cannily sought the favour of the winner. Arran's inhabitants had submitted to Thomas, who besought Edward to confirm the Bisset claim to Arran in perpetuity; Edward granted his petition. Later, in 1301, a Bisset fleet was patrolling the waters around Bute, and again in 1307, on the look-out for the fugitive King Robert the Bruce. That fleet may have been at least partially based in Arran, and in 1307 was operating in conjunction with John de Menteith, who had betrayed William Wallace to the English in 1305, and subsequently obtained possession of Arran.

The Great Cause of Scotland

At the end of the thirteenth century and the beginning of the fourteenth Scotland was plunged into a vortex of bloodshed and uncertainty caused in part by the failure of the very feudal system which David I and his successors had been at such pains to establish. In 1286, as the result of a riding accident, King Alexander III died and left no heir. The nearest likely descendant was an infant grand-daughter, Margaret, 'the Maid of Norway', the child of Alexander's daughter Margaret who had died after marrying King Erik II of Norway. Feudal institutions in Scotland had come to require the preparation of a 'tailzie', a structured plan of entailed descent: in 1284 such a plan had been prepared and agreed, recognising the Maid as Alexander's successor. By chance, however, King Alexander's second wife, Yolande, believed that she was pregnant, and any child born to her would take precedence over the Maid of Norway. No formal confirmation of the Maid as Queen of Scotland was immediately possible.

In the meantime a hornet's nest of claimants to the throne had been aroused, and the young parliament of Scotland appointed a committee of Guardians to protect the kingdom and to keep the peace. Among the Guardians were two Comyns, Alexander and John, and James the Steward (= 'Stewart'); excluded from the committee were two very powerful magnates, John Balliol and Robert Bruce of Annandale, each a claimant hostile to the other. In pre-feudal times, a 'tanist' might well have been chosen beforehand from among the Guardians or from the wider circle of claimants, some at least of whom were within the extended family of Alexander III. Such a solution, however, was impossible in 1286, and, in the circumstances, the Scots decided to appeal for what we might now call 'international arbitration', in this case the judgment of a senior monarch, Edward I of England.

This was the first of many gross blunders committed by the harassed and bewildered Scots. Edward, a great king in many respects, was intelligent, wily, violent, vindictive, patient, legalistic, aggressive, expansionist, opportunistic, energetic and as hard as nails. Moreover, back in 1174, King William I, 'the Lion' of Scotland, had been captured by Henry II in the course of a very ill-judged raid into England and, in the course of fast-talking his way out of an exceedingly embarrassing situation, had been obliged to swear fealty to the English King. Although various wriggling manoeuvres had been performed by William's successors, the hard fact remained: the Scots were legally and feudally vassals to the King of England. Now Edward I could not help but look on the Scots as targets for annexation. Yet the Scots, perhaps naively, applied to him rather than the Pope or any other prince to help them out of their difficulties.

There were many obstacles to the succession of the Maid of Norway, not least the rooted objection of some claimants to the succession to royal honours of any female. Procedures for the recognition of the Maid were cautiously organized, but the squabbling of the Guardians and of the other claimants continued apace. John Balliol was supported by the very powerful Comyn clan, and the Bruces (no less than three Robert Bruces, grandfather, father and son, carried the claim in succession) lost no time in making a secret treaty or 'band' between themselves, James the Steward, Richard de Burgh, Earl of Ulster, and others. Queen Yolande failed to produce an heir. Immediately civil war broke out between the Bruces and the Comyns, but for the time being the Guardians called out the 'host', an embryonic national army, and restored peace with some difficulty.

The question of the Maid of Norway was settled decisively in 1290 by the death of the child, a girl of six, en route to Britain. In the meantime, by a crafty series of legal manoeuvres, Edward I had contrived to wrong-foot the Scots, who were compelled willy-nilly to recognize him as their feudal superior, with the right of intervening in Scotland in return for his arbitration between the various claimants to the Scottish throne. In 1290 Edward had already made use of his overlordship to annex to England the Isle of Man, previously part of the Scottish kingdom. Apart from that, he had recently demonstrated his muscle by breaking Welsh independence once and for all, confirming his mastery by building a series of very strong castles in order to keep the Welsh down permanently. The Scots could see the writing on the wall: union with England was looming.

On the death of the Maid of Norway, the Bruce–Balliol rivalry erupted again. Civil war in Scotland threatened once more but there was no actual outbreak. The Bruces placed themselves under the protection of the English crown, and Edward proved his diplomatic skill by securing the handover of the main Scottish castles, including Edinburgh Castle, without shedding a drop of blood. He backed his moves with menacing military preparations south of the Border. All the claimants to the Scottish throne caved in, accepting Edward as the final adjudicator of their claim in his capacity as lord superior of Scotland. Finally, on 2 August 1291, the lawsuit or Great Cause of Scotland, determining the country's kingship, opened in Berwick. Sixteen months later, on 17 November 1292, after tortuous argumentation, John Balliol was adjudged King of Scotland and was enthroned at Scone, the traditional coronation site of Scotland. All accepted him as king except the Bruces, who retired muttering to their strongholds in Annan and Carrick.

King John opened his reign auspiciously enough, but it soon became apparent that he was no more than a puppet ruler at the beck and call of Edward, subject occasionally to humiliating treatment. The Scots became restive again and, in 1296, demonstrated their claim to independence by allying themselves with Philip IV of France, then at issue with Edward I; this was done under the unwilling leadership of King John, who soon had cause to repent: no sooner did the Scots summon their own army than Edward I attacked and sacked Berwick with awful atrocities, and Carlisle, under the governorship of none other than the senior Bruce, successfully resisted a weak attack by the Scots. Scots and English traded atrocities for some time, but in the end, after the Battle of Dunbar on 27 April 1296, English arms prevailed. On 2 July 1296 in Kincardine Castle, John Balliol earned himself the nickname of Toom Tabard ('Empty Surcoat') by being physically stripped of his royal regalia in a ceremonial demotion.

Robert the Bruce

After this episode it was indeed war to the knife. King Edward no longer sought to govern through a vassal king: when Robert Bruce the senior ventured to put forward his claim now that the Balliols had fallen, Edward replied, 'Have we nothing to do but win realms for you?' Scotland as a kingdom seemed to be at an end. Edward I imposed direct rule.

In 1297, however, a Scottish rising took place at Scone, in which William Wallace had a leading part, and when as a result the English justiciar Ormsby fled, a general revolt followed under the revived banner of King John Balliol. At this point Robert Bruce 'Junior', Earl of Carrick, son of the quondam Governor of Carlisle, and future King of Scotland, turned his coat, joining the insurgents including Wallace – but, after gathering their forces at Irvine in June 1297, they gave no fight. Bruce swapped sides again, fearing for his own landed estates and also unwilling to take part in fighting for Balliol, the rival of his family.

The Scottish coalition as a whole came to terms with Edward, but William Wallace was so disgusted that he withdrew from it and instead joined with a young nobleman from the north-east of Scotland named Andrew Moray, who was still in revolt. Together they rose in insurrection, gathered an army and in September 1297 inflicted a crushing defeat at Stirling Bridge upon the English forces under the Treasurer Hugh Cressingham, who was literally cut to pieces – which were distributed throughout the country as souvenirs; throughout his career William Wallace was capable of the most appalling atrocities. However, during the battle, Andrew Moray had been mortally wounded; Wallace, no doubt a species of hero but a strategic flounderer, was left in charge and was trounced in a set-piece battle at Falkirk in 1298.

Though he survived Falkirk, Wallace never regained the initiative and faded from the scene, continuing as a low-key brigand ultimately to be betrayed to the English and in his turn subjected to an atrocious death in London in 1305.

In the meantime, however, Edward I equally did not succeed in establishing permanent government in any but the south-east of the country – in Edinburgh, Roxburgh and Berwick; in the rest of Scotland the Guardians re-established control. They included both Robert Bruce, Earl of Carrick, and the 'Red Comyn', a long-time supporter of Balliol, hated by Bruce. Strains within the Committee of Guardians straightway showed themselves: on 19 August 1299 near Selkirk, a knife fight broke out, Bishop Lamberton came to blows with the Earl of Buchan, and the Red Comyn 'leapt upon the Earl of Carrick and seized him by the throat'.[3] Peace was restored by James the Steward and the other Guardians, but it is not surprising that by May 1300 Robert Bruce was no longer a member of the Committee and again came to terms with Edward I in 1302, clearly in the interests of retaining his estates as Earl of Carrick and in England. At that stage war had resumed between the Scots and the English in particular in south-west Scotland, where Bruce held much of his land.

In 1303, then, the English had two factors in their favour: Bruce was or seemed to be on their side, and the long-standing war with France was at an end. Edward, taking advantage of the situation from his redoubts in the south-east, struck northward, to areas such as Perth, and Kinloss Abbey in Moray, which had been reservoirs of Scottish resistance previously. This time the English had at least limited success, and the Scots came to terms once more, in effect bowing their necks to the English yoke.

Scotland, even as a part of the English kingdom, had to be governed, and in 1305 King Edward tried the expedient of 'power-sharing': in September, 10 Scotsmen and 21 Englishmen, under the aegis of the respective Parliaments, drafted a plan for the administration of the country. But the still-seething hostility between Bruce and the Comyns put an end to any dreams that Edward had of peaceful absorption of Scotland by England.

Bruce had been secretly laying plans to seize the Scottish crown for himself, and in order for these to succeed, the Comyn rivalry had to come to an end. In February 1306, in front of the high altar in the Dumfries Greyfriars Kirk, seemingly after an altercation, Bruce stabbed the Red Comyn, and someone else ran in to 'mak siccar'.

This murder may well have been unpremeditated, to judge by the reports of Bruce's own horrified reaction, but it provided an unrepeatable opportunity: it was now or never. With astonishing speed Bruce leapt to fortify and provision castles, including his own at Turnberry in Carrick, Dunaverty in Kintyre, and Loch Doon Castle; set in motion the mechanism of appealing for absolution for the murder; and had himself crowned King of Scotland at the coronation hill at Scone; all this in spite of the fulminations and threats that issued from Lanercost where Edward I, by that time lying mortally stricken with disease, had been both thunderstruck and enraged by the news of the murder.

In spite, however, of Bruce's display of virtuoso crisis management, organizing genius, and decisive action under pressure, his luck deserted him in June 1306, when his forces were overwhelmed outside Perth by Aymer de Valence, who was obeying King Edward's ferocious instructions to 'byrn and slay and rais dragoun'.[4] Bruce's men were cut to pieces or scattered, he experienced a sudden haemorrhage of allies, his womenfolk were captured and subjected to imprisonment under appalling conditions in some cases lasting for years; Bruce himself escaped by the merest whisker and spent many months on the run, hiding in locations that have yet to be identified.

Bruce and Arran

During the Bruce wars Arran was a halfway house between Ireland and the Scottish mainland, and was useful as a depot for the commissariat of King Edward's armies. Provisions were brought in large quantities from Ireland during the 1301 campaigns to an unidentified Arran port (probably Brodick), and sent on from there to Glasgow.

When Bruce disappeared so completely after the Battle of Perth in 1306, he is vaguely rumoured to have visited Norway and Orkney among other places. In the early part of 1307 he seems to have turned up in Rathlin Island off the coast of Northern Ireland within sight of Kintyre. The island is said to have been a Bisset stronghold, but this does not appear to have deterred Robert Bruce, who, according to the poet John Barbour, easily secured the submission of Rathlin's inhabitants.[5]

According to Barbour's great poem, 'The Bruce', it was while sojourning in Rathlin that one of Bruce's companions, Sir Robert Boyd, was approached by James Douglas, who proposed a surprise attack on Brodick Castle in Arran.

Barbour's account of the ensuing adventure is as follows. Boyd and Douglas and their party reached Kintyre and then at nightfall rowed across to (the west coast of) Arran, where they hid their 'galay' and marched through the night to a concealed position on the east of the island near the castle, which was occupied by Sir John de Hastings and his men. As dawn broke the men in ambush saw English soldiers unloading provisions and arms from three boats which had arrived in Brodick Bay the night before. The Scots broke ambush and came down upon the soldiers without warning, terrifying them and killing about forty men. A further show of force made the remaining English garrison retreat and bar the entrance to the castle. In the meantime the provision boats had put to sea but two of the three were sunk in very rough water. James Douglas and his party retrieved food, arms and clothes, and retired well pleased with themselves to a strong point, perhaps one of the old Iron Age forts in the neighbourhood.

After ten days, Robert Bruce himself, accompanied by 'thretty small galayis and thre', landed in Arran and lurked for a while in a small '['ferm]-toune', a collection of dwellings and outhouses forming the headquarters of a communal 'runrig' farm. He 'speryt syne specially

> Gyff ony man couth tell tithand
> Off ony strang man in that land'

– 'were there any strangers in the locality?'
   'Why, yes,' said a woman – 'Schir perfay

> Off strang men I kan you say
> That ar cummyn in this countre,
> And schort quile syne throu thar bounte
> Thai haff discomfyt our wardane
> And mony off his men has slane . . .'

– 'the strangers have alarmed our warden and killed many of his men.'

The woman was then persuaded to lead King Robert to the strongpoint where she had seen the strangers, but the site was deserted. Robert 'wound his horn' in the traditional Robin Hood manner, commanded his men to hide, and then wound it again. Not far away 'James off Douglas herd him blaw

> And he the blast alsone gan knaw
> And said, "Sothly yon is the king.
> I knaw lang quhill sine his blawing."
> The thrid tym thar-with-all he blew
> And then Schir Robert Boid it knew
> And said, "Yone is the king but dreid
> Ga we furth till him better speid." '
>
> (Barbour, 173–5)

So the two parties met, possibly in the Lamlash or Whiting Bay area, and King Robert started to lay plans. His objective was to get back to his own lands, to his earldom of Carrick; Turnberry Castle, the principal military strongpoint in the region and Bruce's home base, lies on the other side of the Clyde estuary, about twenty kilometres south-east of Holy Island, and Robert sent across one Cuthbert, a native of the area, to spy out the land. If all was clear, Cuthbert was to light a bonfire as a signal and Bruce was to cross the Firth of Clyde with his cohorts and land at Turnberry. Cuthbert departed and Bruce gathered his forces. When Cuthbert arrived in Carrick, however, he found Turnberry Castle heavily garrisoned with English soldiers and a new Earl of Carrick in possession, Percy, an appointee of King Edward I. Cuthbert did not think it wise to light the fire and remained lurking. However some fishermen lit a bonfire like the intended signal, and King Robert duly came across leading his men.

When Bruce landed on Turnberry shore, Cuthbert ran down as it were waving his hands and attempted to dissuade Robert from further adventure: the place was swarming with English. But King Robert decided that, having brought his men across the water, nothing was going to make him withdraw them again, and instead ordered them to fall on. Many of Percy's garrison had been billeted out in the local village and were sleeping when the king's soldiers burst in on them and slaughtered them without mercy. The men in Turnberry

Castle were so startled and terrified that they barred the doors and sent to Ayr further up the coast for urgent assistance.

Whether the Turnberry garrison ever received any succour is uncertain, just as the ultimate fate of the Hastings garrison in Brodick is wrapped in mystery. It seems that Bruce spent some time simply calming the people of Carrick themselves, for they too had been scared out of their wits by the sudden invasion, and King Robert was not exactly renowned for avoidance of 'collateral damage'. But King Edward I died in early 1307 and under the new king, Edward II, the enterprise against Scotland lost much of its aggressive edge. After seven more years of patient, often guerrilla-style, warfare, Bruce triumphed at Bannockburn and ultimately came into his own.

This narrative is largely based on the poetry of John Barbour, whose epic 'The Bruce', although written about seventy years later than the events it describes, has been accepted as a reasonably reliable account of the War of Independence. But several important details are disputed, including the involvement of Arran itself. It has been suggested that it would have been much more convenient for Bruce to have crossed direct from Kintyre, and that his meeting with Douglas in Arran has been invented.[6] From my own observation I doubt whether even a large shore-line fire at Turnberry would have been visible from Bruce's traditional embarkation site at King's Cross Point (the site of an Iron Age fort and a Viking boat-grave between Lamlash and Whiting Bay), although I am told that it would have been. A. A. M. Duncan's doubts about Rathlin Island have been referred to in reference note 5 for this chapter.

There is, of course, the legendary spider whose indefatigable efforts to spin its web – 'Try, try, and try again' – inspired a despairing Bruce to yet another attempt to win back his kingdom. Some versions of this tale (which does not occur in Barbour) place it in the King's Cave on the west side of Arran north of Drumadoon Cliff. This is rather a dreich spot, where Bruce could indeed have shared accommodation with a spider or, come to that, several spiders. But the deep gloom suggested for Bruce by the story hardly goes with the exhilaration and tension of his brief springboard visit to Arran, if it took place. The King's Cave – a name dating only from the eighteenth century – is more interesting for the ancient carvings that adorn its walls (see p. 53).

Ownership under the Bruces

Bruce gained the kingship in 1306, although he had to fight for it for many years afterwards. Possession of Arran, both as a unit and broken up into smaller properties, became very complicated, depending upon an intricate political game of patronage. All took place within the framework of feudalism, whereby, as explained above, the king was deemed to own the whole land including the island of Arran, but gave away portions of it to local or national magnates who became landowners in their own right under the king – a rather ambiguous relationship. Confusion was heightened by the misfortunes of the kingship – a lengthy succession of incompetent, weak, wicked, under-age, or simply unlucky monarchs.

Before Håkon IV's departure after the Battle of Largs, he gave the rule of Arran to a man called Murchard or Margad, who may be the progenitor of the Murchies, a name still known in Arran. However, this was an empty gift, and it is likely, as we have seen, that the Bissets were already established and pre-dominant in Arran before 1263. That their ownership was at least contested may be inferred from Thomas Bisset's plea in 1298 to Edward I for confirma-tion of Bisset ownership in perpetuity. But Alexander Stewart had established some sort of a claim to Arran following his marriage in 1210 to a grand-daughter of Angus mac Somerled, who had been killed during a dispute with his brother Ragnvald. After this marriage there was an interlude involving the Comyn family in partial ownership of Arran, but by another marriage the whole territory was reunited under a cadet branch of the Stewarts. This branch received the earldom of Menteith and the Islands. The Menteith Stewarts may have been responsible for the construction of Brodick Castle.

By 1307 Edward I, acting as ruler of Scotland, had granted the earldom of Menteith and the Islands to Sir John de Hastings, one of the unsuccessful claimants to the Scottish throne in the Great Cause of Scotland in 1291–92; at the time when Robert Bruce was being hunted in the Clyde area, it was Hastings who was occupying Brodick Castle. But, of course, the Hastings ownership fell after Bruce's triumph, and the Bissets vanished from the scene.

Possession of Arran should probably have reverted to Angus Og MacDonald, a descendant of Somerled, but instead Bruce regranted Knapdale and Kintyre to the Stewarts as a reward for their services, and the Menteith branch of that family took back Knapdale and Arran in particular. After 1309 the new owner of Arran, the younger brother of the Earl of Menteith, was none other than Sir John Stewart of Menteith, who betrayed William Wallace to Edward I in 1305, and who had been operating a fleet for the English in the Clyde estuary in 1301 and 1307 together with Hugh Bisset. His son, also Sir John, became the first Lord of Arran and Knapdale. And apparently it was a third Sir John Menteith, as Lord of Arran and Knapdale, who granted 'penny-lands' at Clachland, Kilbride and (Kin)Lochranza, all in Arran, to Gillespie Campbell of Lochawe. However, after 1357 the line of the Menteith Stewarts failed, and the head of the senior branch of the Stewarts, Robert the Steward (later King Robert II), 'repossessed' Arran and Knapdale before 1371 (the date of his inauguration as King of Scotland). The Menteith line – then represented by Sir Thomas Erskine and his successors – was compensated for the loss of Arran by annual payments of £100 drawn on rents and fisheries of the Burgh of Aberdeen, as arranged by Robert II. These payments continued for nearly two hundred years, from 1387 until 1582. The compensation may have been arranged or unofficial before 1387, and Robert, still only Steward of Scotland, may have been in possession of Arran, also before 1371, since he was in a position before that date to make a grant of land at Knightsland (between Kildonan and Levencorroch in the south of Arran) to Sir Adam de Foulartoune.

In 1391 Robert's son John, now King Robert III, granted Strathwhillan ('Erqwhonne') to Fergus of Foulartoune of Arran, and in 1400 Kilmichael to the son of Fergus. The Fullarton family play a significant part in the subsequent history of Arran, if slavishly subordinate to the Stewarts.

Church affairs

It is from the late thirteenth and early fourteenth centuries that the church arrangements in Arran begin to come into focus, with the Menteiths as agents of change. During the early period of the Wars of Independence, perhaps about 1294,[7] a 'Sir Maurice'[8] is mentioned as the vicar – a substitute for a parson – of what may have been a single parish covering the whole of the island of Arran. Later, in 1326, during the reign of Robert I, 'Sir Benedict' was still 'rector of the [one] Church of Arram [sic]'. In 1337, however, the last

Sir John de Menteith granted the two churches of Arran, of St Mary and St Brigid, together with their parishes, to Kilwinning Abbey, of which he was a patron. The grant, 'in perpetuity', was confirmed by David II in 1357,[9] and later by Robert III, but in 1503 (half a century before the Reformation) the 'advowson' (patronage) of these two parishes was included in the grant of the lands of Arran to the Hamiltons.

The modern village of Lamlash includes the original parish church, now in ruins, of Kilbride Parish near the ancient farm of Margnaheglish at the north end of the village. Standing in the present graveyard, the church can be seen to have had arched doorways and windows, but it is roofless and in a very ruinous state. It is likely to be the remnant of the original fourteenth-century building. Various relics have been recovered and some of them have been lost, but a mediaeval grave-slab is attached to the east wall, and a cross with a crucifixion, probably dating from the sixteenth century, was found east of the church and now stands in front of the present parish church.

It is possible that the change-over from one to two parishes in Arran took place as a result of King Edward I's annexation in 1290 of the Isle of Man to England, which broke the former Norse connection of Man with the Scottish Western Islands – the Nidaros-based bishopric of Sodor and Man. It would be natural for a Bruce/Stewart religious ascendancy to reconnect Arran, one of these isles, with a mainland Scottish abbey. As Mackenzie states, 'The line of division is significant [between the two parishes, Lochranza to Dippin, one parish church in the centre of the island at Kilbride, and the other at Kilmory in the south]':[10] the best means of communication was by water, avoiding the difficult mountain passes.

It is of some interest to note the fierce competition for office and income and also the standards of conduct shown up in the surviving records of one of these parishes. In the fourteenth and fifteenth centuries the income of Kilmory Parish was good, at £18–20 per year, and consequently much sought after. In 1357, the rector of St Mary (Kilmory) was one 'Bean' and before 1391 the office was held by another of the same name, Beanus Johannis (Bean Johnson or MacIan). It appears that on Beanus Johannis's promotion to archdeacon, prolonged and unseemly squabbling ensued, clearly about the stipends payable to the Kilmory rector, and revealing that most of the would-be successors to the vacancy had fathered or were themselves natural children, had not been ordained priest or had at some point had 'unbecoming relations with his housekeeper' (*cum quadam sua comatre concubuit*). At length, perhaps about 1407, a certain Duncan MacBean, almost certainly the son of the Bean MacIan mentioned above, comes briefly into view and then vanishes. The place remained vacant for a long time, during which the income from it could be drawn by the local patron, until in accordance with normal practice the living lapsed to the Pope. Finally, in 1433, when an instruction arrived from the Apostolic See directing the assignation of Maurice MacNeill to Kilmory, it was discovered that during this period one Dugald M'Molmicheyl had been illegally in possession of the parish and had to be removed. The name M'Molmicheyl means 'son of the slave ["tonsured one"] of Michael'.[11]

Administration in Arran

When at last King Robert the Bruce was relatively secure on his throne, he seems to have crossed to Arran several times for relaxation, probably hunting. A payment was made to the crew of a yacht for conveying the king to Arran in 1326.[12] Local traditions state that Bruce rewarded various families for their support during his visit, but no grants of land or anything else to Arran people are recorded for his reign.

Already after 1266 a Scottish administrative framework had begun to appear for the governance of Arran. Under King John Balliol some effort had been put forward with regard to the establishment of new sheriffdoms in the west, probably covering Arran as well as other areas. As a result of this legislation, James (the) Stewart was designated Sheriff of Kintyre and in all likelihood of Arran too. To attempt to extend royal control to the west of Scotland was both necessary and brave but, like all King John's endeavours, doomed to failure because of the crushing effect of King Edward's micromanagement. We have no record of any law-suits or actions concerning Arran during King John's short reign.

A sheriff was the king's man for a given locality, with responsibility for collecting taxes and tributes in kind, regulating trade, keeping the king's peace and administering justice. A depute sheriff might be appointed for a discrete territory like Arran within a wider administrative unit – in this case the Sheriffdom of Bute. Also in Arran there was a subordinate officer known as the coroner or crowner, whose functions were quite distinct from those of a modern English coroner: he had responsibility for the direct collection of taxes, with powers of enforcement; if anybody refused or was unable to pay he could summon the assistance of neighbours of the defaulter, and could set up the crowner's staff outside the affected property.[13] It has been suggested that in the case of Arran the crowner's tasks might originally have included quelling disobedience to the Norman masters on the part of the indigenous population, and keeping a weather eye open for warlike incursions from the isles or elsewhere. It appears that the Fullartons, hand in glove with the Stewarts, were holders of the office of crowner, which became hereditary.

OS References

Ownership under the Bruces
Strathwhillan or Erqwhonne NS 024 355
Kilmichael NS 002 350

Church affairs
Margnaheglish NS 033 323

10. Arran under the Stewart Dynasty

The continuing wars

The line of the first King Robert failed after the turbulent reign of his son David II. The Scottish kingship passed to the Stewart family via the marriage of Robert's daughter Marjory to Walter the Steward's son, which produced a son called Robert in 1316 at the same time as the death of Marjory: that Robert became King Robert II in 1371, in line with the provisions of the kingship's 'tailzies' drawn up in 1315 and 1326. This, and the splitting up of the Stewart family into several lines distinct from the royal stem, is a major factor in the subsequent history of Arran. No later than 1385 'Black John Stewart', an illegitimate son of Robert II, became the Sheriff of Bute, of which Arran was styled a 'bailiary': the lands of Corrygills in Arran belonged to the Sheriff of Bute. The Bailie of Arran, the 'Sheriff-depute' installed in Brodick Castle, was also normally a Stewart. Another illegitimate son, this time of Robert III, was John Stewart of Ardgowan, who in 1406 was granted lands including Kildonan Castle (perhaps at one time a stronghold of the MacDonald Lords of the Isles); he may also have had at least temporarily the Shiskine lands originally belonging to Saddell Abbey in Kintyre. Thus parts of Arran fell under the bar sinister of the Stewarts, who developed their own hereditary successions, while the remainder of the island in large part remained specifically Crown land.

For this reason the whole of Arran, in a vulnerable position on the western fringes, became a target for the Crown's enemies.[1] These included England, still hungry for domination of Scotland. Already in 1335, during the second

War of Independence, while Robert Stewart was still only the Steward of Scotland, trying to sustain government in the absence of his king, a host of 1500 men in fifty ships from Ireland fell upon his lands in Bute and Arran at the command of Edward III of England, and Stewart came promptly to terms.[2]

Brodick Castle was the subject of repeated destructive attacks, not only after the capture and imprisonment by the English of the young King James I of Scotland in 1406, but also from the descendants of Somerled, who felt that they had been cheated of their patrimony, and acted accordingly. Angus Og MacDonald's son, 'good John of Islay', who had married Robert Stewart's daughter Margaret, was made the first Lord of the Isles by his father-in-law when the latter became king in 1371, but this did not produce the required pacification.

Open hostilities between Scotland and England dragged on for more than 150 years after Bannockburn. Meanwhile the leadership of the nation tottered to such an extent that its survival must have seemed miraculous. David II, five years old when the first King Robert died in 1329, had to flee into exile in 1334, and all the gains won by his father were reversed; Edward Balliol, son of 'Toom Tabard', was a powerful man backed by the new and energetic English king Edward III: after taking the Bruce loyalists off guard at Dupplin he was actually crowned king of Scotland at Scone in 1332; Edward III of England then defeated the Bruce loyalists at the Battle of Halidon Hill in 1333 – but the struggle was indecisive, with first one side and then the other claiming temporary victory. In 1341 King David came back from France, seventeen years old, and began a period of personal rule – but was captured by the English in 1346 after a disastrous battle at Neville's Cross, and endured eleven years of imprisonment before being ransomed for the enormous sum of 100,000 marks in 1357. Three years previously Edward Balliol, worn down by more than twenty years of continuous warfare, had handed Edward III a lump of Scottish soil at Roxburgh, signifying that he was finally resigning his claim to the Scottish crown. On the other hand David, freed at last, proved a relatively good, even energetic ruler. Alas, he died unexpectedly and childless in 1371. Robert the Steward then became King as Robert II, the first Stewart ruler of Scotland.

An ill-starred dynasty

The Stewarts were, even for their times, an unusually unlucky set of royals, which makes it remarkable that they survived as monarchs at all: concentrated, almost uninterrupted disaster was to dog their footsteps for more than three centuries. Robert II, who inherited the throne at the age of fifty-five, was feeble and timid, and soon became a shadow monarch, delegating his authority to successive cabals of haughty magnates; his son John, crowned as Robert III in 1390, was even feebler and became a mere figurehead, on his deathbed in 1406 cursing the day he had been born – 'the worst of kings and the most wretched of men in the whole realm'. Just before he died, news had been brought to him that his twelve-year-old son, succeeding him as James I, had been captured by the English, to spend the next eighteen years languishing in the Tower of London.

James I, ultimately released in 1424, started as a vigorous and cleansing ruler but became arbitrary and tyrannous, made enemies and was horribly assassinated in 1437. Scotland suffered another prolonged minority and period of regency, until James II, a boy of six when crowned, grew up into a sinister and violent man. He had powerful examples to follow. Since his earliest days he was surrounded by ceaseless intrigue and murderous strife; his mother had to flee Edinburgh Castle with him in secret, and in 1439 he was abducted by the Chancellor of Scotland, William Crichton, in the furtherance of a power struggle between magnates; Crichton, a major influence in James's early life, perceived a danger to his plans in the young Earl of Douglas, invited him and his brother to Edinburgh Castle on 24 November 1440, and gave them a good dinner; then, at the end of the meal, Chancellor Crichton placed a bull's head on the table, 'quhilk was ane signe and taikin of condemnatour to the death'.[3] Both the Douglases were summarily beheaded.

Such was the atmosphere in which King James grew up. Twelve years after the Black Dinner another Earl of Douglas, Earl William, was openly murdered by James II in front of his own courtiers, who enthusiastically helped him finish the victim off. Besides such villainy in high places, Scotland had to contend with the plague, papal schism and unremitting English hostility. Even after Bishop Kennedy's skilful diplomatic and military manoeuvring during the reigns of James II and James III, which proved decisive in settling the issue of Scottish independence, warfare between the two countries erupted time and again right into the sixteenth century; the 1500s opened with the disastrous Battle of Flodden and continued under the English King Henry VIII with the 'Rough Wooing'.

In all these hostilities Arran was involved, more often than not as a pawn in the complicated three-cornered game played out between England, Scotland and the semi-independent Lords of the Isles.

Arran: rent structure under the Stewarts

The ownership of the land in Arran was complex in structure. Overall there was a chief landlord, usually the representative of a great family such as the Stewarts. He would determine the divisions of his land according to their money rent – merklands, pennylands, farthinglands and so on – or rent in kind ('grassum'); as mentioned earlier, in Arran the place-name Feorline occurs, and this comes through Gaelic feóirling from the Norse fjorðing, 'farthing', based upon the Viking rental of a quarter of a penny, eighteen or twenty pennies making up an ounce of silver.

Having once decided on an appropriate value for a given portion of land, the landlord would fix it as a permanent rent or firma, and the person who took on the responsibility of paying a firma as a rentaller or tenant was known by the Latin term firmarius, whence the word farmer. It should be noted that what we now call a 'farmer', an individual who farms land, is different from the original meaning of one who pays a fixed rental for anything. Mediaeval farmers or husbandmen often did not work the land at all but simply collected the rent from the basic peasant, the labourer who sowed the crops and tended the cattle.

Tenants as such were formally rather different from rentallers: the latter, sometimes also known as kindly tenants, held the farms as life-renters on easier terms, transmitting the property directly from hand to hand by hereditary or similar means of succession. Later (under James IV in 1506), rentallers in Bute were transformed by Act of Parliament into actual landlords who paid feu-duty rather than rent, and they locally acquired the title, though not the full status, of barons.[4]

From about the middle of the fifteenth century we begin to have records of tenancies and rents of the royal holdings in Arran. None of the rents are in money and the produce from which the 'grassums', the rents in kind, are derived is insignificant. This tells its own tale. From 1406 onward and probably from long before, Arran had been subjected to repeated batterings including destruction of crops and property, cattle-rustling and regular assaults on Brodick and other castles.

Grassums for Arran, set at Martinmas, were paid in fixed quantities of barley or in the proportion of one mart (head of cattle) to every five merks (1 mark=13s 4d) of money rent. Earlier, no later than the reign of Robert I Bruce, there may have been a payment in swine. The cattle, very small and meagre, were landed at Arnele (Portincross) and driven at royal expense to Stirling. There was also a proportion of grassum rent paid in salted fish, whiting (whence the Arran place-name Whiting Bay). In the fifteenth century there were no sheep in Arran and no wool, and under the conditions of a general wool impost dating from the time of David II the Arran people had to contribute extra barley and cattle to make up the deficit – under penalty of having to entertain the king and his court during his 'peregrinations' throughout the kingdom. Since no royal visit is recorded during the period, we can conclude that Arran met its obligations or was excused.

These rents, fixed and non-competitive, largely persisted throughout the fifteenth century. For any given year in the half-century recorded in the Exchequer Rolls, the value of Arran, taking into account only about 35 royal holdings, was 85 merks in money (£980 today) and in kind 17 marts and 3 chalders 1 boll 2 firlots of barley, i.e. altogether 104 merks (£1,218 today), as contrasted with the contemporary rental for Bute of 214 merks in money (£2,485 today) and in kind 40 marts and 11 chalders 15 bolls of barley. This difference indicates a brutal reality: Arran was subjected throughout the fifteenth century to repeated attacks and scorched-earth devastation from the west. Bute is in close proximity to the protective mainland, whereas the west coast of Arran, with most of the good agricultural land, faces the hostile territory of Kintyre just across the Kilbrannan Sound.

The tribulations of fifteenth-century Arran

During the anarchic period of the minority of King James II and later, the MacDonald Lords of the Isles, who were now also Earls of Ross, were associated with the turbulent Douglas barons and their friends – and the Kintyre MacAlisters. To these families must be attributed the attacks and losses on Arran inflicted by 'cursed invaders from Knapdale and Kintyre' and recorded for the years 1444 to 1447. The exchequer authorities had no option but to grant 'abatements' in rent for the year July 1445–1446 totalling 76 merks out of the rental of 86 merks in respect of more than thirty properties besides barley and marts for the whole island. But this represents no more than a fraction of the loss and desolation that Arran suffered during the whole period, extending from 1437 into the 1460s.

One resident of Arran, the first ordinary individual whose name we have and whose story we can surmise, was Ranald MacAlister ('Reginald MacAlexander'), the 'farmer' who, in spite of his name, was opposed to the MacAlisters of Knapdale, and who leased nine holdings in the north-west of the island from Lochranza to Machrie Bay. The farms were Kin-Lochransay, Catacol, the two Thundergays, Penriach, Alltgoblach, Machriemore, Auchagallon and Machriebeg, with a combined rent of 22 merks (£252 today), 12 bolls of barley and 4.5 marts. These farms, on the coastal strip between the northern mountains and Kilbrannan Sound, were directly exposed to hostile action from across the narrow sea. Between 1440 and 1453, MacAlister either had the rent abated or cancelled altogether, or simply refused to pay, to the dismay and wrath of the royal accountant ('the Comptant'). An attempt in 1452 to have the farms taken over as military holdings by a soldier, Alexander Lord Montgomery, – sending in the troops to restore order – was forcibly resisted and overcome by Ranald MacAlister himself. This was the time when Lochranza Castle was built – or rebuilt – by Montgomery, who was made overlord of a substantial part of north-western Arran and Glen Sannox in the north-east; in spite of the equally tough MacAlisters, the Montgomerys continued as proprietors of these lands until 1705.

Later in 1452 King James II of Scotland, in urgent need of money, borrowed 800 merks (nearly £6,000 today) from Glasgow Cathedral against the rental or customs duty from six areas including Arran; the Bishop of Glasgow, William Turnbull, promptly leased the entire island to none other than Ranald MacAlister. In 1454, then, as might have been expected, no Arran rent of any sort filled the episcopal coffers, and this impasse persisted, with the Sheriff of Bute being petitioned repeatedly for recovery of rent by distraint – until the Bishop died in 1457; the Chamberlain could 'find nothing of Ranald MacAlister's to distrain'.

During the long struggle between King James and the Douglases, the Earl of Douglas fled to the protection of the Lord of the Isles, who in turn sent a battle fleet in 1454 under Donald Balloch to the Firth of Clyde: this fleet laid Arran completely waste and destroyed Brodick Castle, with the aim of depriving the Bishop of Glasgow of his rent. The vicinity of Brodick was devastated and could not be let: it was assessed as 'waste'.

In 1458 the 'heroic debtor' Ranald MacAlister died penniless, and the arrears, by then amounting to 256 merks (nearly £3,000 today), must have been written off as a bad debt. In 1459 Fergus Fullarton, holding Clachlanbeg of the Crown, was unable to pay his rent 'because the said Fergus lost his goods in the service of our lord the King, in great quantity'.[7] And so it went on. Another dreadful devastation took place in 1462, resulting once again in wholesale debt cancellation, in spite of the protective patronage of powerful friends of the king, namely Lord Montgomery and Colin Earl of Argyll (1466).

The Boyds and Hamiltons

In 1460 the Kilmarnock family of Boyd appeared on the Arran scene in the following intricate manner: King James II, besieging Roxburgh Castle in the Borders, and wishing to have a *feu de joie* for the arrival at the siege-works of his Queen, Mary of Guelders, stood too close to the artillery during the salvo and, when one of the guns exploded, was struck in the thigh by a piece of flying shrapnel and died there and then. James III, eight years old, was crowned at Kelso a week later and promptly fell victim to the usual tug-of-war between magnates (and the Queen Mother) struggling for control of the person of the king and of power within the kingdom. The tussle extended itself over the next seven or eight years, and was exacerbated by the deaths of the Queen Mother and of Bishop Kennedy, a wise statesman who had been been a power behind the throne since the time of James II. Then, on 9 July 1466, the Boyd family kidnapped the young king and spirited him away to Edinburgh Castle, which was held by Sir Alexander Boyd. Under duress, the king consented to the marriage of his sister Margaret to Sir Thomas Boyd, whom he created Earl of Arran, and to whom in 1467 he granted the whole of the royal property in Arran (not that the Arran lands would be a great prize in their desolate and ruined condition).

Earl Thomas, however, did not last long in possession of his earldom or his wife: by a palace revolution in 1469 King James III assumed personal power and denounced the Boyds as traitors: all save one, who was caught and beheaded, fled abroad, including the earl and his countess, who was soon summoned home, divorced and married off to James, first Lord Hamilton – a rather elderly gentleman who had retained royal favour by deserting the cause of the Douglases after 1455; thus another more permanent element would be introduced to the story of the ownership of Arran. For the moment, however, after the fall of the Boyds, the Arran lands were simply added to the already extensive patrimony of the heir to the Scottish throne. The island as a whole was leased to a succession of 'farmers' (firmarii) – Sir John Colquhoun of Luss, Lord John Dalmeny, Lord John Kennedy, Lord Montgomery and last but not least Ninian Stewart, hereditary Sheriff of Bute and Arran,[8] a descendant of 'Black' John Stewart (mentioned on p.86) Robert III's illegitimate son, John Stewart of Ardgowan in Renfrewshire, also possessed the 'Tenpenny Lands' of Arran (most of the south-east part of the island, including Kildonan Castle)[9] until, in 1503 the Bute family, wishing to consolidate their possessions in Arran, arranged to transfer their Perthshire lands to the Ardgowan family in exchange (*excambion*) for the Arran lands.

Flodden: the Earl of Arran's politics

In the same year, 1503, Lord Hamilton's son James was Master of Ceremonies at the wedding of King James IV to Margaret Tudor, daughter of Henry VII of England. Hamilton appeared in a white-and-gold uniform and exhibited great prowess in tilting in the accompanying tournament 'with the illustrious foreigner Antoine d'Arsie de la Bastie'.[10] He was handsome, a fine archer and horseman, and the bridegroom king was moved to confer on him 'the whole lands and Earldom of Arran, lying in the Sheriffdom of Bute' in heritage to heirs-male as a 'free barony for ever' . . . 'because of his nearness of blood, his services, and especially his labours and expenses at the time of the royal marriage in Holyrood'.[11] These services and labours notwithstanding, he exhibited sterling incompetence when put in charge by James IV of the Scottish battle-fleet during the Flodden campaign in 1513. This man, however, was the founder of a line of Earls of Arran and Marquises and Dukes of Hamilton that has lasted down to the present day and until recently possessed a large portion of the territory of Arran (although the family had several ups and downs in fortune, and several other families – the Montgomerys, the Stewarts and the Fullartons – continued to own significant parcels of land in Arran).

We are now approaching the major events – or traumas – in Scotland's six-teenth-century history, starting with the Battle of Flodden, continuing with Henry VIII's 'Rough Wooing', and culminating in the twin upheavals of the Reformation and the disastrous reign of Mary, Queen of Scots. Somehow the Stewarts held on to the monarchy, surviving for more than two hundred years. Arran itself flits in and out of historical notice and is affected by major changes.

Loyal to the spirit of the Auld Alliance, James IV decided to make a diver-sionary attack upon the North of England when Henry VIII quarrelled with Louis XII of France; the fortunes of war, however, were against James, and he fell at Flodden on 9 September 1513, along with many of the senior nobility and clergy of Scotland. He had an heir, born to Margaret Tudor, Henry VIII's sister, but this son, James V, was about eighteen months old when his father died, and the Scots saw unfolding in front of them another long royal minor-ity. Who was to rule the country while the king was under age?

After making his curious and inconclusive voyage round Scotland, punctu-ated by the sack of Carrickfergus in Ireland, the Earl of Arran had found his way to the French court, where he got news of the Flodden disaster. A nephew of James III, John Duke of Albany, who had been born in France and was to all intents and purposes a Frenchman, stood very close to the Scottish throne, and the Earl of Arran in concert with others at the French court proposed that Albany should become Governor of Scotland. This proposal was accepted, Albany came to Scotland in 1515, and the Earl of Arran – also in line for the throne because his mother was James III's sister – became a great man in the kingdom, heading one of the two principal factions in Scotland, the Hamiltons, ranged against the Douglases.

He had a roller-coaster ride of a career, in and out of favour, gaining and losing power. Hard on the heels of Governor Albany's arrival in Scotland, the Earl of Arran became involved in a dispute about the custody of the king's person (then held in Stirling Castle by his mother and her new husband, the Douglas Earl of Angus), and this came to an actual battle near Glasgow, which Arran lost and Albany won; Henry VIII of England had backed the Douglas party but that was 'the wrong horse'. Angus and the Queen Mother were exiled, and Albany took possession of the infant king, proving himself to be an efficient and conciliatory administrator.

The Earl of Arran was speedily restored to favour, was appointed to the commission of regency in 1517, and after the murder of Albany's principal agent in Scotland in September of that year, was effectually in charge of Scottish affairs. However, in Albany's absence, and after a series of anarchic events which showed that the government was losing control to the Douglases, the Earl started to drift out of favour again. In 1524 he offered his support to the Queen Mother, who had left the Earl of Angus, and brought the young king into play by a virtual coronation ('erection'), which spelt the end of Albany's power. This did not end the woes of the Scottish government, and in February 1525 we find Edinburgh divided into armed camps, with Arran and the Queen Mother holding the Castle while the town was controlled by her estranged husband the Earl of Angus and John Stewart, third Earl of Lennox. Arran and the Queen called to arms in vain.

Angus consolidated his power, and held the king in 'protective custody'. Several attempts to rescue the king were made, including one armed attack at Linlithgow in 1526, when Lennox was forced to surrender and then slain by one Sir James Hamilton of Finnart, a supporter of the Earl of Arran. It is fairly obvious that Arran himself, still in government, was trying to be all things to all men, or playing one end against the other, for he is reported to have fallen into a 'deep decline' at the news of Hamilton's treachery – yet, when eventually James V himself, seventeen years old in 1528, managed to escape and reaffirm his royal authority, Arran was one of the party who accompanied the king on his triumphal re-entry to Edinburgh, where he had previously been detained. The Earl of Arran withdrew from public affairs after 1526, and in 1529 he died.

Meanwhile, James V grew up into another dark and sinister – though relatively successful – Scottish monarch with a pronounced taste for cruelty: he once ordered a criminal to be burnt alive at the stake (rather than strangled beforehand in the normal manner of these executions) – 'whilk deid was never sene in this realme of befoir, nor will be heireftir'.[12]

Arran as a pawn in the game: more tribulation

While all this was going on in the mainland, the Isle of Arran had not escaped unscathed. In the late 1400s the attacks on Arran from the west had continued, from Kintyre and Knapdale. The island had been so heavily devastated that once again, in 1480, it was impossible to assess the farms for returns. After the suppression of the Lordship of the Isles by James IV in 1493, the persecution of Arran increased, in 1496 and later. No rent was paid up to 1503, when the Hamiltons were awarded the Earldom: consequently the personnel of the persecutors was expanded to include the Stewarts. The depredations went on.

In the operations against the Lord of the Isles, the king had been materially assisted by Ninian Stewart, Sheriff of Bute, and for this support Ninian was made Hereditary Captain and Keeper of Rothesay Castle in 1498. Already in 1505, a certain 'Watte Stewart' had evidently taken possession of Brodick Castle and was therein bombarded by the warship Colomb, although details of the siege have not survived.[13] Now, after the murder of Lennox, the bitterness of the Stewarts increased, and in 1528, contemporaneously with certain feuds on the western mainland,[14] two sons of Ninian Stewart took Brodick Castle by storm, again burnt it down and killed the keeper George Tait; they later escaped to Galloway, where they took shelter with the McDowells, traditional foes of the Scottish monarchy since the days of Robert the Bruce.

Also in 1528 the new King found time to confirm or renew certain charters, including one to Hugh Montgomery, first Earl of Eglinton, in respect of the lands in northern Arran, including Lochranza in the north-west and Sannox in the north-east, which had been owned by the Montgomerys since the days of James II and Ranald MacAlister. This grant was probably connected with the losses sustained by the Montgomery in Ayrshire in one of the feuds mentioned above, when Eglinton Castle had been burnt down by the Cuninghames in 1527.

James Hamilton, the second Earl of Arran, succeeded his father in 1529 and was made Governor of Scotland following James V's death in 1542. The infant Mary, Queen of Scots became the subject of the usual tug-of-war about custody, but this time the principal contenders were England and France, both of whom offered bridegrooms. Henry VIII offered his five-year-old son, Edward, and suggested that Arran should become King of the old Alba, Scotland north of the Forth–Clyde isthmus; the corollary being that England would absorb all the southern part of Scotland. This ingenious proposal and others were rejected by the Scots, and Henry, often a petulant and inept statesman, decided on a policy of armed intervention, 'the Rough Wooing'. In 1544–55 the Earl of Hertford descended with fire and the sword on the southern Scottish mainland, and the Earl of Lennox, supporting Henry, came up the Clyde in 1544 with the object of capturing Dumbarton Castle.

According to Mackenzie, in 1543 a French sea-captain had outlined to Henry VIII a plan for sea-borne operations against the Clyde coast; the proposal included a scheme to use Lamlash Bay, relatively undefended, as a haven for 100 large ships, just as Håkon IV had done 280 years before. Dumbarton castle remained unconquered, but Lennox fell upon the Earl of Arran's lands in the west in 1544, once more destroying Brodick Castle.

This castle seems to have been phoenix-like, rising from the ashes time and again: it was sorely battered during the sixteenth century, while the castle at Lochranza in the north-west of the island was subject to repeated assaults from Kintyre and Knapdale. At times the only operating castle in Arran was Kildonan in the south, in the lands belonging to the Bute Stewarts.

Sheriff Ninian Stewart of Bute died in 1539, and his successor as Sheriff of Bute, his eldest son, Sir James, had been one of the two raiders who had devastated Brodick in 1528. In 1544 this Sir James Stewart, as Mackenzie says, 'was unhappy in his politics' in 'the troubled time of Queen Mary's minority, when political activity craved careful walking'.[15] Together with an Ayrshire adventurer called Thomas Byschop, he threw in his lot with the new Earl of Lennox against the Hamiltons. Together they harried and burned Arran as well as Bute and Cowal. In 1549 Sir James Stewart had to answer to the Scottish Parliament for his treason; in spite of his defence (mainly that the Earl of Argyll had conspired with others to deprive him of his property), he was compelled to sell most of his lands in Arran and elsewhere to the Earl of Arran. This, however, was not the end of the story. Some parts of the property (Corriegills) were retained as an 'appanage' for the sheriffdom of Bute, which Sir James Stewart kept.[16] The Tenpenny Lands – the south-eastern part of the island – according to Mackenzie, continued to be 'shuttlecocked' between the Stewarts and the MacDonalds until the beginning of the nineteenth century, when they were finally acquired by the Duke of Hamilton, probably in connection with the agricultural enclosures then being implemented.[17]

In 1548, the Earl of Arran had arranged for the infant Queen Mary to be transferred to France in anticipation of her marriage to the Dauphin Francis (much later, in 1557), and as a reward, was created Duke of Chatelherault in France in February 1549. King Henry VIII had died in 1546, succeeded by his son, Edward VI, a tubercular adolescent imbued with strongly Protestant ideas. He died in 1553 and was succeeded (after the nine-day wonder of the

Lady Jane Grey episode) by his half-sister Mary Tudor, who was as fiercely Catholic as he had been Protestant. She did her best to restore Roman Catholicism as the state religion of England, in the process executing so many people that she earned the title 'Bloody Mary'. Mary Tudor was also unhealthy, and she died in 1558. She was followed by her half-sister Elizabeth, a much more intelligent and cautious woman, who favoured the Protestant side once again, and who resisted English involvement in European entanglements (unlike her late half-sister, who had actually married King Philip II of Spain).

Right at the end of Mary Tudor's reign, in 1558, after the marriage of Mary, Queen of Scots to the heir to the French throne, and consequent English hostility to Scotland, the Earl of Sussex swept up from Ireland with a fleet, came into the Firth of Clyde, did terrible destruction upon Arran and Kintyre and continued to wreak havoc on the region until the identical fate fell upon him as had fallen on Håkon IV three hundred years before – a great storm in the region of the Cumbraes.

The Reformation: consequences for Arran

In Scotland meanwhile a Protestant Reformation – or rather, Revolution – was gathering pace in the late 1550s and early 1560s, and in a very short period of time the Roman Catholic version of Christianity was almost entirely swept from the board, with destruction visited upon the buildings and other physical signs of the religion, its establishment abolished and the celebration of Mass made into a capital crime. At the head of the nation Mary Stewart, a devout Roman Catholic, returned to Scotland as Queen Regnant after the death of her husband Francis II in 1561, failed to cope with Protestantism, and after a series of disastrous misjudgments, came out of Scotland like a cork from a bottle in 1568. A horde of asset-strippers descended upon the lands previously owned by Roman Catholic religious corporations, and it was as if David I's own reformation four hundred years previously had never taken place – except in the matter of the parochial divisions of the country, which were subject to only minor modifications.

In Arran the ecclesiastical lands were being disposed of even before the Reformation. The founder of Saddell Abbey in Kintyre, probably Ragnvald King of the Isles (see above) in the twelfth century, had bestowed a very fertile area of Arran, twenty merklands of Shiskine in the west, upon the abbey. Now, in about 1556, this area became subject to the usual haggling and bartering as between three parties – the Hamilton Bishop of Argyll and the Isles, James Duke of Chatelherault (Earl of Arran), and James MacDonald of Dunvegan Castle who, after the Lennox episode in 1544, had made a claim to the lands belonging to Sir James Stewart in the south of Arran and had been bought off. Now in 1556 the Bishop transferred all the lands of Saddell Abbey 'in feu farm' to the Duke for forty-nine marks per year, and in turn the Duke gave MacDonald ('infefted' him with) all the Kintyre lands of Saddell Abbey in return for the latter surrendering his Arran claims. This was subject to the condition that MacDonald and his friends and allies should refrain from 'ony invasions, reiffis, slauchterie, sorningys or oppressions' in Arran and should help to defend the island against the depredations of others. A centuries-old problem was thus intended to be laid to rest, and the Hamiltons secured even more Arran real estate. They had already extended their Arran possessions by acquiring the old Fullarton lands, Kilmichael and Whitefarland, in 1563. This they did, it is alleged, by making the former owner, Allan Fullarton, drunk.

The whole transaction could not be carried through without the co-operation of the principal tenant, a descendant of the 'heroic tenant' Ranald MacAlister, who grimly held on to the north-western portion of Arran in the face of multiple depredations in the fifteenth century: now, in the sixteenth century (25 November 1563), Angus M'Ranald Moir M'Allister had to sign a bond to be a good tenant, to be loyal to the Bailie and Captain of the Isle, and to help to evict any tenants who withstood the will of the Duke.

Arran, owing to its position on the western coastal fringe, was still of national strategic importance. The Hamiltons were supporters of Mary, Queen of Scots, and during her imprisonment in Loch Leven Castle in 1568, a scheme was hatched for the French to liberate her by sailing up the Clyde estuary, using Arran and Dumbarton Castle as stepping stones. This fell through after her forces were defeated at Langside in May of that year.[18] Mary fled to England, her infant son was made King James VI of Scotland, another long royal Scottish minority began, and a regency was established. In 1570 James Hamilton of Bothwellhaugh assassinated the Regent Moray and took refuge in Brodick, as did the Duke of Chatelherault himself (i.e. the second Earl of Arran) in May 1570 along with the Commendator of Kilwinning after they had been forced to stop besieging Glasgow.

From the English point of view, on the other hand, Arran was a useful staging-post for operations against Ireland later in the century and at the beginning of the next; the inhabitants of the island and of Kintyre, both Stewarts and Hamiltons as well as MacDonalds and Montgomerys, might be expected to rally – and to spy – against the great O'Neill, the Earl of Tyrone, who was then in rebellion. After the Union of the Crowns in 1603, the Irish troubles were even gaining in turbulence, and in 1608 King James VI and I was apprehensive enough to command that 'the castellis and fortressis in Arrane [be] weel gairdit and provydit'.[19]

The third Earl of Arran had succeeded his father the Duke of Chatelherault in 1575. (The French title had been withdrawn after the second Earl had turned against Mary, Queen of Scots, but was used on a strictly illegal basis in Scotland for some time afterwards.) The third Earl had been considered at one time as a possible husband for (a) Mary and (b) Elizabeth of England, but in 1562 he was declared insane. In 1581 he resigned the Earldom to none other than James Hamilton of Bothwellhaugh, the 1570 assassin of the Regent Moray, but in 1586 the Court of Session in Edinburgh deemed this resignation the act of a madman, and restored all his titles to him; his younger brother, Lord John Hamilton, was appointed curator bonis, legally in charge of the Earl's estates. The third Earl died in 1609, and Lord John became fourth Earl of Arran and first Marquis of Hamilton.

Crime and punishment in seventeenth-century Arran

In 1606, Arran served as a place of exile, if not exactly a prison island, for a 'contumacious' Presbyterian minister. But within the island itself, according to Mackenzie,[20] the Privy Council in Edinburgh was informed in 1608 that murder was 'verie frequent', together with mutilation, theft and reset. Later the list of crimes in Arran included 'theft, slaughter, murder, mutilation, witch-craft, sorning [basically, uninvited guests outstaying their welcome] and pykrie [petty theft]'. This crime-wave may have reflected social deterioration following more than two centuries of raiding, plundering and war, as well as the fact that the third and fourth Earls of Arran were both absentee landlords who did not exercise proper care.

Murder and robbery were two of the four pleas of the Crown – the other two being rape and fire-raising – and as such, in respect of Arran, could be dealt with only in the King's justiciary circuit court either in Ayr or in Dunoon, unless special commissions of justiciarship were given to local individuals, as was the case with Thomas Montgomery of Skelmorlie in 1548 in respect of Lochranza and Sannox. At the start of the 1600s neither the third nor the fourth Earl possessed a commission of justiciarship. However, the Privy Council granted two such (temporary) commissions, in 1608 to the Earl of Abercorn and in 1619 to the Marquis of Hamilton, who could appoint deputies and hold district courts.[21] These commissions were later (1633) made permanent and hereditary in the Hamilton family.

Apart from the four pleas of the Crown, other criminal matters were in fact dealt with in Arran by the 'baron-bailie' method as well as by the Coronership, hereditary in the Fullarton family. The bailie of a baron (in Arran the 'Captain of Arran and Keeper of Brodick Castle') had 'police and magistral' functions which allowed him even to impose the death penalty e.g. for theft, as well as to fine heavily, imprison and place in the stocks. The Sheriff (of Bute) himself had more extensive powers, but these excluded the Crown pleas. After 1503 the baron-bailie was always a Hamilton, but the office of Sheriff remained with the Stewart family. A contract has survived from 1593 setting out in detail the obligations in goods and money owed by the Captain and Lord (John) Hamilton to each other, and the duties laid upon the Captain in return for the maintenance provided: in particular he was to: 'diligently keep and defend the castle of Brodick and the whole isle of Arran, and the tenants and occupiers from all reif and oppression, and shall cause the rents and duties to be paid to Lord Hamilton.'[22]

Serious violence seems to have been the order of the day, as for instance when in 1576 six men accused of fire-raising in Bute took refuge in Brodick Castle itself and, when a process-server tried to gain admission to the Castle to serve a summons on them, the whole gang rushed out at him, firing a pistol but 'by Goddis providence' just missing the officer (one Symontoun), and 'stoggit him be chance throw the oxtare' with a sword. Finally Symontoun was knocked out with a blow from the butt end of a pistol and left 'for deid', but survived to give evidence against his attackers.[23] They included three Hamiltons, one of whom was the Reverend Gavin Hamilton, parson of Kilbride.

Twenty years later, a certain Patrick Hamilton, allegedly a villain of the deepest dye, had cut off all the fingers of someone's left hand in, of all places,

St Giles' Kirk in Edinburgh, had been put to the horn (outlawed) and in spite of this, went on with 'his accustumat tred of murthure, slauchter and other odius crimes'. But who was Patrick Hamilton? Although 'mony uther and odius wicked deidis [had been] committit bi him upone his Majesteis peceable subjeitis, and speciallie within the pairtis of Arrane', it transpired that 'he is appointit capitane of Brody [Brodick], oppressand sic as may not resist him baith be sey and land'. Patrick got Lord John Hamilton, his ostensible employer, into trouble too, following the latter's failure to produce him, and they were both put to the horn (outlawed), but Lord John was cleared when he averred that Patrick was neither servant nor tenant, and sent an armed party to get him. Patrick Hamilton dodged retribution until 2 April 1595 when, in Hamilton town, he met an apparently richly deserved fate at the hands of Sir John Hamilton of Lettrick. But lo! Patrick's widow *married* one Paul Hamilton who became Captain of Brodick in his turn.[24] One has the sense of a complicated intrigue just below the surface.

Paul Hamilton reappears in 1602 in the course of a dispute involving the Hamiltons of Brodick and the Montgomerys of Lochranza, when he led a large party against a Montgomery property in North Sannox, stole goods, and animals, and captured a 'servitor' whom they detained for several days in Brodick Castle. This action appears to have been an episode in a typical Scottish 'feud' of a kind that was going out of fashion in the early seventeenth century – a vendetta ultimately based on property rights, perhaps fuelled by the dispersal of church lands associated with the Protestant Reformation.

Paul Hamilton died in 1633, having attained the position of Convener of Justices of the Peace – an apparent character-change that parallels an alteration in national outlook occurring in the seventeenth century.

OS references

The continuing wars
Corrygills NS 034 351 – 036 345

The Reformation: consequences for Arran
Auchagallon NR 894 346
Kilmichael NS 002 350
Whitefarland NR 864 425

11. Heads roll: the 'Good Duchess' to the Rescue

Religious strife in the 1600s

Troubles in Arran did not abate during the first half of the seventeenth century, but they were of a different kind from previously. This was the period of the second major phase of the Scottish Protestant Reformation. During the century the Kirk of Scotland completed its movement towards Presbyterianism and against episcopalianism and Erastianism, i.e. the Presbyterians divorced their church from bishops and the Pope, and resisted state interference in church affairs. The leading men in Scotland ranged themselves on either side of the question – basically for or against the King – and the fifth Earl of Arran, later Marquis and Duke of Hamilton, held out for the King. After the King had attempted in 1637 to introduce an Anglican prayer-book and what were seen as crypto-Romanizing practices into Scottish church services, disturbances broke out in Edinburgh and elsewhere. In February and March 1638, copies of a manifesto called the National Covenant were signed in Edinburgh and throughout Scotland by most leading men. In November of that year, a riotous General Assembly of the Kirk was held in Glasgow, at which, on 8 December, the rule of bishops was voted out of existence ('abjured and removed'). A King's Commissioner was present during the first part of this convention, and he was the Marquis of Hamilton. On behalf of Charles I he protested that the proceedings of the Assembly were illegal, and when he was howled down, he attempted to withdraw with dignity. The keys to the cathedral door were 'mislaid', and the Marquis had to wait in wrath until the door was physically broken down. After that, actual war broke out – the two

Bishops' Wars, of 1639 and 1640, in both of which the Scottish Covenanters out-manoeuvred and defeated the King and his adherents. This was the prelude to the Great Rebellion, in which the King lost his head and Oliver Cromwell came to the fore.

The islanders in Arran would naturally follow the politics and religion of the Marquis of Hamilton, and refrained from supporting the provisional Covenanter government ('the Tables') in Edinburgh. However, at the beginning of the first Bishops' War in 1639, the Chief of the Campbell clan, the Earl of Argyll, who was a leading Covenanter and strong opponent of Hamilton, landed in person on Arran with a strong force, seized Brodick Castle, and compelled the inhabitants to 'take the Covenant'.[1] It appears that the Campbells may have remained in occupation of the Castle, for it was recorded that in 1646, during the general Civil War, a Campbell garrison was being besieged by the inhabitants of Arran, when a large party of Campbells came down upon them in order to relieve the garrison, laid the island waste in the old vicious manner, and stole or killed the cattle and other animals, creating such devastation that it took the island six years to recover from the 'violent wrongous and masterfull depradation & roberie'.[2]

In the first part of the Great Rebellion in Scotland, the successes of the Royalists under the Earl of Montrose contrasted vividly with Covenanting defeats at home and reverses in England, where the shaky alliance that the Scots and the English Parliamentarians had contrived was gradually disintegrating. ('The Solemn League and Covenant', 1643, an international treaty of armed assistance, should be distinguished from the National Covenant of 1638, which was a kind of 'mission statement'.) Montrose won a shattering series of victories, including the great Battle of Kilsyth, and at one stage the only obstacle to a rapid Royalist takeover of Edinburgh was a savage outbreak of plague. Assisting Montrose in his victorious progress through Scotland was a Gaelic soldier, Lieutenant-General Sir Alexander MacDonald (Alasdair MacColla) sometimes erroneously called Young Colkitto. He was a brilliant tactician who took the lead when Montrose's generalship faltered, as it often did. MacDonald was a perpetrator of odious war-crimes, massacre after cold-blooded massacre of defenceless civilians, including one awful episode in which a large number of women and children and old men were herded together into a barn which was then set alight, so that they all perished in the flames. His behaviour during the sack of Aberdeen was also truly monstrous.

Now, when the Earl of Montrose was taken off guard and defeated at the battle of Philiphaugh in the Borders in 1645, MacDonald deserted his ally and retreated, blackmailing and slaughtering his way back to his own lands in the west. The inhabitants of Ayrshire and of Arran were highly alarmed, and the Montgomery owners of Lochranza and Sannox in Arran became refugees, fleeing MacDonald's anticipated arrival. The chief Montgomery was the Earl of Eglinton at Irvine in Ayrshire, a leading Covenanter along with other Ayrshire magnates. In 1645 he was furth of Ayrshire on urgent political business, and on 23 December his wife the Countess wrote to him, fearing that MacDonald would 'come ower and tak all that [he] can gett and burne the rest ... I assur you they ar looking everi night for him in Arrane, for man, wyf and bairne is coming ower to this syd [Ayrshire], and all ther goods that they can gett transportit, both out of Arrane and Bute; for he [Allaster] is veri strong, as I feir we find er it be long.'[3]

The Countess's fears, however, were to be allayed: Alasdair MacDonald and his men were outnumbered by the forces of the Covenanting Government under Lieutenant General David Leslie, and retreated down the peninsula of Kintyre on the other side of the Kilbrannan Sound from Arran. They reached the sinister castle of Dunaverty, perched high on a cliff over the sea at the southernmost point of the Mull of Kintyre, where MacDonald left a garrison of about five hundred men. He himself and the rest of his troops embarked for Islay and Ireland, intending to return with reinforcements; he never came back. General Leslie sat down in front of Dunaverty Castle and besieged it until MacDonald's garrison surrendered. Then a certain Reverend John Nevoy or Neave, the minister of Loudoun in Ayrshire, 'exhorted' Leslie and the army for days to remember what happened to Agag and the Amalekites (I Samuel xv, v.14) – 'What meaneth this bleating of the sheep in mine ears, and the lowing of the oxen which I hear?' At length Leslie gave way to this homicidal badgering, and the entire garrison were hanged, shot or thrown over the cliff into the sea (May or July 1647). It is recorded that General Leslie, wading over his ankles in blood, turned to Nevoy, and said, 'Now, Mr John, have you not once got your fill of blood?'

One cannot examine the detailed history of Scotland without a certain frisson of horror – not alleviated, but intensified into prolonged shudders, at the thought of the greater, even more frequent massacres perpetrated in our own times in the name of one ideal or another.

Oliver Cromwell's occupation

In the course of the complex politics of the 1640s in Scotland, a party came to power which supported King Charles I even after his capture and imprisonment prior to his execution. This party signed an agreement or Engagement with the deposed king, and its supporters were known as Engagers. They gathered a fighting force with the intention of liberating and restoring the king and marched south from Scotland under the leadership of the same Marquis (now Duke) of Hamilton; they were met and defeated by Oliver Cromwell at Preston in 1648; the temerarious Duke lost his head shortly after his master, on 9 March 1649. He was succeeded by his brother William, Earl of Lanark, who was mortally wounded at the Battle of Worcester in 1651 when King Charles II was defeated and had to flee.

After Worcester, Brodick Castle in Arran still held out for Charles II. In 1652, however, Oliver Cromwell's man in Ayr sent a party of soldiers across the Clyde to take it over; the soldiers landed at Lamlash, marched to Brodick and received the not entirely willing surrender of the castle. The Arran people seem to have cherished a dislike of the Earl of Argyll even twelve years after they were compelled to submit to the Covenant, and they do not appear initially to have been hostile to the English occupiers. However, these too stole or confiscated large numbers of cattle and 'insulted' Arran women. A tradition states that at last English rule became too much to bear, and the inhabitants are said to have massacred a foraging party returning with their ill-gotten booty.

The story is supported by place-names: the slaughter is claimed to have taken place at Allt-a-Chlaidheim ('Sword Burn') between South Sannox and Corrie on the east coast, and one survivor is said to have been killed at the Clach a' Chath ('Battle Stone': a huge erratic block whose Gaelic name has been misinterpreted as 'the Cat Stane'). Another version of the story has the tenantry getting together with pitchforks and hoes and chasing the Cromwellian governor, who escaped in a small boat with his men, except for one soldier, who died at the Creag an Stobaidh ('Stabbing Rock').[4] This story is unconfirmed but the existence of two versions roughly similar tends to indicate that there is some truth in the tale.

Presbyterian vicissitudes

From the end of the sixteenth century, Presbyterian ministers had been appointed to parishes throughout Scotland, including Kilbride and probably Kilmory in Arran, which were at first, in 1600, subordinated to the new district authority, the Presbytery of Irvine in Ayrshire, but are recorded in 1638 as belonging to the Presbytery of Kinloch (Kintyre). The finances of the Kirk of Scotland, to begin with, were scanty, and even when the situation improved, parish ministers were driven to 'moonlighting' to maintain their standard of living. Some expedients were less reputable than others. The very first minister of Kilbride, a man with the famous name of John Knox, was 'deposed' in 1649 for keeping an ale-house. In Kilmory, on the other hand, James McQuiriter or M'Kirdy continued as parish minister from at least 1626 till 1648, when he finally gave up his charge through extreme old age, to be succeeded by the Reverend Alexander MacLaine (McLean).

Kilbride Parish may have been left without a minister for about two years after 1649, since it was only in 1651 that the same Alexander MacLaine of Kilmory Parish was transferred to Kilbride. Kilmory was left vacant for some considerable time, probably because that part of the island was still lying derelict after the ferocious Campbell assault of 1646. Both parishes were administered from Kilbride, since Kilmory had no regular Kirk Session.

Perhaps, too, Kilbride Parish suffered a second vacancy, from 1652 to 1655, since it is only in the latter year that the Reverend John Cunison is recorded as succeeding MacLaine, who left in 1652.

Both MacLaine and Cunison were 'outed' along with hundreds of other western ministers in 1662 for resisting the Act of Presentation and Collation; this statute was intended to impose episcopal authority upon the Kirk by making each minister apply through a bishop for 're-registration' before being permitted to continue his work. The mass resignations in opposition to the Act in the west of Scotland surprised and alarmed the Government: they had to assemble a large scratch team of substitute ministers or 'curates' in a hurry, and some of these were no better than they had to be.

In Kilbride Parish the curate substituting for the Reverend Cunison, Archibald Beith, overstepped his official duties in 1671 to the extent of shooting at a vessel in Lamlash Bay and killing two men, a crewman and a worthy merchant from Irvine in Ayrshire. The ship was part of an illegal meal-smuggling operation between Ireland and Arran, and its crew regained possession of the contraband after Beith had seized it; they then made off with it again, Archibald Beith firing his guns in hot pursuit. Yet he was arrested, taken to Edinburgh, tried for murder and sentenced to be hanged. King Charles II's system of justice reprieved him and turned him free, and after an unsuccessful appeal to Rothesay Town Council for a beggar's licence, Beith simply vanished.

The year 1688 was the year of the so-called Glorious Revolution, in which the Presbyterians in Scotland triumphed, and the appointment of a curate, Alexander Cameron, to Kilbride in that year must have been one of the last actions of the episcopalian Church in Scotland before King James VII and II was forced to flee by the advent of William of Orange. The curate was no sooner installed than he was dispossessed and the Reverend Cunison, by then an aged man, was restored. In 1692 Cunison finally retired, succeeded by the Reverend Archibald MacLaine, perhaps the son of the previously mentioned Alexander MacLaine. The second MacLaine, who was a Gaelic scholar, was occupied from 1655 to 1660 in translating Old Testament texts and psalms into Gaelic for the Synod of Argyll – a Synod being the next step up from a Presbytery in the hierarchy of administrative bodies in the Kirk of Scotland.

In Kilmory, an episcopal Rev. MacLaine was also installed in 1688 and was turned out in 1690, the year in which Presbyterianism was formally recognised as the state religion in Scotland. No minister of Kilmory is recorded after the departure of the curate until the advent of the Reverend Dugald Bannatyne in 1701.

It is from about the time of the Civil War that particular families and names become more distinguishable, with individuals and individual groups coming prominently into focus. We have already met the name MacAl(l)ister in connection with raiding in the fifteenth and sixteenth centuries, in which one group, based south of Tarbert in Kintyre, raided lands belonging to another MacAlister, the 'heroic tenant', who owned farms south of Lochranza in the north-west of Arran. That MacAlister held on grimly in the face of devastations and destitution. Raiding as a Kintyre MacAlister habit died hard, and men of the family seem to have participated in the 1646 raid, together with Browns, MacDonalds and Campbells, some of whom seem to have come from Cowal. Some raiders settled down in the island, and (in Mackenzie's time, about a century ago) MacAlister burials were visible in the old cemeteries at Shiskine and Kilmory;[5] so also were burials of Browns in a little graveyard south of Lochranza. There appear to have been two sharply distinguishable MacAlister groupings, Sallow John's ('Sliochd Iain Odhar'), the Arran family, and Black John's ('Sliochd Iain Dubh'), from Loup in Kintyre (not the place with the same name in Arran).

Mackenzie tells of a rumour that there was an outbreak of the plague in Arran in 1666, a year after the Great Plague of London, and that the MacAlister settlement came in that year to fill the places of the victims. Mackenzie rather discounts this tale, on the grounds of there being no report of the London outbreak having spread to Scotland.[6] However it is known that at least in Edinburgh, there was just such an outbreak in 1645 or 1646, at the time of the Campbell incursion into Arran, and devastation/depopulation caused by the plague could easily have become confused with the destruction accompanying the raid. Similarly, the chronology could have slipped a decade or two in folk memory – and there is a hillock in Arran, Cnocan Ceusaidh ('The Hill of Torture'), traditionally associated with the burial of plague victims, although no clear record has survived. It could be that the MacAlisters of Loup stepped into the shoes of their Arran relatives after the latter had been wiped out by disease.

Duchess Anne and afterwards

After the execution of Charles I in 1649, and various failed experiments in parliamentary government, a military dictatorship was brought in for Britain and Ireland under Oliver Cromwell. It was during the period of the Commonwealth, when Arran had been devastated and was desperately poor, that the first conspicuously able owner of the island, Duchess Anne, came to the fore. She was the daughter of Duke James, who had been beheaded after the Battle of Preston. James had pawned his estates in order to supplement the financial resources of Charles I, and the family were heavily fined by Cromwell's 'Commonwealth' government. Yet Duchess Anne was able to pay off the whole fine and redeem the property by 1657 – a feat which involved praying in assistance Cromwell himself, who intervened to prevent the dismemberment of the estates by a greedy relative. One of the keys to her success was that she had married William Douglas, second son of the Marquis of Douglas, who took the surname Hamilton. Another, after the Restoration of Charles II, was that she persuaded the king to repay the loan that her father had raised for Charles I by pawning his lands. Duchess Anne was successful in identifying the perpetrators of the 1646 raid on Arran, mentioned earlier, and, through parliament, in obtaining compensation for the loss of livestock and the six-years' misery endured by the islanders following that Campbell raid.

The Duchess took thought for the future commercial viability of Arran as a community, and had a small harbour – a pier and basin – built at Lamlash. Mackenzie tells us that the cost was £2,913, then an enormous sum. She showed business acumen in choosing the sheltered location, but it fell into disuse during the following century. The stonework was plundered at the beginning of the nineteenth century during the development of Lamlash village, but some remnants can be seen at low water to this day.

The portrait of Duchess Anne by David Scougal, now in Brodick Castle, shows her in her youth as a thin-faced sardonic beauty, obviously hard-headed if not hard-hearted, and with lines of bad temper about her mouth: a formidable woman. In spite of the fate of her father and her success in securing compensation from the Campbells, her sympathies were with the Protestants, something that earned her the title of 'the Good Duchess'. When the Covenanters were defeated at the Battle of Bothwell Brig in 1679, she made the purlieus of Hamilton Palace, near the scene of the battle, a 'safe area', barring the Government forces from entering the grounds, and providing sanctuary for the vanquished Whigs; she provided escape routes for several of these to Arran and elsewhere, and the Davidson family of Glenrosa are said to be descended from Bothwell refugees.[7]

Duchess Anne's husband, Duke William, died in 1694, after having summoned and presided at the convention in 1689 in which William of Orange and Mary Stewart were officially recognized as joint sovereigns of Scotland. Duchess Anne resigned the dukedom to her son James in 1698[8] but lived on till 1716, patronizing the Presbyterian church in Arran and performing 'good works' such as the 1705 presentation to the church of two communion cups.[9] Two preaching houses, at Clauchan and Lochranza, were built in 1708 and 1712 respectively, replacing earlier chapels; these buildings were placed at either end of the island, the one at Lochranza for the assistant preacher of Kilmory Parish, to whom Duchess Anne gifted Coillemore Farm as a 'glebe'.[10]

In addition to these ecclesiastical works, Duchess Anne increased the Hamilton estate in Arran in 1705 by the addition of the Montgomery possessions at Lochranza, after they had failed to redeem a mortgage amounting to £3,600. Meanwhile her son, the fourth Duke of Hamilton, inherited from his father the chief role in Scottish politics. The fourth Duke might actually have been able to avert the virtual extinction of Scotland's national sovereignty in the bribery-fuelled Union of the Parliaments in 1707, but seems to have played a dirty trick upon the opponents of the measure by turning against them after leading them to the last instant. Perhaps, however, he simply became confused in the maze of ever-changing party loyalties. This weak and indecisive man, created Duke of Brandon in 1692, and vividly depicted in the novel *Henry Esmond* by Thackeray, was killed in a duel in 1712, four years before the death of his mother.

OS references

Oliver Cromwell's occupation
The Sword Burn, Allt-a-Chlaidheim NS 020 445
Cat Stane NS 020 444
The Stabbing Rock (Creag an Stobaidh) NS 020 384

Presbyterian vicissitudes
The Hill of Torture, Cnocan Ceusaidh NR 935 221

12.   The Eighteenth Century: Squabbles and Sin

The times of the Jacobites

From 1688 up to and including the time of the 'Forty-Five', Arran life was comparatively uneventful. The fifth Duke, succeeding after the fatal duel, was a staunch supporter of the Hanoverian succession against the Stewarts, and his tenants and dependants in Arran as elsewhere did not raise a finger at the time of the 'Fifteen', when the Earl of Mar tried to raise the Highlands in support of the Old Pretender. Later, in 1745, apathy is said to have thwarted the efforts of a Jacobite recruiter, one Hector Mcalaster (MacAlister), to rally the men of Arran to the cause of Bonnie Prince Charlie. The Arran MacAlisters were undoubtedly Jacobite in sympathy, but Hector had no success to report by the time that Culloden had been fought and lost. He spent some time after the collapse of the rebellion in dodging the Redcoats near his hideout at Auchagallon: there is an Arran version of the well-known legend in which the fugitive, in this case Hector, hides under a pile of straw while soldiers drive pikes or spears into it around him. Later, all apparently forgiven, Hector appears as a douce tenant on the Hamilton estate, noted in Mr Burrel's list of 1766 as holding 'Glaster and Mony Quil' farms. (See chapter 13.)

There is a possible confusion in the story of Hector McAlister – two men may have had the same name – but that name appears in an official list, from which we learn that the number of islanders known to the authorities to have been actively associated with the rebels of the 'Forty-Five' was precisely six.[1]

International politics apart, the Jacobite insurgencies of the period represent the last efforts of the Celts to assert a leading role in Scottish political and military life: their failure had already been foreshadowed in the fate of Alasdair Mac Colla and the Earl of Montrose in the Civil War. After Culloden, Gaelic language and civilization, the 'clan' way of life, were in full retreat before the frightened and vengeful British military establishment and the relentless Anglicization of Edinburgh-based Presbyterian evangelism. In Arran, Hamilton dominance and other Lowland influences ensured that the island would take no part in the Jacobite risings.

The Church in the eighteenth century: disputes and patronage

Ministers of the Kirk tended to form dynasties. In Arran, the Reverend Archibald MacLaine referred to earlier (see p.108), held the pulpit of Kilbride Parish until 1698. Sometime later (? 1703)[2] his son Daniel became minister of Kilbride and continued until 1722. Thereafter a Stewart dynasty under the patronage of the Duke held sway in Kilbride: James Stewart, after a stint as catechist at Lochranza, was presented and ordained minister in May 1723; after no less than thirty years he was transferred to Kilmory, succeeded in Kilbride by his son Gershom who remained incumbent there until 1796 when he died at the age of seventy-eight; Gershom's son John held Kilbride in his turn until he died in 1825 aged seventy-one. In the meantime a Bannatyne dynasty held the western parish of Kilmory, Dugald Bannatyne from 1701 until 1748, and his son Charles from then apparently only until about 1753, when James Stewart from Kilbride took the parish over for the remaining nine years of his life.

The general longevity of the ministerial establishment in Arran seems to indicate a standard of living contrasting with that of the parishioners, who probably had no greater life expectancy than the average for the eighteenth century (about thirty-five to forty years). Ministers and their families led a privileged life in accordance with their position as leaders of the community, far more powerful perhaps than even the wealthy but often absentee landlords and their representatives. A genuine feeling of reverence and humility before the manse-dwellers would be widespread among the Presbyterian congregations of Arran and elsewhere. But evidence of a different spirit, resistant to

113

and defiant of authority, and in particular of patronage, often surfaces in eighteenth-century Scotland.

Following the 'Glorious Revolution' of 1688, when Scottish Presbyterianism seemed to have triumphed over the English form of Church government, the newly established Kirk forbade the practice of patronage – the right of landowners to choose a minister for a particular parish rather than the congregation concerned. This right, however, was revived by an Act of the British Parliament in 1712 – and the Kirk of Scotland began to fragment as a result of its application, in the frequent 'secessions' and schisms in the post-Revolution Kirk – harbingers of the Great Disruption of 1843.

In Arran in 1758 Kilmory parish demonstrated its hostility to patronage in no uncertain manner. At that time the Reverend James Stewart, who had been transferred from Kilbride at an already advanced age, was now felt to be too old to carry the burden of an entire parish on his shoulders, and the Duke of Hamilton as Patron cast about for an assistant who should in time become Stewart's successor. He pitched upon another man named James Stewart, previously minister of Kingarth in Bute, 'presented' him to Kilmory, and in February 1758 the Presbytery of Kintyre, to which Kilmory belonged, sustained the presentation by a majority. Ructions ensued. This second James Stewart was in fact a criminal and an arsonist: he had threatened, while in Bute, to burn down a house in the Kilwhinnick estate whose tenant, a cottar woman, had disputed the notice of removal which he had just handed her. The woman responded by handing him a burning slab of peat and challenging him to carry out his threat. This Maister Sheumas did on the spot, reducing the house to ashes.

His reputation had gone before him and he was obviously unacceptable to the Kilmory parishioners, but the Duke and the majority of the Presbytery of Kintyre seemed oblivious. However, two members of the Presbytery appealed against the decision to the Synod of Argyll (the body next in authority above the Presbytery), and the original and blameless James Stewart appealed directly to the General Assembly itself – the supreme governing body of the Kirk of Scotland.

On 23 March 1758 Kintyre's Presbytery met again, under the Moderatorship of none other than the son of the first James Stewart, the Reverend Gershom Stewart of Kilbride. The Presbytery divided equally, Gershom Stewart leading the opposition to the Duke's choice. Then, while the Presbytery itself dithered at sixes and sevens, three of the ministers of the Duke's party or faction went ahead with a formal admission ceremony for the discredited Stewart.

Such a ceremony had to be performed in the church in question – but the supporters of old Stewart had the keys of the building, so that the ceremony had to take place in the churchyard. The General Assembly came down very heavily against the instigators of the churchyard admission, suspending the leader, the Reverend John Hamilton of Skipness, for three months and severely censuring his two allies, for a high-handed act amounting to defiance of the will of the Church. It is a fact, however, that when the original Stewart died three years later in 1761, who should be chosen as his successor in Kilmory but the same Reverend John Hamilton – who ministered to Kilmory for no less than thirty-six years, dying in 1798 full of years (seventy-seven) and honour. What happened to the Bute James Stewart I do not know. Hamilton was forward with good works all his ministry, and kept on applying pressure to build a new Kilmory Parish Church until it was done in 1785.

The moral guardianship of the Kirk

Scottish churches in the eighteenth century took upon themselves judicial functions, often concentrating upon sexual offences, 'profane swearing', Sabbath-breaking and disputes between neighbours – besides making provision for charitable assistance to the poor. By the second half of the century, indeed, communal disapproval as exercised by ministers and elders in the name of the congregation was not feared as it used to be; Presbyterians no longer burnt witches as they had done during the Cromwellian occupation a century before, and the attitude of the Church towards minor transgressions began to be satirized by sophisticates like the poet Robert Burns. But in Arran the Church still retained at least a modicum of the old-style moral control, at least judging by the surviving Kirk Session Records of the eighteenth century. While incomplete, these records are fairly continuous, for Kilbride 1704–49, and for Kilmory 1702–29 and 1762 onward. In them the researcher finds a succession of petty fornications and sexual misdemeanours (sometimes exhibitionist in type) as well as domestic slanging-matches, superstitions and disputes involving strayings of cattle. In 1705, a dispute concerning the spilling of snuff from a snuff-mill (-mull) was brought before the Session. An

Auchencairn man was condemned to stand in sackcloth on the 'cutty stool' in front of the congregation for shouting at his mother and sister. More serious but less frequently imposed forms of punishment involved money fines, or even banishing from the parish.[3] In 1712 the farm-toun of Blairmore was notorious for noisy quarrelling and Sabbath-breaking: one woman was guilty of throwing stones at the neighbours' cattle on the Lord's day, to drive them out of the (unenclosed) 'corn and grass' – and Kilbride Kirk Session did 'think fitt to rebuke ...sessionallie' all the inhabitants of the toun because they had been engaged in 'continual strife' about the matter; they promised to live in peace thereafter.[4]

The Kirk Session took its judicial functions very seriously and in some respects acted as an arm of a social control that would now be regarded as infringing on civil liberties. In the eighteenth century there was a system of inter-parish 'testificates' that was very similar to the internal passport system imposed upon serfs in Czarist Russia up to the late nineteenth century. In the Kilbride Session Records of 30 March 1735 there is an entry concerning a woman who 'having gone to Ireland four years agoe without a testificate from this, and being summoned . . . did produce a certificate from Ireland, with which the Session was not satisfied . . . '[5] They could and did apply to the civil magistrate to have people expelled from the parish, as happened in 1738 in the case of one Alex Campbell who had been excommunicated by the Synod of Argyll.

Sabbath-breaking was considered a grave matter, and Mackenzie mentions a number of cases meriting public rebuke in front of the congregation – including one of 1710 in which the two-man crew of a yawl smuggling 'meall' from Ireland had had to put to sea during a dangerous storm on a Sunday: the smuggling was not nearly as wicked as the profanation of the Sabbath. People got into trouble for spinning on the Sabbath, or bringing home a horse – or drying malt in a kiln for fear it would spoil, on a Fast Day.[6]

With regard to 'superstition', Blairmore in particular seems to have been reprehensibly credulous: in 1712, there were rumours that some people in the vicinity had seen 'ane apparition', and among the milkmaids, one girl had said, 'It is the spirit of some person deceased who left some money hid – God send it in my way to inform me where the gold is!' Then the next day she was accused of being 'a poor wretch who for the love of gear prayed God to send the Divell in her way to inform her of money or a treasure'. She attempted to pass off her wish as a joke, but the Session took it very seriously and censured her.

Later there is a record of a peculiar happening: one Blairmore woman complained that another had claimed to have seen her and others 'sitting upon the highway and that they had a dish of her flesh among them, meaning that they were backbiting her'. On the Lord's Day the daughter of the complainant had commented, 'Mother, if they had a dish of your flesh, the Divell give them bread to it'. The young woman was publicly rebuked for 'prophanation of the Lord's day by impious unchristian expressions'.

Accusations of witchcraft were frequently made in Arran in the early days, some on more serious grounds than others. In our day it is often assumed that witches were punished only for evil deeds, whether real or imagined. That this was not always so is demonstrated by one case which came up in front of Kilbride Session on 3 June 1705. A man called Robert Stewart was accused of calling Mary Stewart (a relation?) a witch. He defended himself on the grounds that what he had said was the truth, since Mary had used charms when curing sick people. When asked what words she used while exercising her art, Mary recited the following poem:

> Togidh Criosd do chnamhan
> mar thog Muire a lamhan
> nar thuireadh golann faoi nemh
> mar chruinnigh corp a chuimigh
> Togidh Peadar, togidh Pol
> Togidh Micheal, togidh Eoin
> Togidh Molais is Molinn
> enamhan do chinn suas an fheoil.

> *Christ will raise thy bones*
> *even as Mary raised her hands*
> *when she raised the wail of lamentation towards heaven*
> *as she gathered the body of the bound One.*
> *Peter will raise, Paul will raise,*
> *Michael will raise, John will raise,*
> *Molais and Moling will raise*
> *the bones of thy head up out of the flesh.*

What was wrong with that? (Note the occurrence of Molais in Mary's list of saints.) The words were used for healing 'migrims and other distempers in the head'. But '[t]he Session after holding furth to her that all charms proceeded from the Devil's invention, let the words be never so good, and that they were expressly forbidden in the word of God, they appoynt her to make publick confession of her guilt before the congregation next Lord's Day.'[7] So much for white witches.

Similarly, on 13 June 1708, two women, Janet McIlpatrick and Effie McKallan, were 'delated' to the Session for being absent from church while melting lead, moulding it into a heart shape and hanging it round the neck of Margaret Taylor, in an attempt to cure her of chest pains. On 9 December 1716, Ferguhar Ferguson got into trouble for curing 'Elf Shot'[8] with herbs and particularly one kind of herb that had to be plucked in the name of the Father, the Son and the Holy Ghost: that case was referred to the Presbytery.

William Mackenzie made a unique collection of Arran superstitions, super-natural tales and other folk elements still current in his day – giving the originals in the Arran dialect of Gaelic, which was spoken up to about 1950. These were published with their English versions in his Volume II of *The Book of Arran* (1914), and I have reproduced some of them in Appendix II of this book, in order to make more familiar to the public – or simply to conserve – these now rare examples of Gaelic folk-lore and mythic thinking.

Perhaps this is the right place to mention a Western Islands practice noted by the late seventeenth-century traveller Martin Martin: the 'force-fire' or Needfire (Neatsfire, from neat, 'cattle'), a ritual against witchcraft or the plague or the cattle-murrain or other serious infection. If such a spell or disease came to the parish, all the fires in the community were put out, and a 'force-fire' was generated by the well-known Boy Scout technique of rubbing two pieces of wood together: this task was performed by the men of the parish in relays. When the fire was lit, it was used to light new fires throughout the parish – or to heat water which was sprinkled over the suffer-ers, to their instant relief. The ritual is said to have been performed in Arran as recently as 1820. The Kirk's displeasure seems not to have been in evidence on this occasion – or, at least, I have found no record of it – presumably because it involved animals rather than human beings and did not invoke saints or demons.

The eighteenth-century Church had its forward-looking intellectuals, bred up in the fertile union of education and religion, in Arran as elsewhere. They often excelled in the field of philology. The Reverend Duncan Smith of Kilmory was an Orientalist, i.e. he was interested in Hebrew and related languages. He, however, died young, at the age of twenty-nine in 1801, after only two years in the parish. More important was an earlier figure, the Reverend William Shaw, born but never ministering in Kilmory (Clachaig), who published the successful *Analysis of the Gaelic Language* in 1778 and, in 1780, a book with the long title typical of the time – *A Gaelic and English Dictionary, containing all the words in the Scottish and Irish dialects of the Celtic, that could be collected from the voice and old books and MSS, followed by an English and Gaelic Dictionary* ... This, however, ran into trouble: Shaw took the wrong side in the controversy over Macpherson's Ossian (1765) – a linked series of poems which purported to be translations from Gaelic about the exploits of 'Ossian' (the fabled Celtic hero Oisin) and his son Fingal. Because of the polished eighteenth-century style of the English versions, many critics took the view that they had no Gaelic originals and were faked up out of whole cloth: in fact Macpherson had adapted the characters and ideas of his stories to suit contemporary literary sensibilities, yet the poems rest upon genuine Gaelic manuscript and oral sources, and have poetic power of their own.

Following the lead of the famous English critic Samuel Johnson, William Shaw took the sceptical side – and lost the favour of the more romantically inclined part of the reading public, mainly Scots and Irish (some of whom recognized the authenticity of Macpherson's sources). Poor Shaw was assailed by indirect means: the Ossian controversy was not mentioned; instead, he was accused of lexical false pretences – overloading his dictionary (which was a subscription edition) with Irish as opposed to Scottish Gaelic; this was partially true, since he had found it easier to get data from the Irish peasantry than from the mercenary Scottish Highlanders, who tried to extract cash payment from him per vocabulary item; the case was taken as far as the Court of Session, where a decision was given in Shaw's favour – and indeed Irish and Scottish Gaelic had been identical until the fifteenth century. But William Shaw's real offence was to impugn Macpherson; he was effectually ruined in Scotland, went south in disgust, and joined the Church of England, where he found a living probably through the influence of Dr Johnson.[9]

The Kirk and education

Education was a responsibility of the Church in Scotland from the earliest days; in pre-Reformation times, education had slowly developed from the times when educated men and copyists were needed to disseminate the message and the sacred texts of Christianity among the pagan masses, to a more complicated organization where training of choristers was required for church music and where centres of learning prepared aspirants not only to the priesthood but – cautiously at first – to learned professions such as secular law and diplomacy; the predecessor of Ayr Academy in 1233 was headed by an ecclesiastic important enough to be a witness to state documents, and the diplomat Hugh Kennedy had learnt his grammar from the Dominican friars of Ayr.[10] Schools and universities expanded to teach not only theology but canon and civil law, medicine and the arts – including grammar, rhetoric, logic and philosophy; later, from the middle of the sixteenth century, the Reformation in Scotland brought an entirely new if still religious element into the equation: that every person in the land was equally entitled to absorb the Christian message from its sources, and therefore should be able to read the Bible, which itself began to be translated into the vernacular. Not only ministers should be able to read and expound in Latin and increasingly in English, but 'ordinary people' should be trained to read and write: the school-master became more important in the local community – not necessarily as a cleric, though schoolmastering was often a preliminary step to the ministry.

However, the greater spread of education was very patchy in early Scotland. Arran was too poor and remote to attract a concentrated educational effort such as one might find in Edinburgh or Aberdeen. John Knox had envisaged a school in every parish, but it was more than a century after his death, in 1698, that an Act of the Scottish Parliament required there to be at least one school and schoolmaster in each parish, the upkeep being laid upon the local landowners – 'heritors' and tenants alike. Almost a century again elapsed before this requirement was fully met; it had no very willing response any-where in the country, the landowners dragging their heels in respect of any financial contribution at all. Educational provision often fell by default upon the Kirk Sessions alone. Thus, in Arran in the eighteenth century as elsewhere, education was heavily slanted toward religion: everybody in the parish should

120

at least be literate in his or her profession of religion. In 1731 we find Kilmory Session stipulating that anybody wishing to get married in the parish must at least have the Shorter Catechism (the printed series of questions and answers whereby the individual confirmed his or her Christianity in public) by heart, 'under penalty of five merks Scots'.

Of course the educational responsibilities of the Sessions ranged beyond the strictly religious. They had not only to license schoolmasters but also to ensure the provision of premises on a very restricted budget – mainly composed of the small fines that they were entitled to levy in their capacity as guardians of the parish morals. In Kilmory in 1704 they laid down strict specifications for the building of the schoolhouse, which the selected schoolmaster was apparently expected to supervise personally. It was to be of two rooms only – one for living quarters for the master and one schoolroom; 'sufficient lights', according to McLellan,[11] amounted to unglazed windows opened or closed depending upon the direction of the wind. It would be a draughty place for learning. The building was to be thatched with divot and heather, and would have a hearth in the middle of the floor with a hole in the roof above. The sources do not state whether there were to be two hearths, or whether it was the children or the teacher who would have to shiver in the snell winds of Arran. The cost was to be £40 Scots – perhaps not too much for the fines exacted for casual immorality within the parish.

Similar buildings were to be found near the old St Brigid's chapel at Lamlash (probably built in 1709) and in the Glenashdale area (South Kiscadale, Whiting Bay), where an assistant to the main (parochial) Kilbride schoolmaster was required. Some far-flung communities, where the distances to the main school were too great for the children to walk, provided micro-schools ('petty schools'). These did not have custom-built schoolhouses, but took advantage of the private dwellings of the teachers or local barns or even shoreline caves. In the Shiskine district pupils used to stuff holes in the walls with moss to keep the draught out.[12] By contrast, the Preaching Cave near Kilpatrick was draught-proof and warm, and was used as a schoolroom until 1843.

The Kilbride Session also arranged for monthly school inspections by the minister and an elder; in the 1704 enactment they warn the teacher, Mr Angus Ker, to be more attentive to his duties and to make sure that his lessons 'profite the Children', under penalty of instant dismissal (eighteenth-century 'payment by results'). The schoolmaster at Arrantoun in Kilbride is admonished for his intemperance (with rum) and for drunken quarrelling with his wife (26 September 1714).

Many if not all of these schools were run on the basis of one individual teaching a full range of ages in all the then available subjects, in a single room often under wretched conditions. Nothing like universal comprehensive education was thinkable, although each group of children may have vaguely resembled a 'mixed ability' class, perhaps with the more able assisting the slower or younger pupils. In 1800, in Shiskine, only two girls were taught to write. Some children, perhaps numbers in each catchment area, would never attend school, although truancy was probably less frequent than today because of the fees demanded from the parents. 'Special educational needs' would of course be met with exclusion from any kind of education at all.

Before the turn of the century, parochial schools were few and far between (only two in Kilmory), and the heritor (the Duke of Hamilton) and the tenants contributed equally to the masters' salaries; this was probably in addition to provision of free housing and supplementary fees for teaching individual subjects (quarterly: 1s for reading, 1s 6d for writing, 2s 6d for arithmetic). In continuation of the link with the Kirk, schoolmasters also received a substantial annual fee – £6 – for acting as 'session-clerks', with 1s for each marriage and 6d for each baptism (from marriage-couples and parents).

Pay for the teachers at side schools came from the same three sources – the Kirk Session, the heritor, and the children's fees.

The Great Revival

Towards the end of the eighteenth century and the beginning of the nineteenth, in Arran as elsewhere there began to appear a new spirit in religious observance, not always respectful of existing institutions. In the case of the Haldane brothers, who preached in Arran in 1800, the Kirk of Scotland could not satisfy their missionary urges, and they set up independent 'tabernacles', small meeting places where the new vision was preached with fire and vigour: both the Haldanes were young, tough, rich ex-naval officers who had distinguished themselves in the service. The model of church government enjoined by the Haldanes became known as Congregationalism, or 'Independency' – a rule where each congregation is sovereign over its own affairs. This style of church government had an obvious appeal for those dissenting from the official Church of Scotland line on patronage.

After their initial plan of setting up a mission in India was frustrated by the Honourable East India Company, they set out to revive Christianity throughout northern and western Scotland by a combination of preaching and tract-distribution. Their territory included both Arran and Kintyre. In order to call as many as possible of the faithful to renewal they undertook a punishing schedule, sometimes undertaking as many as four preachings in different places in one day, in a time when communications were very poor. They often walked from place to place (or travelled with a pony and light cart filled with tracts). The result of these methods was that large-scale meetings took place out of doors, with crowds trekking miles to hear the addresses; some people thought the old field-conventicles of the seventeenth-century Covenanters were being revived – and were alarmed. Certainly the landowners, as patrons of the official Kirk, were nervous, and on one occasion in Kintyre one of the Haldanes was actually arrested and avoided having to take an Oath of Loyalty only because the Sheriff could not find the correct form of words.[13]

In Arran, the Haldanes' mission resulted directly in the setting up of a Congregationalist church in the Sannox locality. Generally the anti-patronage implication of the mission, together with its charismatic evangelism, spread to the whole of Kilmory Parish and beyond, creating the spiritual conditions leading to Arran's Great Revival. It was an important stage in the journey, ultimately leading to the 1843 Great Disruption of the national Church.

In 1800 the Kilmory parish minister was the 'Orientalist' Duncan Smith, who died in 1801. He was succeeded in 1802 by the Reverend Neil McBride, a man with a fire in his belly, whose preaching was in tune with the powerful pessimism of the Haldanes. His call to repentance prompted, among the parishioners, a salutary sense of sins weighing on their souls. From the first beginnings in 1804–5 to the summit of the Great Revival in 1812–13, a sense of being unworthy sinners grew darker and darker among the population. According to the Reverend Angus M'Millan, 'In 1810 and 1811, many were lower and more abandoned in wickedness than they had been at any former period'.[14]

Guilty self-knowledge held the parishioners of Kilmory in thrall; 1812 saw a characteristic outbreak of 'outcrying', very recognizable in our own time. The estate factor John Paterson wrote, 'Almost at every meeting, when a clergyman or other person, who they judged to have the Spirit, presided, great numbers, especially of women and children, were moved in a most extraordinary manner, uttering strange cries, trembling and falling into convulsions, so that the service could not go on with regularity'.[15] 'Multitudes' packed the churches, people trudged miles to hear the preachers, and the services became longer and longer and more disorganized. The Reverend Andrew Bonar relates how '[a] plain lad, whose heart was filled with joy in believing, was heard praying at one of these meetings: "Lord, pity the people in Kilmory who are content with tatties and sour milk, when they might have their soul satisfied with fatness."'[16]

Neil McBride ministered in Kilmory until his death in 1815. Thereafter the congregation clamoured for the Lochranza catechist, Angus McMillan, an evangelist of the same temperament as McBride, but once again the old obstacle arose: the Duke of Hamilton as Patron presented Dugald Crawford (formerly assistant to the Reverend Hamilton in Kilmory), in 1815 the minister of Saddell in Kintyre, a man well stricken in years. The congregation deserted the parish church and the douce Crawford in droves, setting up their own unofficial church in 'The Preaching Cave' (Uamh Mhor) below Kilpatrick under the leadership of an ex-farmer called William MacKinnon. But in the end, in 1821, the Reverend Crawford was drowned crossing the Firth of Clyde, and Angus McMillan came into his own as it were, becoming the parish minister of Kilmory in 1822.

The 'happy-clappy' style of worship[17] began to pall from the beginning of 1813, and some of the most conspicuous converts showed a lamentable disposition to back-slide. McMillan notes with regret, 'Like the stony-ground hearers, the religious impressions of many were slight and transitory ... coldness, deadness, and formality in religion are now too prevalent among us'. In fact, religious observance simply reverted to more traditional forms, in which there was not as much breast-beating and trouble of conscience among the ordinary people as in more fervid times.

In the Arran of 1823 there was still a division between the Congregationalist Reverend Alex MacKay of Glen Sannox (directly succeeding to the Haldanes' mission), and the preferred, more fiery Gaelic preaching of the now established Mr McMillan of 'The Tent'. But in that year we get a sense of a more relaxed, happier religious atmosphere in the island, in the mildly disapproving description of a Congregationalist flock gathering for communion sent by a lady visitor in a letter to a relative on the mainland:

> The church is six miles from this, but notwithstanding the roads hereabouts were covered with people going to church today, some in carts, some on horses, double, and many walking . . . The red cloaks and tartan plaids gave vivacity to the scene, and could we have thought them all animated with a spirit of devotion the spectacle would have been truly gratifying, but I fear many make of it too much a ploy and an occasion for the display of new clothes; for in many of the houses we found tailors making clothes for the occasion, and in one house a fine red cloak for the gude-wife . . . The road to church exhibited to us a novel spectacle – cart after cart in thick succession conveyed the aged and those unable to walk – many were on horseback, and many on foot – all seemingly impressed with the sacredness of the day and the solemnity of the ordinance about to be celebrated. The common in front of the church was covered with vehicles, and with the horses which peacefully waited the return of their owners from the services of the day. Perhaps, two hundred horses were on the common[18]

Eleven years after this, the celebratory, almost party atmosphere is even more marked:

> The distance from Shisken to Kilmory Kirk across the moor would be six or seven miles, by the road farther. The people in ascending the hill going south frequently formed into squads and got merrily along; the lasses clean and tidily dressed would take off their shoes "with an eye to economy" and skip along, and on nearing the Kirk sat by the Burn-side and put on their White stockings and shoes and then marched into the Church. The elder folk went on Carts or on horse-back by the road, those who rode having their wives seated behind them, and with their scarlet mantles they commonly formed a picturesque sight.[19]

OS references

The moral guardianship of the Church
Blairmore NS 028 325

The Kirk and education
South Kiscadale NS 040 256
Arrantoun NS 024 306

The Great Revival
The Preaching Cave, Uamh Mhor NR 900 265

13. Enclosure, Clearance, Disruption, Famine

The Agricultural Revolution

From the beginning of the eighteenth century a whole series of radical and fundamental changes took place in Europe, in Britain and in Arran. Kings and queens themselves were being transformed into so-called 'enlightened despots' and even constitutional monarchs, although, like Frederick the Great of Prussia, they sometimes combined greater understanding of the needs of their peoples with continued ferocious warlordism. Correspondingly, lesser aristocrats were metamorphosed from barbarous tribal chieftains lording it over semi-autonomous private domains to wealthy proprietors, anxious to maximize profits from their landed estates. In Britain, following the mood-change that came about with the conclusion of the Civil War, and the aftershocks of the Restoration and the Glorious Revolution, landlords turned their attention away from martial arts and confrontation, to apply instead the techniques of a different kind of revolution – the agricultural one. In Arran, the most important feature of life to be reshaped in the melting-pot of the eighteenth century was agriculture, both pastoral and arable.

Arran, in 1766, was probably still in a depressed state after the devastation of the Civil Wars more than a century before – especially perhaps on the west side, which had been exposed to depredations from Kintyre. The island had never been a particularly fertile spot after the forest clearances of the Neolithic and Bronze Ages, and the subsequent blanketing of peat extending over the whole terrain. However, since about the tenth century, Arran had benefited by improvements in climate and also by new methods of farming, including soil fertilization, perhaps introduced by the Vikings. Although the island was mountainous, low-lying pockets of good soil existed all round the southern coastline at the mouths of rivers and up the valleys, as well as the extensive plain of the Blackwater in the south-west: in these areas, arable farming could be pursued. At a greater altitude in the interior, mountain and moorland provided rough (summer) grazing for cattle, sheep and horses. In some parts of the coast, ledges of fertile soil made for what is still almost a series of terraced farms in steep cliff faces. Rough grazings, however, accounted for the greater part of Arran: Martin Martin said in 1695, 'The whole isle is designed by nature more for pasturage than for cultivation.'

Whether nature or the Vikings designed Arran for the last millennium is perhaps a moot point, though Nordic place names such as Glen Scorrodale and Chalmadale may lead us to suspect that Viking owners were responsible for the mediaeval organization of the land. It is also worth considering that an analogous if more dramatic pattern of farming is to be seen in the Norwegian fjords, where patches of fertility are to be seen grouped along the shoreline and up the steep cliffs, while the sæters, or summer grazings, are often seen at an astonishing height above the farms. This style of farming may go back a long way.

Farming was paramount in Arran, and although fish were plentiful in the seas surrounding, fishing as an activity always took second place, to be carried on during the agricultural off-season.

Runrig

Now, for many centuries before the eighteenth, mixed agriculture had been carried on in the island by a system of runrig, based on small settlements – groups of dwellings and associated agricultural land: communal units known as [ferm-] touns or clachans.

Each clachan provided subsistence for a number of families, multiple tenants sharing ownership of livestock and strips of cultivation, runrigs ('runrig' = roinn, 'share' + rig, 'ridge'): plots of land adjacent to the clachan were divided into strips, furrowed and banked by the plough in such a way as to give a corrugated appearance to the land: the top surface of the bank was cultivated with oats, barley, potatoes or whatever. The dividing trench, or baulk, between each strip provided necessary drainage. Each tenant sharing membership of the clachan community was allocated one or several strips, from which his or her share of the crops would be drawn, although the land was worked on a communal basis.

These rigs or strips were worked in two different kinds of area in relation to the clachan: the infield or 'croft-land' and the outfield, which was a wider area surrounding the infield and clachan. Beyond the outfield lay common pasture. The infield was subject to unremitting cropping, leading to major soil exhaustion in spite of being constantly manured (principally, in Arran, with kelp). The outfield was subject to a three-fold rotation, cropping year in and year out to the point of exhaustion, after which it was abandoned to lie fallow with grass and weeds, or for milk-yielding cattle to graze, enriching the ground with dung. After some years, the outfield would be judged to have recovered, and would be broken up again for cropping. However, the tendency was to convert a greater and greater part of the outfield into infield, which led to intense cultivation of all the productive land in the holding, with inefficient fallowing. As yet, at the beginning of the eighteenth century, permanent fencing was a rarity, even between the areas claimed by the respective farms, and proper drainage was unknown.

Beyond the outfield again, the mountainside was used as common pasture, into which all animals – cattle, sheep, horses and goats – were driven. In this area, the sheiling, at a higher elevation than the rest of the farm, animals were grazed during the summer months, and the members of the community who tended the herds there lived in rough structures, sheiling huts. Remnants of these huts, and of the ruined clachans themselves, are still to be found scattered across the landscape. This method of stock transfer to higher ground in the summer is known as 'transhumance'.

The sheep and cattle were undersized and meagre compared with today's animals, in spite of forming a substantial part of Arran's exports to the mainland. Horses, also exported, were necessary adjuncts of day-to-day labour, but were again undersized, akin to the kind of horses known as *garrons*. They were expensive and sometimes had to be shared out between two or more peasants. (The normal team for ploughing consisted of four horses.) Sometimes human traction took the place of horse power and it was not uncommon for gangs of people, women and children as well as men, to labour together to pull the heavy primitive ploughs over the ground.

The strips were subject to annual redistribution among the tenants of the clachan. The yearly allocation of the rigs was determined by an adaptation of the 'short straw' method, drawing lots, by the toun 'tacksman', the principal tenant, known as the *fear a bhaile*: he was responsible for collecting tacks (rents) from the other tenants and in turn paying a tack for the whole clachan to the superior landlord.

Villages as such, small urban centres, did not exist in the early eighteenth century in Arran: clachans or ferm-touns were mere clusters of primitive dwellings in the fields, perhaps the rough equivalent of 'hamlets' in other parts of the country. The characteristic style of ferm-toun architecture, common throughout Scotland, was the black house or long house, in which human beings shared the accommodation with the animals: one end of the house was a byre for cattle and the other was the living quarters (a kitchen, and, divided from it by a partition, sleeping accommodation).[1] The building would be roofed by a thatch of heather or equivalent material, probably weighed down against the fierce winds by a tarpaulin with lead weights hanging round the edges. Sometimes under the thatch there was a garret supported by rafters and reserved for the children. The house was lit by unglazed windows covered by heavy wooden shutters which were open or closed depending on the direction of the wind. Perhaps some idea of the living conditions in these buildings may be obtained by visiting the so-called Burns Cottage in Alloway, south of Ayr, on the mainland. Museum specimens of black houses are to be found in Skye and elsewhere, but not in Arran.

John Burrel's plan for enclosures

The death of the Good Duchess Anne of Arran had taken place in 1716. Anne, as we have said, was the first really capable owner of Arran, rescuing and consolidating the Hamilton estates, and taking thought for the social, commercial and religious life of the island. Just fifty years after her death, there came forward another strong individual with a modernizing, improving mission: this was the estates manager John Burrel, who was given specific instructions by the young Duke of Hamilton's trustees in 1766 to undertake a wholesale shake-up of the Arran estates. He went at his task with a will but had very limited results: yet, however unsuccessful, he set the trend for a transformation which ultimately gave us the Arran landscape of today.

The whole style of runrig agriculture was primitive, low and uncertain in yields, and obviously uneconomical. Yet even peasants with very little capital resources could survive in this context. It was not so secure for them after Burrel's arrival.

He came from Kinneil in West Lothian, where he had acquired a wealth of practical experience in running landed estates, and, from books, a deep knowledge of the philosophy and background of the agricultural revolution. Both personally active and scientifically meticulous, he based his campaign on his own fact-finding investigations and painstaking gathering of data. He was the first person to attempt, for instance, to estimate the value of Arran land by soil analysis (carried out by himself) as well as by statistical assessment of the number of animals supported on the land and the production of a given quantity of grain.

All the farms in Arran were visited by Burrel himself and reported upon. In accordance with his template, he sought two things: radically improved farming methods, but, above all, a rationalization of farm holdings – the division and enclosure of farm land, with a correspondingly drastic reduction in the number of tenants. Herein lies the germ of his ultimate frustration: he was so set upon this ideal of streamlining the farms, with increased profits for *the noble proprietor*, that he forgot to take into account the human cost as well as the sheer practical difficulties of stripping away the agricultural 'deadwood'.

In 1766, there were about 100 runrig farms in Arran, the majority spread along the coasts of the island. Most of these were extensive, but each 'fermtoun', because of the inherent inefficiencies of runrig farming, still had to struggle to support a large population of clachan-dwelling peasants and their families. Burrel disapproved of the communal features of runrig and was prejudiced in favour of a single farmer's independent control of an enclosed holding. He hoped to eliminate all the 'commonty' of land by the time all the leases in the estate had run out (mostly in 1772).

After his research and assessments, John Burrel put forward and tried to implement the following scheme: each of the holdings should be divided into smaller farms commensurate with the labour and financial resources of one lessee with a family and dependants; the old rigs should be replaced with enclosed fields for both arable and pastoral purposes; the former open common ground on the mountain and hillsides should also be enclosed in blocks corresponding to the extent of the nearest farm below.

Proper rotation of crops should be observed; in particular, potatoes should be grown only on new and newly turned ground; adequate manuring should follow ploughing; lime (a form of manure) should be obtained from quarries opened for the purpose (and carted and paid for by the peasants). Each farm enclosed its former infield and outfield together as one parcel of land, which was then to be divided into three parts, 'not more than one of which was to be ploughed and sown, the rest to lie under grass; and not more than two crops to be taken in succession'.[2] Within these fields the quality of crops was to be raised, good seed (and stock) hopefully being obtained.

Burrel's plans for enclosure were only minimally realized in his lifetime.[3] He had to struggle against inertia, even in those who had invited his schemes; a proposal that the Duke himself – the Hamilton estate – should undertake the reshaping of each farm and elimination of runrig was speedily dropped. The work was then assigned to each tenant, but it was soon downgraded from compulsory to merely optional, and much of Burrel's time thereafter was spent trying to cajole individual groups of farmers into giving the new ideas a chance.

Burrel did succeed in having walls ('head dykes') erected between each farm to prevent the straying of cattle from one property to another. But it proved impossible to enclose the high common pasture beyond the fields themselves: there had been, since the earliest days, a custom of annual 'souming' – of assigning so many animals belonging to each peasant to a given extent of pasture – and the variations from year to year in the pasture assigned proved impossible to reconcile with the fixed limits of an enclosure.

The new lessees (mostly the former tacksmen of the old clachans) were forbidden to sub-divide their new tacks, which were to be non-transferable either in whole or in part, except under licence: there was to be no backsliding into the old-fashioned multiple tenancy typical of runrig.

It had been common practice in north-west Scotland as elsewhere for a section of a farm to be divided off for a child or children of a tenant to run as a separate unit as subtenants; besides, there were very small plots of land or single houses ('cottages') occupied by cottars who sometimes, without paying money rent, bartered their services to the main tenant in return for accommodation and other perquisites; and of course there were some cottars who were simply squatters on the land and were maintained without rent as an act of charity.

If customary practice were forbidden and one tenant became responsible for an entire formerly communal farm, the rent became far too burdensome for a single individual.

The factor that frustrated his reforms was precisely the one that should have occurred to this methodical, forward-looking, money-minded man, John Burrel: his new valuations, expressed in terms of rent, were simply beyond the means of most of the lessees. Those who were left in possession were thus unlucky – and those who were not were doubly so. According to one of Inglis's sources, 'Those who were in arrears with their rents got [no portion of land], while those who had their rents paid up got lots [parcels of land], but they had to pay up the arrears of their unfortunate neighbours.'[4]

The number of tenant families on the island would be reduced from about 1,000 to around 250, leaving at least 750 families out of work, with no prospect of local re-employment save as very depressed agricultural labourers in the service of their former neighbours. Looking for other work elsewhere was often checkmated by the sheer lack of transport, one of many factors tying the Arran peasantry to their native soil; another was linguistic – work for Gaelic men and women was not easily found in the Scots-speaking parts of the country, where employment opportunities were greatest.

John Burrel believed that high rents equalled high agricultural yields, and therefore should be applied as encouraging improvement. Tacks were to be calculated partly from the anticipated yield in terms of farm produce and livestock, and partly from the (newly enclosed) acreage of the farm – taking into account the then rising value of farmland in Ayrshire and other mainland areas; in these areas land was being transferred at ever-faster rates from the ancient aristocracy to the new bourgeoisie, successful businessmen anxious to attain the rank of landed proprietors.[5]

The principle of competitive tenancies destroyed the security of tenure on which the peasant way of life had originally depended. In 1775, the traveller

Thomas Pennant observed, 'The succeeding tenants [in Arran] generally find the ground little better than a *caput mortuum*; and for this reason, should they at the expiration of the lease leave the lands in a good state, some avaricious neighbours would have the preference in the next setting, by offering a price more than the person who had expended part of his substance in enriching the farm could possibly do. This induces them to leave it in the original state.'[6]

Burrel's rents were exorbitant. But, supposing a provident and improving sitting tenant was somehow able to meet the rent and thereby increase the value of his farm, by that very fact he might risk being outbid and dislodged at the end of his tenancy by any person with a deeper purse than his own – whereas, with the 'kindly tenancies' of the Middle Ages, a single family could retain a lease, or hold a clachan together for several generations. Now the peasants were in a no-win situation: if they could not meet the rent they were evicted; if they could, they risked being outbid. And, with Burrel's reforms, one tenant per farm had to meet the new rent on his own resources. Bankruptcy succeeded bankruptcy, and several farms were abandoned and fell into ruin.

The basic philosophy was flawed from the beginning – the assumption was that the lack of productivity was directly associated with the indolence, ignorance and racial inferiority of the native peasantry. The cart was put before the horse: since high rents seemed to be associated with high productivity, these rents were demanded before yields could be raised, on the hallowed principle of a boot up the backside.

An example quoted by Margaret Storrie gives a clear picture of how and why Burrel's streamlining designs were frustrated.[7] She examines the case of the fairly large runrig holding of Bennecarrigan in the south-west of the island. In 1766 the place was listed as having one tacksman, Robert McCook, and ten sub-tenants. In 1772, Burrel planned to sub-divide this farm into seven separate holdings, each with its own tenant operating the holding independently. In 1773, it is obvious that the offer of the separate farms had simply not taken, and all seven newly defined properties were leased as a single unit – to the same Robert McCook. In 1776 the lease had passed to John McCook (Robert's son?), and in three more years Bennecarrigan went bankrupt: the abolition of the runrig collective farm and the efforts to enclose and improve it had proved too much of a strain on what were probably very meagre financial resources. In 1779, therefore, the whole process started again, and Bennecarrigan was this time divided into twelve holdings, each with its own tacksman. Once again, however, the cost of redeveloping each holding was too much for a single man even on the reduced scale, and, despite the clear prohibition of further subletting, the twelve farms were each divided in two. So, in the end, in the place of one tacksman and (ten) subtenants, Bennecarrigan became a mosaic of twenty-four holdings – twelve tacksmen and twelve subtenants, who reportedly spent their time quarrelling among themselves.

In the case of Glencloy, Burrel's 1773 division was into four farms, East, West, Mid and South Glencloy, tenanted respectively by 'Hector (MacAlister), Al. McBride, Alln. Fullarton, Pk. McBride'. Yet, by the time of Bauchop's map (1811), at least seven tenants are listed, and by 1815, when the general enclosure plan was to be implemented, only one tenant is indicated for Glencloy, Dr John Stoddart. The same kind of fate as at Bennecarrigan seems to have befallen Glencloy; that Stoddart was the sole tenant in 1815 may be explained by the fact that this man would be one of the richest men in Arran, as the Duke's personal physician and one of the two JPs on the island (the other being the estate factor).

In perhaps a majority of cases, the former headmen of clachans were transformed into sole tenants of enclosed property which was too expensive for single families to run. The rent demanded was just too much for one farmer: it had to be shared, and subdivision of the land with subtenancy appeared to be the only option. Burrel's plans were bound to be frustrated by this factor alone. Most of the farms on Arran remained in multiple occupancy and communal tenancy with runrig cultivation and associated inefficiencies till at least 1815. In the meantime the population of the island actually increased, in part due to the introduction of potato farming with its superior cropping per plant and relative ease of cultivation.

By 1792 (according to a report of 1800) the blame had been decisively laid at the door of Mr Burrel and his 'original plan', which caused 'the tenants ... [to] run into great arrears, of no less than Three Years rent, and of necessity [they] soon became bankrupt ... When William Stevenson commenced Factor on the Estate at Whitsunday 1792 the whole tenants on the Estate were one and a half years rent in arrears; he by persevering, care and exertion ... brought the whole Tenants ... to liquidate arrears. At Martinmas 1795 when the Leases of about two-thirds of the Estate came to be expired, it was for the interest of the Duke of Hamilton deemed highly necessary, not to let such a large proportion of the Estate for Leases of nineteen years at one time to Arran tenants, and especially to those who were not likely to improve in their mode of farming.'[8]

After Burrel: implementation of enclosure and clearance

In 1784, already a new factor, John Cochrane, had reported on Bennecarrigan and other properties and tenants, mentioning 'bad tenants', tenants being replaced by others, and describing how tacksmen and subtenants were 'rouped' (their farms were auctioned off over their heads). He was of the opinion that 'the hurt arising to the real interest of the Duke' stems from there being too many tacksmen in the farms and 'the houses being almost always in a cluster together' (i.e. settlements were still in the pattern of the ancient clachans, where the newly 'promoted' chief tenants lived cheek-by-jowl with their less fortunate brethren.)[9]

The Hamilton possessions in Arran were more and more fragmented, in spite of the retention of the boundaries of the former larger holdings. It seemed to the administrators of the estate that further adjustment of the whole land-holding system was urgently required, and to begin with there was much uncertainty about which direction to take.

At last, however, starting in 1814, John Burrel's basic ideas began to be systematically realized, though possibly not in the form originally conceived: the Hamiltons marked out larger farms and invited more progressive and 'industrious' farmers from the mainland (Ayrshire, Renfrew and Lanark) to take up leases upon them; enclosures began to be effectively implemented and the runrig system to be eased out.

Enclosures could imply a policy of wholesale eviction, and removing tenants legally became easier after 1804. In Arran, 'decreets of removal' were served against no fewer than 708 tenants in eighty holdings.[10] Yet the number of farming units increased almost fourfold in the years after 1814. Until 1815, the number of farms in the Hamilton estate had remained at 113, and each of these had multiple (four to twelve) sub-tenancies, created by the process outlined above. But in the 1814–15 shake-up the sub-tenancies were transformed into separate holdings, i.e. their numbers quadrupled to 458.[11] As

Storrie points out, the multiplication of smallholdings was the most tangible, almost the only real result of the Agricultural Revolution in Arran.[12]

Of these 458 (or 448) post-1815 farms, fifty-three were large and the others were from two to forty acres in extent. Arable farming was concentrated in coastal regions in the south of the island and in the plains of the south-west; the northern half of the island and indeed much of the hillier parts of the south was given over to sheep-farming – seemingly more profitable than arable and requiring far less staffing.[13]

Decisive action had at last been taken – and similar action nationwide over this period led directly to the agricultural and social upheaval known as The Clearances. These gave rise to terrible suffering in some parts of Scotland. In order to accelerate the conversion of allegedly useless land to profitable sheep-walks, men like the notorious Sutherland factor ('Commissioner') Patrick Sellar did not hesitate to burn people's homes over their heads and turn the inhabitants out in a destitute, homeless condition. The people of the interior of the district of Strathnaver, driven almost literally naked from their homes, were told that they could set up such housing as they could physically build on tiny, unsuitable plots of land on the north coast. We read of whole districts with 250 or 300 houses aflame, crops burnt, smoke clouding the countryside, cattle untended or destroyed – and even of marriage itself being forbidden by decree of the Countess of Sutherland, as it were to cut off the supply of new unwanted Highlanders at source.

The motives for such forced removals were not just economic. In Scotland at large, landowner and (more frequently) estate factor hostility towards the natives stemmed not only from the ideology of enclosure and the 'inconsiderate rage' for sheep farming, but also from intemperate anti-Celtic racism. This was often expressed as a conviction that nothing could be done for the ordinary Highlanders unless the Gaelic language were completely eradicated. In Arran, the factor John Paterson, one of the more sinister of Burrel's successors, was highly prejudiced against Gaelic, and he expressed himself in openly racist terms in a paper presented to the Royal Highland and Agricultural Society in 1837: he described Arran feet and limbs 'especially of the females, [as] very clumsy, the former being large and flat, the ankles thick, and the heel projecting considerably beyond the limb'. He declared that 'although generally honest in their dealings with one another [Arran folk] frequently, like the Jews, think

137

it no great crime to get as much as they can from strangers, or those in a situation above them in rank'.[14] In this light, the Clearances can be seen almost as a kind of 'ethnic cleansing'.

William Aiton, in his report for the Board of Agriculture in 1810, describes the then inhabitants of Arran as 'blamefully ignorant, indolent, and wedded to many prejudices and bad habits . . .'[15] He says that these attributes are 'the fault of the proprietor alone', but he points the finger of blame at the defective style of land management, by which he clearly means the failure at that time to adopt fully a policy of land enclosure – this policy including the dual principle already referred to: high rents to encourage improvement and low wages to stimulate harder work;[16] both leading to the expulsion of the ignorant and indolent of Arran.

The character of the Sutherland monster, Patrick Sellar, may be gauged from the eyewitness account of an episode of June 1814, in which the house of a certain William Chisholm was to be set alight in spite of the desperate appeals of the inhabitants that an old bedridden woman of ninety or a hundred years was still inside the building: before the fire was lit, Sellar arrived, was told that the old woman was unfit to be moved, and said, 'Damn her, the old witch, she has lived too long; let her burn.' Immediately the house was set on fire, but some of the younger women managed to get her out, although flames were actually enveloping the bed and sheets: she cried out, 'O teine [O the fire].' She was parked in a little shed, from which the family repelled the arsonists with difficulty, but she never spoke again, and died after five days.[17]

That, together with more general accusations, brought Patrick Sellar to the bar of justice, but he was supported by character references and witnesses who swore to Sellar's limitless benevolence: he was incapable of cruelty or malice! In the Court at Inverness, the Lord Commissioner of Justiciary, Lord Pitmilly, after receiving the unanimous verdict of the jury, dismissed him from the bar.

This episode brings to mind the sinister example, above recounted, of Maister Sheumas of Bute and the resistance to his appointment put up by the Parish of Kilmory in Arran; that episode took place in 1758, more than sixty years before the Sutherland case, but it resounded darkly in the annals of the time.

It is, however, an ill wind that blows nobody any good. The Clearances, harsh and oppressive as they were, relieved suffering in another way. The great

Potato Famine of 1845-50, which began in Ireland and spread to Scotland, created starvation conditions in the north-west Highlands and Islands. Large Scottish estates had been in a parlous condition for many years, and famine had threatened or actually visited the nation several times before 1845, the last occasion as recently as 1835–37. The tenants and cottars were often simply unable to pay any rent at all, and were living in desperate conditions. When these tenants were cleared away, the strain upon local resources relaxed to some extent. Clearance of the land could be a way out both for the owners and for the displaced, and not all clearances involved forcible eviction. Many of the richer landowners met a part or the whole of the cost of shipping the people overseas, as did the Duke of Hamilton in Arran: as related below, he paid half of the travel costs of the 'Megantic' settlers – timeously, seventeen years before the Scottish famine, thus minimizing the pressure placed upon the island when the dearth arrived, as well as maintaining the productiveness of the land through sheep farming.

Megantic

'every man paddle his own canoe . . .'[18]

There were extensive clearances in Arran, leaving some parts of the island completely depopulated. Particular details of these mass evictions are scanty, and, one suspects, hushed up. However, one episode was outstandingly successful – and consequently highlighted in Arran lore: the Odyssey of the inhabitants of the Sannoxes (South, Mid and North), the Laggantuine, the Laggan, the Cuithe and the Cock, all in the north-east of the island.

The families 'were evicted in 1829 to make way for a single large sheep farm at Mid Sannox, and a smaller enclosed farm at the Cock' at the instance of the Duke of Hamilton. The Duke proposed that the residents should emigrate to Canada, and in his benevolence offered to pay half of the fare: he even made arrangements for their reception on the other side of the Atlantic, in what used to be French Canada.

The chosen area was south of the St Lawrence River near Quebec, and north of the border with Maine in the United States. In 1829 it was largely untamed forest, and the authorities were still at the stage of welcoming settlers through a system of agency whose representatives were offering land squared off into lots at advantageous prices. The existing population of the land was predominantly French, and the British, who had conquered Montreal and Quebec in 1759 before the American Revolution, were anxious to attract loyal settlers from Britain and particularly from Scotland.

The crossing by sailing-ship from Britain was always difficult and could be dangerous, but the settlers from Arran, eighty-six of them to begin with, came through comparatively scaithless. They were clearly not destitute, unlike the later sufferers from the Scottish potato famine, and they were able to raise a collection to meet a Greenock stowaway's fare by having a ceilidh on board. However, hardships were endured during a voyage lasting two months, in a brig (the *Caledonia*) of only 196 tons burden; it is almost incredible to think of such a tiny ship, driven only by wind power and laden altogether with 180 persons, tumbling and tossing for so long over the broad Atlantic. They were all violently seasick while they were yet off Ireland, and the length of the voyage imposed a severe water-shortage on them; washing, both of clothes and bodies, was strictly forbidden. Yet no-one actually died on the voyage or from its after-effects, and they reached Canada safe and sound on 25 June 1829, exactly two months after having left Lamlash on 25 April.

The *Caledonia* was towed by a steam tug up the River St Lawrence to Montreal, whence they were to travel to a site in that neighbourhood in the so-called Renfrew County. The Duke of Hamilton had arranged with the land agency for them to settle in that county. They disembarked near a place called Point St Charles, and the women did a monster washing of clothes by the side of the river: in those days there were not even any steam laundries and the clothes had to be washed by hand in the river, and spread out to dry on flat stones – the method going back at least to the time of Homer.

While this was going on the original Quebecois land agent approached the party, vehemently warned them against the Renfrew site and advised them of a site named *Megantic*, south of the St Lawrence. This man may have had a personal interest in selling the site, but he convinced the leaders of the party sufficiently for them to go and have a look.

A leader had now emerged among the emigrants, Archibald M'Killop, a man of strong character and devout Christianity; he and three others trekked about fifty miles south of Quebec to the Megantic region, where they decided that they liked the place.

Back they went to Montreal, and persuaded the other members of the party to take the trouble of re-embarking on barges and to travel back to Point St Nicholas on the south bank of the St Lawrence opposite Quebec city. From there the leaders organized an expedition with pack-horses whereby the whole party, and such equipment as it had, came down to a spot near the small Lac St Joseph (not to be confused with the St Joseph Lake west of Quebec). This place is north of the big Lake Megantic but within Megantic County. It may have been only a temporary stopping place, because the city nowadays called Scottstown is west of Lake Megantic and of the Megantic Mountain. Wherever it was, the settlers determinedly set to work in an allotted area initially called New Hamilton and later simply Scotch Settlement, in which the areas of land to be cleared of forest were fewer than originally promised: there had been an understanding that all the men in the party were to be allocated a free portion of land, but initially this happened only to heads of families.

These settlers in Canada certainly gave the lie to the myth of the worthlessness and idleness of Highlanders from Arran or any other part of Scotland. Under the direction of their self-appointed leader, Archibald M'Killop, they set to work with a will, creating an entire community from scratch, in the middle of primaeval, trackless forest. With our hindsight, we moderns may deplore even the beginnings of forest felling, mirroring the slash-and-burn methods of Neolithic farmers which led to the complete coating of Arran in deep peat thousands of years ago. But the Megantic colony took root long before the world started to be aware of global warming and the other frightening goblins: we cannot withhold admiration from the sheer rugged strength of character, mind and body of these pioneers. They felled great tracts especially of maple and spruce, cleared roots and undergrowth, and prepared ground for both arable and pastoral farming. Each man had a unit of 100 acres; 'Captain' M'Killop had 200 acres.

In the first six months, the average rate of forest clearance was four acres, M'Killop having eighteen acres to his credit. They had only tents or 'wigwams' to live in at first, but by the spring of 1830 log houses had begun to be built, roofed and internally walled with birch-bark, floored with balsam or spruce.

The difficulties that these people had to overcome were daunting in the extreme. For a self-sufficient colony, they had to import food over long distances in almost trackless country; in some respects they had to revert to a hunter-gatherer model, shooting deer and bear and fishing for trout. They had to learn woodcraft and the art of making and paddling canoes.

Communications were primitive in the extreme, and shopping even in the nearest store was a gigantic ordeal involving a round trip of at least seventy miles, undertaken on foot by men and women alike, who had to carry the goods by hand or on their backs. Mackenzie tells of a 'John Sillars [who] bought a hundredweight of flour at Quebec, had it ferried across to St Nicholas, and then carried the load on his back for forty miles to his home'.[19]

The rigours of the Canadian winter were appalling, especially as an efficient method of heating was only painfully evolved: the green wood of the forests was unsuitable for the old style of 'black house' which had for chimney just a hole in the roof above a peat hearth: the Megantic settlers either choked or froze. Before they developed the use of stoves, two of the older women died.

There was employment in the area – lumberjacking and sawmilling – and many of the younger men were able to supply money in this way for food and clothing. But sheep and cattle were introduced, and crops grew in the fertile cleared soil. The colony became permanent, solidly built, economically sound, creating its own sense of community. The spiritual needs of the colonists were attended to, because Captain M'Killop was active and enthusiastic in his Christianity, and, though not ordained, preached strongly to his flock. Marriage ceremonies, however, had at first to be performed in Quebec, meaning that all participants had to tramp forty miles in each direction. Later a log church was erected, and a resident clergyman was found. Similarly, a teacher at first went from house to house, until a regular schoolhouse could be erected. Later still, in the next generation, Mackenzie says that the colony provided its own professional workers – 'doctors, ministers, lawyers, schoolmasters and artisans'. The Megantic colony was a success.

The 1829 *Caledonia* travellers were only the first group from Arran to settle in Megantic County. Others came in successive years, and by 1833 the Arran colony was estimated at 222 individuals of altogether twenty different families.[20]

The situation back in Arran

By contrast, statistics and records of the other large-scale clearances in Arran are defective or non-existent. We are told that, mysteriously, there is no record of the natives of Arran who went to the British mainland to find work, nor of those who were cleared and went to Canada from 'Margareoch, Glenree, Burican, Gargadale, Corriehiam ... Glenscorrodale in the Sliddery glen ... Cloined, Aucheleffan, Strathgail, Ballygonachie, and Auchareoch on the Kilmory water'.[21] That list seems to represent a large number of people to vanish without trace, especially when it is considered that each of these place-names represents at least one 'ferm-toun', one entire small community. McLellan tells us that 'the bulk of the people are said to have gone to Chaleur Bay, opposite Nova Scotia' (some distance away from Megantic). But numbers of indigent Arran people emigrated to ghettos in early industrial Glasgow and must have endured indescribable living conditions there. No record seems to survive.

As for the evictions themselves, we have to glean information from fragments and hints; Mackenzie mentions, in passing, that runrig cultivation 'came to a violent end on the Hamilton lands'[22] but does not elaborate. 'The resolution of these discords is ... possible, but this is not the place for it ...' He hints that Arran folk were angry and bewildered: 'It was not easy to understand why the full economic use of land should mean the amount of produce and cattle it could raise without reference to the number of human beings thereby occupied; why, indeed, greater productiveness should mean fewer producers; why, too, redeeming waste land on the one hand should go along with turning cultivated land into pasture on the other, so that the net result should be less under tillage than before the improvements had begun.'[23]

People saw a judgment in the fate in 1825 of one Captain McKirdy, on the way to take up his new tenancy of the Glenree farm in the south-west of the island, from which the original inhabitants had been evicted. The captain was knocked off his sailing yacht when the boom gybed unexpectedly, fell into the Firth of Clyde and there drowned: '[t]his accident was burdened with a significance appropriate to the occasion,' as Mackenzie delicately puts it.[24]

Before the times of the Clearances few of the island's poor had to apply for assistance to the Kirk Sessions of Kilbride and Kilmory, because they were supported, albeit at a low level, within the communal runrig system; when enclosure came in, the numbers on the parish poor rolls went up: in 1793, for Kilbride there were twelve poor out of 2,545 of a population and for Kilmory forty out of 3,259, but in 1835, for Kilbride the figures had risen to fifty out of 2,397 and for Kilmory to seventy-five out of 3,779.[25]

1843: The Great Disruption of the Church of Scotland: another kind of Clearances

Mass eviction appears again in an unexpected context at this time in Scotland: people were evicted not merely from farms and living quarters but from their spiritual homes throughout the country, and at the instance of the same people – the landowners. Behind the relaxed picture of the country folk in 1822 going to church in their finery, there rumbled on the old discontent over patronage, finally and fiercely exploding in the Great Disruption, in which a large body of ministers literally walked out of the General Assembly of the Church of Scotland in Edinburgh in 1843, and set up their own Church. This was the culminating schism in the Kirk, a protest against the landowners' right to appoint parish ministers. The landowners, of course, reacted strongly, and the creation of the Free Kirk of Scotland resulted in many congregations being expelled with their preachers from the revered parish kirks, which for centuries they had held in as much affection as their ancestral farms.

Painful and often pettifogging arguments broke out over the ownership of individual church buildings and lands. Ministers who had transferred their allegiance to the new Free Kirk preached in buildings and resided in manses on glebe lands which in law belonged to the old established Kirk of Scotland; after 1843 they were expelled – or withdrew voluntarily – with their congregations, and set adrift without a roof over their heads, just as so many farmers were driven from their lands in the same period in the agricultural Clearances – and, of course, many landowners, including the sheep-farming ones, were fiercely against the schismatic Free Kirk and refused its adherents sites for new buildings.

Even temporary premises were denied, and tenants who were bold enough to offer to accommodate the schismatics were often evicted. The result was that the dispossessed ministers and congregations were frequently reduced to conducting services in the open air, like the field conventicles of old, in all weathers on patches of waste ground or by roadsides. Notorious were the cases of Duthil and Wanlockhead in central Scotland, where 'sometimes the congregation met on the bare hillside, sometimes in one of the valleys, changing the locality so as to escape as far as possible the fury of the blast, though no change could free them from the cold benumbing wind, and the frequent showers of rain and snow'.[26] The Duke of Buccleuch was responsible for the Wanlockhead misery, in 1845–46.

Especially vexed was the question of the *quoad sacra* church buildings, formerly 'Chapels of Ease', which the congregations had built and paid for themselves, i.e. frequently cutting the patron landowner out of the loop. The Established Kirk tried to claim these buildings and lands – and in some cases leave the outstanding debt on the building to be met by the recusant congregation; such disputes went to the courts and even to the House of Lords.

In Arran there was one *quoad sacra* church, at Brodick, whose congregation and that of Whiting Bay followed the Free Kirk, while the Lamlash congregation under the Kilbride parish minister, the Reverend Dr. McNaughton, continued with the established Kirk of Scotland. In the case of the Brodick congregation the Duke of Hamilton did not try to evict them immediately from the chapel, but when the minister, Mr McAlister, died in 1844, they had to leave. However, unlike many other Scottish landowners, the Duke provided a new site for them at a disused sawmill at the site of Old Brodick near the Cnocan Burn and they continued in a building there as before, though they had difficulty in finding a new minister for some time. After three years they found another site at Strathwillan on the other side of the bay on the southern outskirts of the new Brodick village, and besides a church built a rather grandiose manse (now the Carrick Lodge guest house). The Free Church also established itself in Corrie in 1848.

In Kilmory Parish there were three churches, at Kilmory itself, at Lochranza and at Clachan. Under the influence of Angus McMillan and with the memory of Neil McBride before him, all three congregations deserted the Established Kirk. We have already seen how the patron had been repeatedly at odds with the congregation particularly in Kilmory Parish – finally yielding to popular demand in 1822 with the long-desired appointment of Angus McMillan as Parish Minister. Now, in the Great Disruption of 1843, McMillan was one of the 470 ministers who withdrew from the General Assembly, signed the Deed of Demission and helped to set up the Free Kirk. He held Kilmory Parish Kirk – the very building, the physical symbol in which resided the ancient, sacred point of worship for the Kilmory congregation. He was now expelled. The congregation of Kilmory Church voluntarily took up quarters at Clachaig (or Clauchog) Farm. Mackenzie tells us that 'Maighisteir Aonghus', leaving Kilmory in 1843 for the last time, based his sermon on the text "And she named the child I-chabod, saying, The glory is departed from Israel". He held services in the parlour of Clachaig farm while waiting for the new church and manse to be provided under the aegis of the Free Kirk. However his health by then was not good, and he died the same year.

A large church was built in 1847 for the Clauchan (Shiskine) congregation, at the junction of the Shiskine Road with the (present) A841 north of Torbeg; it was replaced in 1957 by a smaller church building. A monument to an early minister, the Reverend Archibald Nicol, stands close by. In Torbeg itself the Old Manse survives. In Lochranza the Free Church building fell victim to the frequent unions and sunderings of the later nineteeth century churches, and the latest version now serves as an art gallery.

In the case of the breakaway 'Preaching Cave' congregation who rejected the patron-chosen Dugald Crawford as their minister in 1815, Robert McLellan points out that their leader, William MacKinnon, had lost his farm during the Enclosures and had been downgraded to the status of a 'cottar': he makes the point that the Enclosures were at least as much a cause of social bitterness at that time as patronage, and that in Arran, as elsewhere, the Disruption may be seen as 'an unconscious outlet for repressed political fury' as well as discontent over patronage.[27] He also traces the disruptive anger in part to the lingering self-accusation and depression left by the ruthlessly bitter tone and railing of the fiery evangelists of the immediately preceding generation.

The Potato Famine: Ireland, Scotland and Arran

When considering the consequences of the enclosures and the clearances for Arran, we should also remember that in the nation as a whole the culminating social and economic cataclysm of the period was the Irish Potato Famine of 1845, which indeed was made more terrible by the policy of the landlords. Only two years after the Great Disruption of the Scottish Church, and at the height of the agricultural enclosures and clearances, the potato crop in Ireland failed with dreadful consequences for the peasantry there, who had a greater degree of potato monoculture than elsewhere; a year later the blight spread to Britain, most acutely to the Western Highlands and Islands of Scotland, including Arran.

For a long time previous to 1845, the Irish peasantry had been in an even worse condition than the farmers of the Scottish Highlands and Islands. Their troubles had been building up since the reigns of Elizabeth and James VI and I – and the mid-seventeenth-century 'interregnum' of Oliver Cromwell, whose anti-Catholic policies carried a whiff of genocide with them. It was the Irishman Jonathan Swift, Dean of St Patrick's in Dublin, who in the early eighteenth century attacked the whole concept of the Agricultural Revolution, lampooning the landowning 'projectors' in the third book of *Gulliver's Travels* in terms which accurately reflect the social consequences of enclosures. Swift also wrote an appalling satire with the seemingly innocent title *A Modest Proposal*: the misery of the masses could be usefully relieved if their swarms of poverty-stricken children could be sold, killed and made into food for profit.

Given Swift's description of the ruling classes, it should not surprise us, though it may shock us, that the 1845 Potato Famine exposed a savage indifference on the part of the ruling classes to the fate of the Irish, and with a lesser degree of cruelty, to that of the Gaelic-speaking Highlanders of Scotland.

While the London government may not have been entirely guilty of criminal or constructive negligence, the underlying attitude of many individual proprietors of estates in Ireland was indeed ugly: Sir Charles Trevelyan, the civil servant charged with such famine relief as there was, remarked that most of the landowners simply wanted 'the extermination of the population'. The Russell government, terrified by the thought that the burden of sustaining the poor might fall upon its shoulders as a mounting, open-ended commitment, was at least being realistic. The British Government in early Victorian times was disorganized, under-resourced and under-financed, vastly more primitive than the modern Welfare State.

On the other hand, many traditional Scottish proprietors depended upon rent as their sole source of income and when the tenants vanished these landowners went bankrupt in any case; many went to the wall. Nevertheless, a spirit of paternalism animated quite a few owners, and some actually beggared themselves in a vain effort to provide food for their tenants. But estates were often sold to absentee landlords, and this increased the trouble.

In spite of mitigating factors, then, Scotland needed relief during the famine years, and the governmental and charitable responses should not escape criticism. But grim Benthamite utilitarianism prevailed, and aid filtered through the recently established Free Church reflected the same conceptions of racial (Gaelic) inferiority and indolence incurring the Wrath of God, as we have noted elsewhere. The indignities of means-testing in our own time are nothing compared with the inquisitorial methods of the Destitution Committees of the 1840s and 50s and their inspectors, who were instructed to present an unyielding countenance to even the most desperate pleas for assistance. The able-bodied had to labour unremittingly for a tiny daily portion of meal, insufficient for a day's work. The intention was to force them into employment, as though the famine were the result of reprehensible idleness. That many more did not die was lucky.

In the Western Highlands and Islands of Scotland the population had increased, in part owing to the adoption of potatoes as a food crop – easily grown under rainy weather conditions, more productive per acre than any other crop, and highly nutritious; other demographic factors were the sudden increase in profitability of fishing and kelping, both stimulated by war conditions from the 1790s. Yet, of course, this prosperity came to an end with the closure of the Napoleonic Wars, and the barren soil of north-west Scotland, intensively farmed by runrig methods at merely subsistence levels, did become overcrowded. When the enclosures produced an 'expulsive' regime leading to widespread clearances, those of the huddled ex-runrig masses who had no other means of earning a living or of travel cowered in sink villages – like Tobermory or Oban. To these, the potato-blight simply was the last straw, immiserating the whole region and bringing famine or near famine to thousands of people.

The blight spread to Scotland in 1846, and famine conditions persisted in the Highlands and Islands at least until 1851. However, Scotland was not as badly affected as Ireland. Few appear to have died in Scotland, although conditions were fraught for many years after 1846, and there was a marked increase in emigration, both internally to the big towns of the south, and to Australia and Canada. The areas of most concern were principally the north-western islands, as well as Sutherland and Wester Ross.

Mackenzie tells us that '[t]he famine of 1846 ... does not seem to have affected [Arran] to an extent comparable with its effects in other parts of Scotland',[28] but this is another statement upon which he does not elaborate, beyond saying that 'it induced the Duke of the time to give liberal abatements of rent for that year [1847], extending to upwards of thirty per cent on the average'.

Governmental famine relief was not as inadequate in Scotland as in Ireland. Sir Charles Trevelyan, Assistant Secretary to the Treasury, said in 1846, 'The people [of the Scottish Highlands] cannot, under any circumstances, be allowed to starve.'[29] The authorities may have felt more capable of coping with the smaller number of people involved in the Highlands, about 150,000. The catastrophe of the Irish millions completely overwhelmed landowners and administrators alike.

A transforming aftermath

The effects of clearance were certainly cruel and devastating during the 1800s. In Arran as in many other cases, however, blanket accusations of deliberate neglect levelled at the landowner would be misplaced. The Duke of Hamilton took thought for those of the community who remained. The alternative of resettlement on small southern farming / fishing units was open to families who were left in Arran after the 'thinning-out' process had been carried out. This kind of land redistribution, of small coastal plots for people displaced from inland holdings by sheep-walks, is to be found right round the periphery of Scotland.

In the case of Sutherland mentioned earlier, these substitute sites, on the stormy north coast, proved to be completely worthless ground, where soil had to be laboriously transported, sometimes on people's backs, to fill up a few hollows between jagged rocks – and where soil and climate interacted to make cultivation of crops almost impossible; to say nothing of the destitution and bewilderment of the bereft Sutherland tenantry, who had no idea of how to go about pursuing the fisherman's trade. Many went through the trauma of displacement and 'resettlement' twice or three times. Thousands simply fled.

However, the evil example of Sutherland was not replicated in every area, and many people settled down quite well to coastal occupations such as fishing. When we come to Arran we find coastal plots of land allocated with relative success: the Hamilton estate made available sites – 'acres' – for homes and smallholdings at the heads of coastal bays and inlets: Brodick, Lamlash, Whiting Bay and right round the south and south-west coasts, in addition to Lochranza in the north-west. These were specifically for fishermen and other maritime workers such as kelp-gatherers. Their purpose is indicated in the number of 'port' names given to otherwise insignificant inlets on the south coast: Port Mor (Whiting Bay), Port na Gallin (Largybeg), Porta Leacach (Dippin), Port Dearg and Porta Buidhe (both at Kildonan), Port a' Ghillie Ghlais near Bennan Head, Port Mor near Slidderywaterfoot, Port na Feannaich (Corriecravie) – all at the base of a formidable series of shoreline cliffs; the two at Kildonan reached by a long, very dangerous series of steps cut into the rock. New tenants in these smallholdings, encouraged by a year's free rent, had to build their own houses (using the Duke's timber and lime), hedge, fence and ditch newly enclosed fields, and observe strict rules with regard to crop rotation, goat-keeping (banned altogether), herds of pigs (movements restricted), and sheep-breeding (banned except on stock farms).

Country-wide, these relatively small plots of land became officially designated as crofts, and their status ultimately became more secure as a result of legislation such as the Crofters' Holdings (Scotland) Act of 1886. The Isle of Arran, however, was specifically excluded from the provisions of the Crofters Act at the instance of the Duke of Hamilton – thus continuing the insecurity of tenure of the tenants of the little farms crowding along the southern coasts of Arran. In the end, many of these were absorbed into larger farming units – in and after the 1860s.

OS references

John Burrel's plan for enclosures
Bennecarrigan NR 943 230
Glencloy NS 004 358
Clauchog or Clachaig Farm NR 949 216

1843: The Great Disruption
A large church built in 1847 – Clauchan (Shiskine) NR 901 300
Torbeg NR 900 295

A transforming aftermath
Port Mor (Whiting Bay) NS 048 252
Port na Gallin (Largybeg) NS 052 230
Porta Leacach (Dippin) NS 043 214

Port Dearg (Kildonan) NS 032 205
Porta Buidhe (Kildonan) NS 025 208
Port a' Ghillie Ghlais (Bennan Head) NS 000 206
Port Mor (Slidderywaterfoot) NR 935 217
Port na Feannaiche (Corriecravie) NR 919 230

14. Napoleon, the Press Gang, the Smugglers

Diversification

There had always been attempts to diversify occupations in Arran. Non-agricultural industries came and went. In the end, the principal economic life-line of the island apart from farming proved to be tourism. But many other occupations were tried and some of them survive to the present day. Fishing had never been greatly developed. It was a seasonal occupation. There had always been a herring fishery, and the name Whiting Bay is derived from the plentiful supply of whiting obtained from that locality. But fishing was secondary, to be engaged in during the slack period by farm workers. It was only when bounties became payable (from 1787) to inshore fishermen, and later, when the Napoleonic wars imposed restrictions on the British fishing industry, that Arran fishing began to become profitable. Throughout the nine-teenth century the industry throve, with a substantial fleet (about a hundred vessels recorded in 1847) based at the main centres (Lamlash, Brodick, Whiting Bay, Lochranza) and smaller ports along the west coast.

During the French Wars kelp suddenly increased in value when European supplies of soda were cut off.[1] Kelp preparation was a traditional, often seasonal occupation. Kelp seaweed, which can also serve as fertilizer in coastal areas, is burnt to produce 'potash', a crude strong alkali, which is useful in the production of commodities as different as soap and glass. Although kelp burning had been practised in Holy Island from the thirteenth century, Arran was not the most favoured spot for this industry. However, it rose to prominence during the Napoleonic wars, when it was impossible to obtain the material from the continent. This continued until 1823, when the tariff barriers on exports of Spanish seaweed ('barilla') were removed, and kelp production in the west of Scotland ceased to be profitable. The industry in Arran and elsewhere finally collapsed about 1836.

War and government service provided new opportunities for a maritime population. Young men – as many as 300 a year in the last part of the eighteenth century – went in for 'life before the mast': customs and excise, and of course the Navy, as well as private mercantile service. During the wars and before, many Scottish landowners became 'military entrepreneurs' (T. M. Devine), gathering fees against the provision of recruits from their estates. Arran men flocked to serve in the navy; there appears to have been a prejudice in favour of the navy, understandable in terms of the background and experience of these islanders; in a wartime navy, they were skilled and trustworthy crewmen. On the other hand, attempts to recruit for the army were largely a failure, as the Duke discovered when attempting to raise a land regiment. Indeed there also was resistance to forced service in the navy, when the press gang operated even in the remote glens of Arran. Many young men took to the hills or hid overnight in isolated sheiling huts to avoid forcible enlistment. There was a largely unsuccessful attempt to assess localities for likely numbers and to pay a bounty for each man recruited. But in the end many returning Arran soldiers as well as sailors had tales to tell from the Continental, Peninsular and American Wars – ranging from the atrocious conditions of Sir John Moore's forced march to Corunna in 1808–09 ('a Fullarton of Lamlash [Kilmichael], a Sym from Tormore, a Nicol from Kilmory, a Murchie from Shannachie ... a Shaw of Shisken')[2] to the successful naval action of the frigate Shannon against the American Chesapeake in 1813 (involving Lachlan Thomson, a Kildonan man still living in 1849).[3]

Some of the stories appear to be legendary: in Arran, we have a version of the tale in which an outlaw – here a smuggler named McCurdy – boldly claims the reward of £500 for his own capture, and so impresses the authorities that he is taken into their service instead of being imprisoned. In this case McCurdy supposedly enters the navy, rises to command his own ship, captures a French warship and dies heroically when the captive French crew blow the vessel up. A nephew of the same McCurdy is alleged to have come across a French warship unexpectedly while he was in command of a small boat feeling its way cautiously in a dense fog: he made a surprise attack, overcame resistance, captured the vessel and battened the enemy crew below; a similar tale is told of a number of naval heroes of the time, including Lord Cochrane of Dundonald (in Ayrshire on the other side of the Clyde estuary) – but this is not to say that the Arran version must be untrue; many ruses were employed and unexpected opportunities seized during the period of the 'wooden walls'. Mackenzie says that the latter McCurdy was still alive in Brodick in the 1850s[4] – something that seems to exclude the possibility that this is the same as the Captain M'Kirdy mentioned earlier as drowning in the Clyde in 1825.

Alcohol and smuggling – and other occupations

Two Arran trades, intimately connected with each other, were smuggling and illicit whisky distilling. We tend to associate both with the period of the Napoleonic wars, but of course smuggling had been rife long before, and whisky in particular had become more popular with the imposition of taxes on other spirits such as gin and brandy from 1725, when traditional home brewing of ale became very costly after a duty on malt was brought in. Whisky distilling was not illegal throughout the kingdom, but in order to maximize their profits the owners of the big southern distilleries succeeded in having Highland distilling prohibited to all intents and purposes. Yet barley, a vital ingredient in whisky manufacture, was being overproduced in places like Arran due to improved methods of cultivation, the rents rose with the level of production, and the still-considerable difficulties of transport meant that it was hard to move the barley to markets even close at hand. Hence illegal distilling was widespread among the farming community, and the smugglers were able to provide clandestine transport for the product. Particular places in Arran were Whiting Bay, Kilmory, Balliekine near Pirnmill, and Lochranza – not that the whole island was not engaged in the trade.

Another commodity which the smugglers used to run was salt, the subject of a tax first imposed in 1702; by 1798 it had risen to 5s a bushel, and later still to 15s.[5] This increase made salt smuggling a phenomenally profitable venture.

Smuggling two hundred years ago was as attractive and ineradicable as, although much less harmful than, the present-day trade in dangerous drugs. Like modern police and customs officers, the excisemen and 'gaugers' used to play cat-and-mouse with the smugglers. Arran in particular was a smuggler's paradise, along with the Cumbraes and the whole south-western seaboard of Scotland, and frequently desperate measures were taken to stem the flow in the eighteenth and early nineteenth centuries.

We have already seen one example of 'preventive' excess even earlier, in 1671, when the curate of Kilbride, Archibald Beith, was sentenced to death, though later reprieved, for killing two smugglers in hot pursuit in Lamlash Bay. In later cases the balance tipped against the lawbreakers, but there was a deal of sympathy for smugglers at a popular level, since it was felt that they were being unfairly targeted by iniquitous laws. In 1796 a young man in a salt boat had been shot dead between Pladda and Arran, and the *Edinburgh Advertiser* laments the persistence of 'the poor people on the coast' in carrying on a trade 'which by the laws of our country subjects their property to seizure, and exposes their lives to destruction if they make any opposition to the officers of Revenue'.

In 1817, there was a truly horrific gun-battle over smuggled whisky in the south of Arran: the whisky was seized by the Revenue men, a mob gathered and tried to retake it, fire was opened and three people, a woman and two men, were killed; but the officer who gave the order to shoot was acquitted of murder by an Edinburgh jury because in spite of his 'firmness and forbearance' it was 'absolutely necessary to defend the lives of those who were under his command'.[6]

Where whisky was concerned, however, the illicit trade was often the only means open to farmers and cottars of paying the rent which contributed to the income of the magistrates and other members of the land-owning class. This meant that the courts often showed leniency in cases of distilling and smuggling.

The smuggling trade ended through being squeezed at both ends: as free trade developed, and as the prohibitions against small distilleries were gradually relaxed, whisky smuggling became less profitable, and the preventive officers grew more zealous. With transport improvement it became easier to ship grain to larger distilleries. The salt tax was also removed in 1823.

Smuggling exploits and the participants in them were still remembered in

Arran more than a hundred years later. There was a particularly famous revenue cutter called *Wickham* based in Arran: one member of the crew, Sandy Hendry by name, built a 'low, thatched, whitewashed house' about 1812 at Cul-na-sgagaid ('Wellingtonia') part of which was still standing and pointed out in the 1930s.[7]

Arran, of course, nurtured numbers of law-abiding 'civil' seafarers as well, and in the nineteenth century many master mariners plied their trades from the island. Inglis tells us that Brodick had the appearance of a thriving shipping port, and recollects the names of some of the 'splendid sloops and schooners' laid up over winter on the now-vanished beach at Strabane: the *Grace Wallace*, the *Speedwell* and the *Annabella*. But this trade, like the beach itself, has now departed. One interesting naval connection is that with HMS *Beagle*, in which Charles Darwin made his South American and Pacific voyage leading to the publication of *The Origin of Species*. Inglis tells us of one Arran sailor, John Davidson, who served on the Beagle as an 'able-bodied seaman' in 1826–27 – before, however, Darwin boarded the ship. Later Davidson joined the mercantile marine as chief officer of the *True Briton* trading between the Clyde and the West Indies, where he led an exciting life and repelled marauding privateers. After this, he settled down to farming in Arran.[8]

Legitimate non-agricultural industries had been introduced on an experimental basis by John Burrel and his successors, but the enterprises were often grossly unsuitable for an island environment, and few survived for any length of time. In particular Burrel's venture into coal-mining at Laggan at the northeast end of Arran and Clauchlands near Lamlash soon ended, the possibilities being very scanty and in the latter site nil in terms of geology.

Other enterprises – not all new introductions – were moderately successful, but did not stay the course. In the early nineteenth century there used to be water-powered textile mills in the island (carding at Brodick and Burican, flax at Lagg, waulking and dye at Monamore), but they ceased to be profitable when steam machinery began to be used on the mainland; when cotton began to be an important element of manufacture elsewhere, a mill for making wooden bobbins ('pirns') was built at Pirnmill on the west coast south of Lochranza, but the supply of wood soon ran out; clay tiles for drains were made at Clauchog, but its raw material was also soon exhausted. Three licensed whisky distilleries were in operation in Arran in 1793, but improved communications enabled the barley growers to send their produce to the mainland – to Campbeltown, Ayr, Greenock and elsewhere – and in 1836 the last of the three had closed at Torrylin. Meal mills were reduced from five in 1811 to two in 1878 (Shedog and Monamore) and these are long gone, victims of technological advance.

Slate mining was carried on successfully but for a short period only in the Lochranza area (Glen Farm). Barytes mining (barium sulphate, mainly used in paint manufacture and nowadays for oil- and gas-well drilling) from 1840 in Glen Sannox was productive for a time (1853–62, when 5,000 tons were mined) until the mine was closed down by the eleventh Duke, who decided that it was too ugly for its beautiful surroundings; later, in the twentieth century, when there was a national shortage of barytes, the mine was reopened and continued successfully until 1938, when the vein was exhausted.

Quarried stone, in particular white and red sandstone, had always had a certain export market as well as providing material for some of Arran's own most prestigious buildings (such as Brodick Castle itself). Large quarries were exploited for red sandstone at Brodick, Cordon and Monamore. White sandstone, together with limestone, was quarried at Corrie and An Sgriob. Limestone was extensively burnt and used in Arran, and many disused limekilns still survive in the island; one of the better-preserved ones is on view at Bridge Farm. Limestone alone was quarried in the Clauchan Glen, and a very fine quality limestone was got from near Corrie (at the Coire nan Larach Burn). Arran sandstone was extensively used in the south-western mainland, for instance in the construction of Troon Harbour, and many of the impressively solid domestic buildings in Ayrshire and elsewhere may have been built using this material. The stone quarrying industry, however, was more or less extinct in Arran before 1930.

We should perhaps mention here that since time immemorial primitive iron-smelting on a tiny scale had apparently been practised at various spots all over Arran; the evidence for this consists of masses of slag or 'bloomeries' reputedly to be found at several locations, although a 1977 OS survey has failed to confirm the existence of these in a majority of cases. Ironstone occurs in several locations in Arran (e.g. near the bridge at Rosaburn). It is reported that in the past the glow from the smelting on these sites at night was to be seen from ships at sea. But Arran's iron micro-industry seems to have had its heyday during the seventeenth century, and it did not survive into the age of the improvers.

Something which is perhaps overlooked is the amount of cottage industries which preceded the age of technological omnicompetence in Arran and elsewhere: weaving and knitting, candle-making and other pursuits.

In the surviving agricultural sector in Arran, although the process of enclosure and reform spelt disaster for many long-established farming communities, new stability gradually asserted itself, and those farmers and ancillary workers who remained or migrated to the island began to prosper at their trades. A true agrarian community began to coalesce in the island, signalled by the appearance of one of the characteristic features of modern farming – the agricultural association: the Arran Farmers' Society was founded in Brodick as early as 19 January 1830, under the patronage of the Marquis of Douglas, who became Duke of Hamilton in 1852. This society encouraged efforts to improve production by means such as competitive ploughing matches and shows offering prizes for best specimens of horses, cattle, sheep, horticulture and farm crops. More robust stock – Ayrshire cattle and the Clydesdale horse as well as blackface sheep – had been introduced by the Duke and the leading farmers, and improved methods of feeding had been brought in with the use of turnips and with the practice of sowing pastureland. Farm machinery – metal ploughs, harrows, horse-rakes, seed drills and the like – made it possible to operate larger farms with fewer agricultural labourers.

By the 1840s, we are told, improvement of cultivation and the increase in the sizes of individual farms had led to a doubling of Arran's produce across the board over fourteen years. Statistics are wanting, and figures of fluctuations in currency values must be regarded with caution, but it is fairly clear that, for instance, where herring fishery in 1772 brought in £300 per annum, and in 1793 £1000 per year, in the 1840s the annual figure had risen to £4,000; that was when the fishing fleet consisted of 100 vessels, counting £40 per boat. Exported cattle (£2/£2 10s per head) in 1793 brought in £1200, but in 1840, when the price per head had risen to £3 10s, 900 black cattle brought in £3,150'.[9] In this case the Napoleonic Wars had obviously had a profound effect on the value of money, and although the numbers sold had clearly gone up, the increase in receipts may not be as dramatic as at first appears. Other exports included pigs, sheep and wool, barley, wheat, oats, potatoes, pulses, shellfish, fowls and eggs, butter, cheese, and freestone and limestone.[10] Often a whole flotilla of boats would arrive at one of the great mainland fairs, for instance at Ayr or Ardrossan, to sell produce and enjoy mainland life. On the island itself, horse and other fairs took on a new lease of life, developing a lively and prosperous internal trade. Arran was becoming a productive unit in the kingdom, although the conditions of life were still rigorous and spartan for a substantial section of the population.

In the first half of the nineteenth century the Duke of Hamilton and the principal farmers on the island were able to improve stock-breeding by the introduction of more robust kinds of animals, and to maintain the quality of cattle by providing turnips for feeding, and sowing good grass and other food plants instead of leaving pasture wild and weedy as had been the previous practice. The old ferm-touns were replaced with 'white houses', white-painted stone buildings for the accommodation of a single tenant farmer and dependants, including farm servants sufficient for one holding. The smaller holdings were gradually taken over by the big farms which used them to extend their capacity for grazing and cultivation, although the territorial extent of the former seems intact; the houses have now often become private residences. These developments have largely shaped the tranquil, well-ordered look of present-day coastal Arran. (The interior of the island, divided between large-scale sheep-walks and extensive forestry plantations, retains the historically shaggy moorland and upland appearance.)

Alcohol and smuggling
Shedog NR 913 302
Glen Farm NR 953 503
Cordon NS 027 302
An Sgriob NS 019 414
Bridge Farm NR 928 319
Coire nan Larach Burn NS 005 430

15.   Development of Services in Arran

Communications

In the early eighteenth century, the Isle of Arran was still a remote place, and isolated from other parts of the kingdom. Sea communications were in a better state than contemporary roads but sporadic and ad hoc. It was only when Arran's status as an improvable and potentially profitable territory began to be recognized that anything like a regular service was brought in to connect it with the mainland – with Greenock, Irvine, Ayr and Saltcoats in particular. A ferry boat linking Arran with Bute had operated for a short time from 1684 but did not pay its way; the *Glasgow Journal* of 12 March 1759 advertised a weekly service by packet boat between Saltcoats and Arran 'for the conveniency of travellers', but this too did not last.[1]

As might have been expected, the prime mover in arranging for a more regular service was John Burrel, who had had a few frustrating experiences in 1768 and 1770 – for example, when he was left on the quayside in Saltcoats in Ayrshire after the revenue cutter on which he had arranged a passage to Arran had dashed off in pursuit of a smuggler. After a public meeting in March 1770 at The Cladach in Arran, at which he and other notables were present, a service backed by the Duke of Hamilton, involving two 'pacquet boats', was set up to ply weekly between Saltcoats in Ayrshire and both Brodick and Imachar in Arran. One boat (Imachar) was commanded by Duncan Sillar and the other (Brodick) by Hans or Hance Banna(n)tyne.

The ungrateful tenantry were perhaps not well-disposed towards this example of ducal bounty, since they had to pay for the upkeep of the boats themselves: on one occasion, in January 1773, when Mr Commissioner Burrel was about to sail for Ayrshire, someone engaged in a spot of sabotage, breaking the rudder and cutting out a section of planking on the starboard side. A new boat was built at a cost of £94 3s 3d, from timber cut on the Castle grounds, but in May 1776, before settlement of the account, the ship was lost with all hands and a consignment of cattle; Hans Bannatyne's children were left to the Duke's charity.[2]

Before the eighteenth century, dry-land communication in Arran had been unimaginably bad – in fact, for the most part, non-existent. The original division of the island into two parishes, east and west, may have been dictated by the fact that the easiest communication between settlements was by water: to get across the central ridge on foot or even by pony or horse was a formidable undertaking. There were a few pony-tracks to south and west from the Brodick-Lamlash area. Wheeled vehicles were almost unknown, and land transportation of loads of any size had to be by pack-horses or primitive sledges.

At length, in the time of the Good Duchess Anne, the creation and upkeep of roads, harbours and bridges by joint labour was laid upon the estate tenants on so many days per year; we have already mentioned the provision of the quay on the Lamlash site. In 1719, three years after the Duchess's death, it was more definitely laid down by statute that the tenantry had to devote six days' unpaid labour per year to road-making – or pay a financial penalty. This species of corvée labour was manifestly inefficient, even after the period was extended to nine days, covering by-roads, embankments and harbours. The system could only at best keep open the wretched pony-tracks and footpaths. In spite of this inadequacy, however, 'statute labour' was not ended till 1881, and in the meantime nineteenth-century estate factors such as the detested Patersons found a way of getting the work done for nothing: in the Baron-Bailie courts the financial penalties mentioned above were augmented by the strict enforcement of fines for infringements of estate regulations, and the funds thus collected were devoted to road-making materials and tools as well as to supervision, so that the upkeep of communications came at no cost to the 'noble proprietor'.

Real road-making began only at the beginning of the nineteenth century, when the state began to take an interest in the provision of communications countrywide: in Arran in 1810 the so-called Parliamentary Road between Gortonallister (near Lamlash) and Brodick was constructed jointly at the cost of the national government and the Hamilton estate. Thereafter road-building was private, done at the Duke's expense, but maintained by the same system of 'statute labour', unpaid work by the tenants supplemented by estate fines. In 1817, the first east-west road, known as 'the String', was built, as an extension of the Parliamentary Road, between Brodick and Blackwaterfoot: the engineer in charge of this construction was none other than the great Thomas Telford, who directed so many important road schemes in Britain during the period. Also in 1817 a northward road was built as far as Sannox from Brodick, and four or five years later the Ross Road was built from the Lamlash area to Bennecarrigan in the south-west of the island. Finally, in 1843, Sannox and Lochranza were connected via the Boguille, a section of the road between Glen Chalmadale and Sannox. These roads form the basis of the island's internal communications to the present day.

The first two nineteenth-century Dukes of Hamilton wanted to retain the 'romantic rural retirement' of Arran, with shooting and hunting facilities for themselves and their close friends. But in 1825 the paddle-steamer *Helensburgh*, carrying none other than the Duke of Hamilton and his friends, showed that it was possible to make the round trip from Greenock by Rothesay, the Kyles of Bute, Lochranza, Lamlash, Brodick, Millport, Fairlie, Largs and Helensburgh, with spectacular scenery all the way, in thirteen hours. The first experiments in steam navigation had taken place in the Clyde, and by the 1820s the estuary was busy with primitive but efficient mechanically propelled craft. These literally expanded the horizons of thousands of town and city dwellers who had never previously dreamt of a day's or a week's holiday 'doon the watter', as the phrase went. Rothesay, Dunoon, Millport, Largs flourished; Arran, further away from Glasgow than these, and intensely scenic, early became a main target for the adventurous holiday-makers, undeterred by awkward landing facilities and by unwelcoming landowners.

By 1829 regular weekly steamboat sailings had been established by the Royal Mail Steam Packet Service, with two small wooden paddle-steamers plying between Glasgow and Arran – the *Toward Castle* sailing for Brodick and

Lamlash on Tuesday returning on Wednesday, and the *Inverary Castle* on Saturday coming back on Monday (Sunday travelling being frowned on in those days). From 1826 a ship called *The Duke of Lancaster*, run by a Campbeltown consortium of merchants between the Mull of Kintyre and Glasgow, also served the west of the island, Lochranza and, until the closure of the mill in 1840, Pirnmill. The MacKellar Company's boats (*Jupiter, Juno* and *Star*) sailed daily between Glasgow Broomielaw and Arran from 1832 to 1864.

In the early 1840s the railway extension to Ayr facilitated the provision of a direct service between Ardrossan and Arran. In 1842 a summer service was introduced involving two ships, a MacKellar boat called *Hero* and the *Leven* owned by Robert Jamieson of Arran. In 1847 the Ardrossan Steamboat Company, formed by the Earl of Eglinton and the Duke of Hamilton, built a paddler named *Isle of Arran* to run between Ardossan and Brodick and Lamlash to replace a sailing schooner, the mail-carrying *Brodick*, for the winter service. The *Isle of Arran* was replaced in 1860 by the iron-hulled *Earl of Arran* built for the same company, and in 1868 an attempt involving the twelfth Duke of Hamilton was made to expand this traffic with a new ship, the *Lady Mary*. This enterprise, however, fell through and for some time the traffic between Ardrossan and Arran was carried on by the *Rothesay Castle*, owned by William Buchanan and skippered by Ronald M'Taggart, and then by another Buchanan vessel, the *Brodick Castle*, which in turn was followed by the *Scotia*. Thereafter the Ardrossan service passed into the hands of the Glasgow and South-Western Railway, with the first *Glen Sannox*.

Medicine

Little is heard of the treatment of illness before the nineteenth century – beyond the superstitious practices frowned upon by the Kirk Session. In Burrel's accounts for 1773 we learn that the housekeeping expenses of 'Doctor Fullarton' amounted to '£18 17/3 1/2'. This is the Dr Lewis Fullarton mentioned below in chapter 16, who sent his three sons to fight Napoleon in the 1800s. In the last part of the eighteenth century he was 'the surgeon of the island', with a salary of 2d per £ gross rental: 'each tenant pays for bleeding and other allowance when sick or sore'.[3]

It is known that Dr John Stoddart was the Duke's physician in 1801; his name is recorded as one of the two justices of the peace mentioned in the Census return for that year. He was probably the father of the Dr Andrew Stoddart mentioned below as one of the two physicians in Arran in 1850. In 1852, after Andrew Stoddart's death, Dr John A. Jamieson was appointed to be the Medical Officer of Health for Arran. Dr Jamieson had been born at The Cladach in 1818.

A Dr McCredy is recorded as living in Cromla at Corrie at the time of Waterloo (1815). He may have been responsible for the 'Doctor's Bath', a peculiar formation carved out of sandstone on the foreshore.

Other doctors obviously practised at various times in early nineteenth-century Arran. But in Scotland as late as the period of the Potato Famine, medical services outside the large towns were amateur and almost non-existent.

Here is an interesting contrast: the Duke of Sutherland employed district surgeons in strategic locations in Sutherland at a salary of £40 as an embryonic health service for those who could not afford medical fees. He also set up an efficient network of relief stations distributing food during the potato famine. On Arran, on the other hand, in 1850 there was only a single official medical practitioner in Brodick: Andrew Stoddart, supported by the grants of both parishes, Kilmory and Kilbride, all of whose parishioners he was supposed to cover. There was one other practitioner, Charles Cook, based in Lamlash, who wrote that:

'[Stoddart] is upwards of 18 miles from many of the paupers and he is not able to attend them all. Often I have to give advice and medicine without any remuneration. There are only two medical men on the island. If the salary of two parishes was divided, as he lives at Brodick and I at Lamlash, the north would answer to him and the south to me. I am sure the poor would get better justice.'[4]

Neither Charles Cook nor Andrew Stoddart had any kind of medical certification. In later years, however, a proper distribution of doctors was organized in Arran and throughout the country. There was an increased output of properly qualified medical graduates, and the care of the poor became much less patchy, although the physicians still had to be paid at the point of service by the patient.

1n 1845 the responsibility for public health had been placed with parochial

Arran seen from *Caledonian Isles* coming in to Brodick

Drumadoon Cliff

Standing Stone at Drumadoon

Above. Courtyard of the Arran Heritage Museum, Rosaburn

Right. Chirotherium ('Hand-monster') (courtesy of Arran Heritage Museum)

Below. Torrylinn Chambered Tomb

Survivors of Megalithic
Ring at Machrie Moor
(with millstone fragments
in foreground)

Megalith at Machrie
showing scale

Excavated and reburied (Haggerty): Circle 11 looking towards Circle 1

Excavated and reburied (Haggerty): Circle 1 looking towards Circle 11

Suidhe Coire Fhionn, Fingal's Cauldron Seat

'Cup and ring' markings at Stronach Wood above Brodick

Torr a' Chaisteil Dun near Corriecraivie

Ailsa Craig and Pladda Isle with lighthouse

Holy Island and Lamlash Bay

Crosses carved on rear wall of St Molaise's Cave, Holy Island

Lamlash Village seen from Holy Island

King's Cross Point Dun and Viking Grave with Holy Island in background

Kildonan Castle

Lochranza Castle

The 'Good Duchess' Anne: detail of portrait by David Scougal.
(Courtesy of National Trust for Scotland)

Old print showing Holy Island and Duchess Anne's Quay at Lamlash.
(Courtesy of Arran Heritage Museum)

The Lagg Hotel, 1791

Typical Arran Cottage, 19th century
(Courtesy of Arran Heritage Museum)

'The Cladach', now Arran Brewery

Brodick Castle

William Alexander Anthony Archibald, 11th Duke of Hamilton: statue in front of Brodick Primary School. Goat Fell in background.

Princess Marie of Baden, wife of 11th Duke of Hamilton: detail of portrait by Francis Grant (Courtesy of National Trust for Scotland)

Un salon particulier à la
Maison Dorée

Glen Sannox paddle-steamer (Courtesy of Arran Heritage Museum)

Ivanhoe paddle-steamer landing passengers by shore boat at the Ferry Rock, Corrie
(Courtesy of Arran Heritage Museum)

Blackwaterfoot Harbour

Arran Postbus at Lochranza

'Heavy traffic in downtown Lochranza'

boards. In 1857 'lunatics' came under the care of district boards (including one in Arran). The Local Government (Scotland) Act 1894 redistributed these responsibilities again, this time to district committees composed of representatives of county and parish councils, in the case of Arran, of Bute County Council, Kilbride Parish and Kilmory Parish. Under this regime, an isolation hospital built of corrugated iron was constructed about 1894, north of the present Lamlash golf course near the Blairmore Burn.

Education

In 1803 Parliament passed 'An act for making better provision for the parochial schoolmasters, and for making further regulations for the better government of the parish schools in Scotland'.[5] This legislation loosened the grip of the Kirk on Scottish Education, and set foot on the path ultimately leading to the great Education Act of 1872. It regularized the payment of schoolmasters and attempted to improve the state of school buildings, including housing for individual teachers. Its effect on Arran can be seen immediately in the following record:

KILMORY KIRK, 2 OCT. 1804

Met here this day.

James Lamont Esq. of Knockdow, Factor to his Grace the Duke of Hamilton on his Grace's Estate in Arran, and Revd. Neil MacBride, Minister of Kilmory parish, and proceeded to consider the Act of Parliament anent the settlement of Parochial Schoolmasters, and considering the extent of this parish and population thereof, proceeded according to the eleventh section of the Act, and in all time coming allow the Schoolmasters, to be paid as follows, to the Schoolmaster at Kilmory twelve pounds Six shillings & Eight pence Sterling, to the Schoolmaster at Shisken Nine pounds Six shillings & Eight pence Sterling, to the Schoolmaster at Lochranza four pound Sterling, to the Schoolmaster at Imachar four pounds Sterling, and to the Schoolmaster at Drumlabarra Mill four pounds Sterling; and to be paid quarterly at the following rates, for reading English alone two shillings Sterling, for reading English and writing two shillings and Sixpence Sterling, for writing and Arithmetic, three shillings and Sixpence Sterling, for book-keeping one pound Sterling, for Navigation one pound ten Shillings sterling, for teaching Latin five shillings Sterling.

That Archibald M'Kenzie is continued as a teacher at Kilmory pro tempore, but that no teacher in future shall be eligible for Kilmory but one who is qualified to teach Latin, and that the whole teachers in the above districts shall teach the Gaelic Language and that the Schoolmaster at Kilmory shall also be qualified to teach Church Musick; and as it has been a custom with the Schoolmasters in this parish to teach two quarters of the year only, it is hereby ordained that they are not to vacate their School at any time of the year except in harvest, and that not exceeding Six weeks, and if they neglect to do so they shall not be entitled to uplift any part of their Salary.[6]

It will be seen that fees still had to be paid to the masters by the pupils in addition to the official salary. In 1804 there are now five 'official' schoolmasters in Kilmory Parish, arranged in descending order of salary (depending upon the number of pupils taught), and the subjects offered against the payment of fees now include book-keeping and navigation. It is interesting that the teaching must include Gaelic – without a special fee for it; presumably, as McLellan points out, this would be necessary for the teaching of English. The agreement set out above stipulates that it should be taught in all parish schools, but Paterson, a very unpopular estate factor, who was prejudiced against Gaelic, says that it was taught only in the non-parochial 'Assembly' schools (see below) set up in 1823.

By 1840 the number of parochial schools was four in each parish, one master for each school, paid as before in descending order of salary depending on numbers of pupils: (Kilbride Parish) Lamlash (£19), Brodick (£16), Lochranza (£6 + [joint school] supplement from Kilmory), Corrie (£4); (Kilmory Parish) Kilmory (£17 10s), Shiskine (£15), Imachar (£5 16s), Lochranza (£10 10s + [joint school] supplement from Kilmory school). The total salary budget for the two parishes was thus approximately £100. In addition each master except the one at Imachar had a free stone-built white-washed house with a chimney rather than the traditional hole in the roof. The children still paid fees to be taught reading and writing, with arithmetic, Latin, navigation and book-keeping as extras.

In addition to these establishments, the Church set up 'Assembly' Schools, one at Whiting Bay in Kilbride Parish. There was also a private school in Lamlash. In Kilmory there were the four parochial schools, two Assembly schools, and six private schools, including one at Blackwaterfoot (under 'Pate Raghill'), Birchburn, Balmichael and Feorline. It was at Feorline in 1845 that a tragic accident took place. The roof of the temporary classroom at Feorline (an old potato bothy) fell in after a hard frost: in the rush to get out, five little girls were trampled and burnt to death. Mackenzie recounts that the schoolmaster, Charles M'Gregor, was nearly lynched because he refused to let the children out although warned by his senior pupils that the walls were giving way.[7] School buildings were obviously not up to standard yet. However, a few years later, the Duke of Hamilton acted with some munificence in Brodick: the previous schoolhouse at Rosaburn had been a small white-washed building (now part of the Arran Heritage Museum), to which the children brought peats for burning during the cold winter. During the removal of the village to its present site, the Duke erected a red sandstone schoolhouse in the centre of the new village (opened 1856). This apparently was at the urging of his wife, Princess Marie of Baden, a typical Lady Bountiful of the nineteenth century with ostentatious philanthropic concerns. The Duke had a schoolhouse built every time new housing was put up in any part of the estate.

The Scottish Education Act of 1872 considerably weakened the link between the Kirk and the schools: although these were still organized on a parochial basis, they were now administered by school boards elected by ratepayers. The boards in Arran bought most of the schools built by the Duke, paying as much as £250 for the Kildonan school, and built some of their own in the characteristic stone-and-slate 'educational' style still recognizable throughout Scotland. The twelfth Duke is said to have retained control of three schools – Brodick, Corrie and Auchagallon – because they had been built by the eleventh Duke exclusively out of estate money i.e. the tenants and parishioners had not made any contribution to the cost; he ran and maintained these schools, but the arrangement came to an end with his death in 1895. The boards also met the cost of school fees (still payable) for parishioners who could not afford them. In the meantime attendance at school was made compulsory for all children between the ages of five and thirteen (fourteen after 1883) and from 1888 a measure of 'quality control' was introduced in the shape of a Leaving Certificate, which came to be recognized as a qualification for University Entrance.

The administration of justice

Heritable Jurisdictions – hereditary judicial powers held by landowners – were abolished in 1747. Thereafter Scotland was organized into more rational sheriffdoms, where sheriff substitutes were appointed to each county town and other principal places. But one remnant of the heritable jurisdictions was still in operation throughout Scotland after 1747 and well into the nineteenth century: 'Baron-Bailie' Courts continued to be under the control of the landowner. In Arran these were held every Saturday. The Baron-Bailie Courts, also known as Factor's Courts, dealt specifically with infringements of Estate regulations and were not popular, since the factors involved were not given to leniency.

JP Courts, in practice also dependent on the land owner, were held once a month. In Arran, a bailiary of the County of Bute, offenders could be imprisoned in Brodick Castle (in 'Jock Bhudis' Hole'[8]) for forty-eight hours before being transferred to the County Jail in Rothesay. Appeals from JP decisions were heard in Rothesay at the Sheriff Court, which itself was subject to the jurisdiction of the Circuit Court at Inverary, the seat of the Sheriffdom of Argyll. Headrick tells us that capital cases (involving the death penalty) were 'unknown' in Arran, but that the Sheriff in such a case would waive his jurisdiction in favour of that of the High Court of Justiciary.[9]

Later, a Sheriff Court was held regularly in Arran. A Court House was built about 1850 in Brodick near the present golf course. There was a Buteshire Sheriff Clerk Depute for Arran and resident in the island. Round about the time of the Education Act (1872) the holder of this office was John Fullarton, who lived at the Alma near the Mayish. He was also an early member of the School Board. Another Fullarton, Alexander, was not only a JP but Clerk to the JP Court in Brodick.[10] It may be recollected that the Fullartons had held the office of Crowner under the Stewart sheriffs since early days.

Political Developments

In 1800 in Arran, the Duke of Hamilton had been the sole political power-holder, and ruled through justices of the peace – his factor and his doctor – appointed by him as Commissioner of Supply. In the County of Bute as a whole there were only twelve parliamentary voters, nine of whom, landowners merely on paper, depended on the goodwill of the Duke of Hamilton, the Marquis of Bute and one other real landowner. But political reform was coming, slowly at first but gathering pace throughout the century. Indeed, the 1832 Reform Act, often regarded as a historic milestone on the road to democracy, was almost purely symbolic, because it extended the franchise only to landowners whose property was valued at £10 or more, or to tenants whose rent was £50 or more – in Arran initially resulting in the addition of just three or four major land-holders as parliamentary electors.[11] However, by 1841, the number of electors had increased: the vote in Buteshire as a whole in that year's General Election totalled 206, returning Sir William Rae as MP by sixty-two votes. Two successive Reform Acts, of 1868 and 1885, widened the franchise much further, the first lowering the property bar, and the second abolishing all property qualifications and extending the suffrage to the entire adult male population. As a result of these Acts and similar legislation the strength of the landlords dwindled steadily, and real control of the various urban and rural areas of Britain, including Arran, passed to expanded local government organizations practically empowered by a population of rate-payers.

OS references

Communications
Gortonallister NS 033 295
Boguille NR 961 482

Education
Birchburn NR 911 296

The administration of justice
Mayish NS 016 358

16. Arran in the Nineteenth Century

Arran's owners

We referred earlier to James, fourth Duke of Hamilton, who succeeded his mother the Good Duchess Anne in 1698 and who was killed in a duel in 1712. The fifth Duke, also James, died in 1743. The principal claim to fame of the sixth Duke, yet another James, is that he married the famous Irish adventuress and beauty Elizabeth Gunning, who went on to become Duchess of Argyll. He died in 1758.

The seventh Duke of Hamilton, James George, inherited another title, Duke of Douglas, and died in 1769, whereupon both titles reverted to a man named Douglas, who was brother of the late Duke of Douglas, and who therefore became eighth Duke of Hamilton. He bestowed a large part of the land in the west upon an illegitimate daughter, Anne, as a dowry when she married the Hon. Henry Westenra, an Irish aristocrat with a Dutch name who later became the second Lord Rossmore. This farmland, on the narrow coastal strip on the island's north-western shoulder, is the same as that repeatedly devastated in the fifteenth century by raiders from Kintyre, and had passed through the ownership of McAlister the 'heroic tenant'. Later, it was owned by the Montgomerys of Eglinton, before it was acquired from the latter by Duchess Anne Hamilton in 1705. The territory also included Glen Sannox in the east. The farms included Catacol (where Rossmore built a minor stately home, now used as a farmhouse), the Thundergays, both Penriochs, Alltgobhlach,

Imachar, Dougarie, and Auchagallon, a line of properties running almost continuously down the north-western coast to Machrie; they had never been improved, and retained runrig and the clachan system until 1838, when Westenra needed money and put them up for sale at £34,000. This group of properties, besides offering what we would now call 'unrivalled opportunities for redevelopment', was said in the advertisement for the sale to be 'the only property in the island to be had by purchase'; the whole of Arran having been 'very strictly preserved, and all intrusion carefully prevented. All strangers have been sedulously excluded, and Arran is almost a terra incognita to its very nearest neighbours. To the sportsman it is invaluable. The hills abound with grouse, and there is a natural preserve in the centre of the property which ensures their protection and food in the most unpropitious seasons. Red deer are becoming more numerous, and the tenants can vouch for the amazing increase of the black game ... '[1]

Thus privacy and gamekeeping were dexterously combined as a supreme selling-point. However, the property was not sold then, and the Hamiltons reabsorbed it into their own estate about 1844, when the surviving runrig was at last made away with.

Game had been carefully guarded in its own preserves in Arran since the days of Robert the Bruce and before, and up to 1700 there were about 400 red deer on the island. However, they seem to have dwindled almost to the point of extinction through the succeeding century, due to human environmental interference, for instance, 'the improvident destruction of the woods'.[2] Roe deer and wild swine were wiped out, and wild goats nearly so. Grouse and black-cock were plentiful, partridge rather fewer (Headrick). As customary, gamekeepers and farmers slaughtered hawks and eagles mercilessly. The Duke and his friends restocked with the animals and birds that it was fun to kill.

When Douglas, the eighth Duke, died in 1799, his uncle Archibald became ninth Duke. When Archibald died in 1819, his son Alexander succeeded to the title as tenth Duke. It was under Alexander's son, William Archibald Anthony Alexander, eleventh Duke of Hamilton from 1852, that the village of Brodick took on its present appearance. The Duke wished to distance himself from his tenants and villagers, even going so far as to demolish the previously existing village of Brodick in 1856–58 and shift it and its inhabitants across the bay to its present site, enveloping a previous settlement known as Invercloy: this removal accompanied a reorganization and improvement not only of Brodick Castle itself but also of the deer park and pleasure grounds. Wholesale removal of a village sited inconveniently close to a great house – the fastidious withdrawal, as it were, of the hem of the great man's garments from the odoriferous proximity of the common herd – was not unknown in the eighteenth and nineteenth centuries: 'Go off; I discard you. Let me enjoy my private; go off.'

The Duke of Hamilton wanted to conserve the entire island of Arran as a very private pleasure-ground for himself and his friends, and for a long time in the early nineteenth century discouraged outsiders from the mainland from settling or even visiting the island – by such stratagems, for instance, as delaying the provision of adequate landing stages for ships at Brodick and other locations. The hilly and mountainous interior landscape not only served for sheep-walks: it provided excellent grouse-moors and other varieties of hunting-grounds, including extensive tracts for deer-stalking. Lord Teignmouth, who wrote *Sketches of the Coasts and Islands of Scotland* in 1836, observes, 'The Duke, being desirous of preserving the game in Arran, does not much encourage the residence of strangers.'[3]

There was one other considerable landowning family in Arran, the Fullartons, who had owned property in the island since the time of David II in the fourteenth century, and were hereditary 'Crowners' (Coroners) of Arran (see pp. 84–5). They gave their sons to military service, as was expected of the class during the Napoleonic and other conflicts. Dr Lewis Fullarton sent his three sons to the wars – Lieutenant John Fullarton RN, later in command of a revenue cruiser, Major Archibald Fullarton, who served in the Peninsular War and was severely wounded at Salamanca, and Sir James Fullarton, who was present at both Corunna and Waterloo, and died in command of the 96th regiment at Halifax, Nova Scotia. The eldest, Lieutenant John, came into the ownership of many farms, including one at Whitefarland interposed between Imachar and Alltobhlach i.e. in the midst of the Westenra property on the north-west coast; this too had been unimproved but was dealt with at the same time as the other farms. Another Fullarton property, Kilmichael on the east in Glencloy above Brodick, had been taken in hand earlier. Generally the island of Arran was swept clean of runrig by the middle of the nineteenth century. The last working communal runrig farm seems to have survived just into Mackenzie's time (1914) at Balliekine, a unit between another two former

Westenra possessions, Dougarie and Imachar, also on the north-west coast not far from Whitefarland.[4]

The lands at Corriegills south of Brodick, which had been kept as an appanage of the Stewart sheriffdom of Bute, were acquired by the Hamiltons at the beginning of the nineteenth century. The other Stewart possessions in Arran, the 'Tenpenny Lands' stretching nórth from Kildonan through the present Whiting Bay to the Clachlands, had been acquired by Ninian Stewart, Sheriff of Bute, in the fifteenth century but were lost again in 1549 apparently as a result of the treason of Sir James Stewart. Their subsequent ownership is uncertain, but they appear finally to have been bought by the Duke of Hamilton from the Marquis of Bute also at the beginning of the nineteenth century during the process of enclosure in Arran.[5]

The changing face of Arran

The villages of Brodick, Lamlash, Whiting Bay and the smaller centres really did not exist as such in the eighteenth century. Brodick in its modern form appeared in the 1850s, Lamlash about 1830. Before then, life centred on the parish structure, its principal kirk and satellite kirks, and within that framework, the ferm-touns or clachans in which the whole population lived, apart from the castle-dwelling gentry, their servants, the parish ministers and schoolmasters.

But in the nineteenth century – as a result of the clearances and voluntary emigration, improvements in both internal and external communications and the development of Arran as an attractive tourist destination – the whole balance of the population begins to change and tip away from agrarian and maritime occupations towards service industries of one sort or another, especially in the eastern segment of the island. A new kind of non-agricultural workers appears in the island. Recognizable village life forms itself, although in the beginning only on the eastern side. In addition to the categories mentioned above and traditional rural workers such as blacksmiths, we find in a table of 1835 two cobblers, three carpenters, seven grocers, three masons, three surgeons (the two referred to earlier in 1850 and another Stoddart, John), three tailors, no less than seven vintners, and one flesher, one dyer and one distiller: interestingly, nineteen of these are in Lamlash as opposed to only nine in Brodick.

Census returns for Arran in the second half of the nineteenth century and later show a gradual rise in employments such as shopkeepers, innkeepers and clerks, corresponding to a fall in agricultural and maritime work, and in traditional rural crafts such as weavers, tailors, shoemakers and bakers. Overall, Arran's population increased from 1755 up to about 1821 with a high of nearly 6,500, and thereafter decreased to less than 5,000 in 1891. Between 1821 and 1901 Kilmory Parish, the western agricultural parish, showed a steeper rate of decline (roughly 4,000 to 2,500) than Kilbride Parish with its four gradually expanding village resorts (say 2,600 to 2,400); the fall for both parishes became more pronounced in the twentieth century. The distribution of the population changes between 1801, when numbers are more or less even right round the island, and 1891, when the population has clustered round the four main eastern centres, Corrie, Brodick, Lamlash and Whiting Bay and a rather smaller concentration in Lochranza in the north-west. Attending to the needs of visitors was becoming the prime employment in Arran, and attracted workers to the east like iron filings to a magnet.

Changing to a tourist economy meant that accommodation all over Arran had to be upgraded or built right from scratch. The first wave of building took place in the 1850s. The eleventh Duke provided lodges – for instance at Dougarie for deer-stalking and grouse-shooting. These recreations came in for a variety of reasons, including the fashion for shooting game birds following the example of Queen Victoria's circle at Balmoral, and a considerable fall in the price of sheep, rendering large sheep-walks economically unviable. But throughout the island a more middle-class clientèle began to be catered for as the islanders came to appreciate the benefits brought by the influx of summer and other visitors.

The earliest tourists were put up in private homes, but as their numbers increased, different kinds of accommodation, including rented housing, began to be built to cater specifically for their needs. In Brodick, villas and hotels were built, including the Douglas Hotel (probably 1856) – on a site on the former croft of the alleged ex-Jacobite Hector McAlister. It appears that the estate factor acted thereafter as a drag on house-building, because a second phase of provision did not begin until 1881, when the second of the unpopular Paterson dynasty died. In fact the building drive did not really develop until 1894, a year before the twelfth Duke died, when improved housing at

Hamilton Terrace in Lamlash replaced the former whitewashed cottages; following 1895 there was a relaxation of restrictions on building, and leases were more readily transfomed into feus i.e. real ownership of land and housing became possible. After 1895 the handsome sandstone buildings characteristic of south-west Scotland sprang up in numbers all over Arran.

Accommodating visitors in estate houses was finally permitted when it became apparent that otherwise the inhabitants would become a charge on the community as paupers. McLellan tells us of an old woman living in Douglas Row in Brodick, who, when the news of the lifting of the regulations came through, ran up and down the street shouting 'Hooray! Hooray! We've got oor leeberty noo! We've got oor leeberty noo!'[6]

The original village of Brodick, just to the south of Brodick Castle, was demolished after 1852 in order to make way for a deer park and other enlargements of the Castle pleasure grounds. In 1856–58 the eleventh Duke built housing at Douglas Row (later Douglas Place) and Alma Terrace in what is now Brodick on the opposite side of the bay at Invercloy for people displaced by the removal of the village. The new Brodick crystallized around the older, smaller village, Invercloy, the 'mouth of the River Cloy' – a stream which runs down from Glen Cloy under the shore-front roadway to issue just beside the 1872 Brodick Pier. This, now long gone, was an elegant iron structure built next to the Douglas Hotel on the waterfront, when the Duke at last consented to facilitate arrivals of visitors and holiday-makers.

Businesses and shops as well as residential accommodation appeared – grocery and provisions merchants, a bakery, a saddlery, a shoemaker, a smithy, and several boarding houses as well as grander houses for prominent residents like John Fullarton. Hans Bannatyne took up tailoring in the winter and hiring out pleasure-boats in the summer; he was a descendant of the unfortunate Hans Bannatyne who was drowned in 1776 while operating a sailing-boat service between Brodick and Saltcoats on the Ayrshire mainland (see chapter 15). John M'Bride, a shoemaker, also 'drifted into the boat-hiring business'.[7] Another shoemaker, Peter Sinclair, established what amounted to a small factory employing several men, and building up a business which attracted the important patronage of the Castle. Fullarton, a tailor in Laigh Glencloy, produced among other things riding habits for the nobility and gentry (Lord Rossmore's family at Dougarie).

Peter Hunter was a village joiner and undertaker. John Currie also had a joinery business; his daughters opened a store selling small household requisites and local seaside picture postcards.

A typical Scottish grocery-cum-Post-Office appeared in Brodick in 1870, run by a Mrs William Gray, with deliveries to Corrie made by a 'post runner', Robert Douglas. Mrs Gray's establishment was succeeded in 1872 by Ernst (Ernest) Ribbeck's post office. Ribbeck was a German who had come to Arran in 1856, sent there by a Glasgow ornamental ironwork firm in order to paint the gate of the Brodick Castle flower-gardens. This was some time after the arrival of the German Princess Marie of Baden, with whom he made contact. A few years later his younger brother Heinrich (Henry) also came to Arran, and the two of them settled, married Arran girls, and prospered.

Ernest also developed a postal delivery service, at first extending only to Corrie but later expanded. Both Henry and Ernest were skilled saddlers and travelled round Arran making and repairing harness for the island farmers. Henry built up a considerable business on his own account.

In the nineteenth century, horse-drawn vehicles served the needs of ship passengers disembarking at the main ports. The earliest we have a record of was a simple van run for hire in 1814 by one McBride (first name unknown). This vehicle needed repair on the mainland, and was lost at sea in 1817 together with the ship and most of the crew. John Hendry, son of old Sandy Hendry the revenue man (see above pp. 155–6), developed a carrier service and expanded it under pressure of the numbers of visitors to Arran.[8] John Davidson regularly operated a two-horse 'charabanc' from 1870, between Brodick and Corrie and along the String Road. He is reputed to have had a third horse with which he would supplement the traction of the other two when taking the hilly road to Lochranza. Davidson died in 1911. Other early haulage and postal delivery contractors included William Currie.

One way of getting around, from the 1830s, has been described as follows: 'vehicles called caravans had been introduced, a kind of luxurious box apartment which was set on cart wheels and used on special occasions by the notables of the time for going to church and other important gatherings. Dr John Stoddart, Mrs Jamieson and Captain Fullarton were local pioneers in this new mode of travelling, each having one of these vehicles.'[9] Of course this was a different kind of vehicle from our traffic-jamming homes on wheels, and yet it seems not to have resembled a roofed travelling coach of the early nineteenth century: I have an impression of something like a western prairie schooner, a pioneer's covered wagon.

Mackenzie's, an early Shiskine firm of coachbuilders, built vans for merchants. The Hamiltons of Whin House, butchers, had a horse-drawn delivery van which did the rounds of the south of the island. Currie of Balmichael acted as a general carrier to the west, and Ernest Ribbeck, the Brodick postmaster, as mentioned above, ran a postal delivery service to and from Corrie: this service was later expanded.

Businesses, of course, grew up spontaneously wherever a need was felt, and not necessarily in the centre of the new villages: Corriegills is only a scattered collection of farms between Lamlash and Brodick, yet in that rural area there was not only a wheelwright's business belonging to Samuel Bannatyne, to which women brought their spinning-wheels for repair, but also a grocery store whence Mrs Bannatyne made deliveries on foot throughout the neighbourhood. There was even an embryonic coffee-house or café milieu in a converted farm-steading at Alltbeag where newspapers and their political contents were discussed in the traditional and respectable style of rural intellectuals before the advent of radio and television.[10] Hawkers toured the island: John Gillan had a donkey and cart from Lochranza, and John Kerany had a wheelbarrow from Lamlash.

It is noticeable that Lamlash steadily grows in importance through the nineteenth century as contrasted with Brodick. The 'factorate', the residence of the factor and the administrative centre of his operations, had been transferred there early in the century, and there, in the (recently demolished) Whitehouse, two generations of the redoubtable Patersons lived, until 1881.

After the failure of the City of Glasgow Bank, the Bank of Scotland opened a branch in Lamlash in 1878, and in Brodick ten years later. Previously the banker had visited Brodick on a weekly or bi-weekly basis, and stayed overnight in one of the new houses in Brodick. Shops opened at various locations in the Whiting Bay area and Lamlash, as well as at Blackwaterfoot, Kilmory, Slidderie and Kildonan. A centre of commerce on the west side of the island was Shedog (Shiskine), with a range of retail and craft outlets suited to the rural character of the area – two general stores, two joiners' businesses, a saddler's and a smiddy, besides a dressmaker and a tailor.

Private houses were often made available for visitors either 'with attendance' (the original family retiring to the rear of the premises from which they would provide services) or on a completely self-catering basis. Houses with attendance were to be found in all the settlements around the coasts, and especially in the larger centres on the east coast, Lamlash and Whiting Bay as well as Brodick itself. The visitors often took the accommodation for several months in the summer and people on the verge of retirement – businessmen and seafarers – began to look for places to settle down in permanently, for instance at Lochranza.

The churches in Victorian Arran

What had started at the end of the seventeenth century as a single national church, now continued its fissiparous career throughout the nineteenth. After the 1843 Disruption, each of the two separated entities, the Church of Scotland and the Free Church, vied with the other in providing magnificent temples in all the principal locations in Arran. From 1845 to 1900 nine buildings were erected by the Free Church (at Brodick, Bennecarrigan, Shiskine, Lennymore, Kildonan, Whiting Bay, Lamlash, Corrie and Lochranza). But these religious bodies kept on performing what was almost a kind of square dance, changing partners, merging and separating with bewildering facility. In 1900 the Free Church merged with the United Presbyterian Church, forming the United Free Church, but some Free Church members refused to join the union, and this led, as in 1843, to squabbling over the ownership of existing Free Church buildings. It became necessary to erect no less than seven new church buildings for the newly amalgamated United Free Church, at Brodick, Whiting Bay, South End, Bennecarrigan, Shiskine, Pirnmill and Lochranza. According to McLennan, this building frenzy was largely tourist-driven: nineteenth-century visitors to Arran may or may not have been devout partisans, but the church buildings, many of which still survive, are witnesses to a competitive fervour unlikely to be equalled today.

Visitors

Arran's holiday industry originally began with health tourism. The island was already famous from the early eighteenth century for one curative commodity – goat's milk, whose restorative properties were then of high repute:

> Good goat milk quarters may be had this season in the island of Arran, in a very commodious slated house [The 'Cladach'?], hard by the Castle of Brodick, consisting of three very good rooms above stairs, and two below, with a large kitchen, some bedsteads, chairs and tables. This house will serve two small families, with garden things at hand. (*Glasgow Journal*, 12 May 1759)[11]

Fashionable people would take goat's milk as others would 'take the waters' at Buxton or Bath. But goats became scarce, and scenery replaced the milk as the main attraction of Arran.

The scenery, of course, was the result of millions of years of geological upheaval, and it was to Arran, later in the eighteenth century, that James Hutton came in search of geological rarities and unusual layering: sorting the island's bewildering jumble of rocks into systems enabled him to formulate the first viable theory of igneous geology. But it was the aesthetic rather than the geological factor, the beauty and terror of the mountains and moors, that acted as a tourist magnet. In the late eighteenth century the Romantic Revolution, every bit as economically important as the French, American, Industrial or Agricultural Revolutions, had transformed people's awareness of the countryside. The non-urban environment had previously been regarded as just a rather smelly if necessary adjunct to the architectural splendours of the Town. The advent of the poets Wordsworth and Coleridge with their *Lyrical Ballads*, and earlier heroes like Gray, Young, Goldsmith and others, had changed all that. Impressive landscapes, mountains and lochs had to be sought out and praised to the heavens.

In Scotland, Walter Scott, the poet and novelist, had led the charge in 1814 with publication of a poem entitled 'The Lord of the Isles'. In his fanciful – and muddled – account of the wanderings of Robert the Bruce 500 years previously, Scott introduces a mythical love interest involving Bruce's sister Isabel, staying where 'yon mountains hide The little convent of Saint Bride' i.e. at Lochranza, from which she sends an urgent messenger:

By many a mountain stream he [Augustine] pass'd,
From the tall cliffs in tumult cast,
Dashing to foam their waters dun
And sparkling in the summer sun.
Round his grey head the wild curlew
In many a fearless circle flew.
O'er chasms he pass'd, where fractures wide
Craved wary eye and ample stride.[12]

Arran was a Gothic-romantic's paradise, with Byronic gloom, wild chasms, and lofty peaks – and it was more accessible than the northern Highland solitudes. Fashionable ladies read, some doubtless swooned with delight, and soon they were excursioning not only around Lochranza but to Brodick Bay and elsewhere.

Other authors added to the island's touristic glamour – perhaps most importantly the Reverend Dr David Landsborough, who wrote *Arran: a Poem in Six Cantos* (1828), and *Excursions in Arran, with reference to the Natural History of the Island* (1847) with reprints and additions, some from the pen of his son, up to 1873. These works are today monumentally unreadable, but in their own time they spread the word.

A tale of passion

With the gentrification of the aristocracy, life was high in Brodick Castle and nothing but the Victorian best would do. In 1844 the future eleventh Duke married Princess Marie of Baden. In order to do the honours, he commissioned a well-known Scottish architect, Gillespie Graham, to extend and refurbish the old castle, parts of which date back to the thirteenth century. There may have been even older forts, including both Viking and Iron Age, on the site but there is no means of confirming this since the present castle has been built right over the suspected location. The earliest visible part is the irregular strip of discoloured stone which runs along the base of the eastern section of the main block: this could well date from the thirteenth century, and in that case might have been built by the Menteith Stewarts. During the two centuries after the end of the Wars of Independence, Brodick Castle was sacked and repeatedly destroyed not only in ferocious inter-family fighting among the Scots but as a result of incursions from England by Tudor fleets. The jumble of roofs, gables and towers at the east end of the building probably represents the *ad hoc* reconstructions necessitated by this cycle of destruction, and dates from the sixteenth and early seventeenth century, as does the superstructure of the eastern part of the main block. East again, connected with the main building, is a low gun-battery associated with the Cromwellian period. At the west end, however, rises a splendid tower with corner turrets above the level of the main block, which is connected with it by a short extension: this is Gillespie Graham's contribution, conferring a Scottish Baronial atmosphere on the whole confection, and transforming the rugged old fortification into a 'stately home' which we now recognize as possessing its own Victorian authenticity. Princess Marie herself laid the foundation stone and Graham constructed a sumptuous interior for the enlarged castle, with a huge entrance hall, a great staircase, an enormous kitchen which still conserves its old-style copper utensils and three ovens built into a single range; an indeed stately drawing room contrasting with a cosy wood-panelled dining-room; a library and a gallery. The building and grounds are now in the care of the National Trust for Scotland.

William Alexander Anthony Archibald, eleventh Duke of Hamilton, was the son of Duke Alexander and Susan Beckford, who was the daughter of William Beckford, the celebrated millionaire, collector, paedophile and author of *Vathek* (1782). This was an astonishing work written in French and translated into English; as scandalous as it was blasphemous, it is perhaps the greatest of all Gothic novels. This literary monster avidly collected silver: his vast hoard passed to his daughter and a portion of it is on display in Brodick Castle. It includes pieces by Paul de Lamerie, a superb London silversmith of the early eighteenth century. Beckford died in 1844, the year of his grandson's marriage.

As for Princess Marie, she was the grand-daughter of Claude de Beauharnais, a cousin of the Empress Josephine, wife of Napoleon I; Marie's mother, Stephanie de Beauharnais, had been married off to Karl Ludwig Friedrich, Grand Duke of Baden. Meanwhile Josephine's first husband, Alexandre de Beauharnais, had a daughter, Hortense, before he was guillotined in 1794. Hortense, later Queen of Holland, had a son, allegedly by her official husband (King) Louis Napoleon, and this son, claiming to be a great-nephew of the first Napoleon, later became Napoleon III, Emperor of the French. In this manner Princess Marie of Baden could claim a certain relationship with Napoleon III, and spent a great deal of time in France, where she met the future eleventh Duke of Hamilton. He seems to have become acquainted with Napoleon III through his wife.

In Paris, at the corner of the Boulevard des Italiens and rue Lafitte, to this day there rises a magnificent building now housing the Banque Nationale de Paris, but at one time the most fashionable and expensive restaurant in the city: the Maison Dorée. The front part of the restaurant gave on to the boulevard, but the rear section was reserved for the Lucullan repasts of distinguished and wealthy patrons, who also had access to the upper floors: these areas contained facilities for high-play gambling, and many *salons particuliers*, whose function could be gauged by the numbers of very beautiful Lorettes who strolled the corridors or sat in curtained, perfumed seclusion. All the world was to be seen in the Maison Dorée; clients and patrons in the second half of the nineteenth century included the future Edward VII of Britain, as well as Emile Zola, Gérard de Nerval, Alexandre Dumas, Henri de Toulouse-Lautrec, Marcel Proust, Paul Claudel, Jules Laforgue, Auguste Renoir – and *la plus belle femme de Paris*, Misia Godebska. In that very Deuxième-Empire, Orphée-aux-Enfers setting, no-one would have been surprised to see the lightly incognito figure of Napoleon III himself stealing up the stairs, though few might have recorded it.

It was in this distinguished if raffish company that the Duke of Hamilton found himself in 1863; he also stole up the back stairs – without, of course, his wife. What could be more natural than that two gentlemen, distantly but cordially related, should settle down together to gamble – or for any other purpose? Again, what could be more natural than that they should become a little over-heated by the excellent wine culled from the enormous cellar (80,000 bottles) kept by the house? That voices should be raised? That the two should suddenly jump up, glare at each other, and march side by side out of the *salon particulier*?

Be that as it may, one thing is certain: the door slammed behind them; followed a strangled cry and the sound of a prolonged, heavy fall. The cocottes dashed out into the corridor and to the head of the stairs, where I think they would discover Napoleon III, Emperor of the French, perhaps dusting off his hands, with a high look in his eye, while at the foot of the stairs sprawled the eleventh Duke of Hamilton, his neck emphatically broken.

Marie of Baden was at the time cooling her heels in the great house of Brodick in Arran. When the news was brought to her, she was very angry indeed. After the steam from her ears had subsided a little, she gathered her skirts around her and descended a flight of stairs – perhaps not so different from those in the Maison Dorée – leading to the Duke's private cellars: there he had stored a priceless collection of rare French wines. She surveyed the serried bins for a while, and then ordered all the bottles to be brought out and piled in a great heap on Brodick foreshore – after which, she took a hammer or a poker, smashed every one of them, and, dusting off her hands, returned in dudgeon to the castle.

Or so the story goes. Some credence may be lent to it by the fact that Napoleon III bestowed the revived title of Duke of Chatelherault upon the eleventh Duke's heir in 1864. Was this a partial attempt to make amends? The French title had been given to the Earl of Arran in 1548 as a reward for support for Mary, Queen of Scots, but had been officially withdrawn when the Earl changed sides. (See chapter 10.)

In spite of the foregoing, the pedestrian who walks past Brodick Primary School today will see a bronze statue of William Alexander Anthony Archibald, eleventh Duke of Hamilton, erected at the cost of his wife and his principal tenants; there on his plinth he sits, bekilted, with a perhaps speculative look in his sculpted eye, looking out over the Bay of Brodick.

The aristocratic penchant for adultery may not have been exhibited only by the eleventh Duke. Marie of Baden may have had her own weaknesses. There was a lady in Brodick by the name of Marion Hamilton, whose presence required some explanation, if one had been forthcoming. One theory is that she was the offspring of a celebrated Brodick beauty named Elizabeth Hamilton and 'a Scottish nobleman' otherwise unspecified. Another theory is that a certain German landscape artist, Baron von Heringen (known in this country as 'Mr Hering'), had come to Arran in search of inspiration, and established himself in the favour of Princess Marie during the Duke's frequent absences in Paris: hence Marion Hamilton. Both Marie and von Heringen were German, and shared a passion for landscape gardening. Often they strolled together through the policies and pleasure gardens communing with nature face to face. But speculation is rather cooled by the facts that the Baron's wife was also present on the island at all times, and that the Duke of Hamilton gave the impression of salving his conscience by building a substantial red sandstone house, Ormidale, in the outskirts of Brodick, for the Heringens: they, who had just lost a child, adopted little Marion Hamilton, renamed her Jeanie Hering, and got the best doctors to treat her for a slight lameness. Whether this was cured or not, Jeanie grew up to be a beauty in her own right, married John Adams-Acton (a fashionable portrait sculptor), and became a leading hostess in St John's Wood in London.

The eleventh Duke of Hamilton, possibly at the urging of his wife, fulfilled his duty of educational care for his tenants and their children as far as bricks and mortar were concerned; he appears in a less socially responsible light in the Maison Dorée episode. His philanthropic stock falls even lower if we believe that he actually issued an edict banishing pauper children ('cairgen weans') from Arran, like the present-day politicians who attempt to brighten the image of our cities by 'forbidding' mendicants to beg in the streets. The following poem was written in the Lagg Hotel Visitors' Book by an otherwise unknown poet in the 1850s, when the order was made:

The Cairgen Weans

O dinna ban the cairgen weans
But meet them wi' a smile;
They come to seek the healing breeze
That blaws o'er Arran's isle.
O let the shielan shield fae harm
The puir wee orphan bairn
An' let them in that kindly care
Thy homely virtues learn.

We brought the pale wee cairgen bairns
The cotter's care to seek
And noo they play among the Glens
Wi' roses on their cheek –
They lo'e the isle that gave them health,

An' sair wid be their pain
If noo ye shut the cotter's door
Upon the cairgen wean.

You see yon sturdy ploughman cheil,
Yon bonny bloomin' lass:
He whistles o'er the furrow'd fiel',
She sings among the grass;
He brings nae curse upon the soil,
Her song a blessing earns,
An' yet they came into the isle
Twa orphan cairgen bairns.

O mither come an' plead wi' me
Against the edict stern
That bids the cotter steek his door
An' ban the orphan bairn –
An' let the cairgen rhymer's lay
Plead not with thee in vain:
Still let thy shielan shield an' bless
The cairgen orphan wean.

James Paul Crawford

I must thank Mr and Mrs Peter Bowers, proprietors of the Lagg Hotel for drawing my attention to this poem, which is not a bad example of mid-century Scottish verse, and which exhibits the same generous humanitarianism as some of the works of Robert Burns.[13]

Celebrity visitors

Members of the upper classes, mainly connections of the Hamiltons and their friends, stayed in Arran for longer or shorter periods in secluded luxury. Lord Cockburn, the celebrated Scottish judge, was a frequent early visitor. Later in the nineteenth century, Lord Kelvin, the electrical pioneer, made several visits to the island, and was responsible in 1872 for the installation of the first electric telegraph in Arran. Jeanie Adams-Acton brought many famous people to

Arran, to Ormidale, her step-parents' home. The poet Robert Browning had known Baron von Heringen's wife, Katie Bromley, before her marriage; he stayed at Blairbeg near Lamlash and visited Ormidale several times. Graphic artists flocked to Arran, as they still do, and Lewis Carroll, the author of *Alice in Wonderland*, came to Lamlash in search of one of them, Sir Noel Paton, the Queen's Limner in Scotland. Carroll (Charles Dodgson) was in search of an illustrator for the book. Paton refused, but recommended him to Sir John Tenniel, who eventually took on the task.

Another famous visitor to nineteenth-century Arran was Henry Herbert Asquith, the Prime Minister who took Britain into the First World War in 1914; he lost his first wife, Helen, to typhoid in Lamlash in 1891. Earlier visitors to Brodick Castle seem to have included none other than Louis Napoleon about 1851, before he became Napoleon III, Emperor of the French.[14] Edward VII and Queen Alexandra visited Arran and Brodick just after their coronation in 1902. Others were the Tsarevich of Russia (which Tsarevich is uncertain), the King of Saxony, and, before the First World War, Winston Churchill.

In the nineteenth century a walking holiday was still enjoyed, or more fashionable than today. In 1886 Jeanie Hering Adams-Acton proposed to walk from London to the Arran ferry terminal at the Broomielaw in Glasgow, and did so, accompanied by her young children – six in all, with a pram for the youngest – and two maids. The pram, we are told, was of curious design, with three instead of the normal four wheels: we wonder whether this vehicle resembled the 21st-century three-wheeler, which is reputed to be liable to tip over under certain circumstances. Perhaps the fact that Jeanie had suffered from slight lameness in youth made the journey into a challenge which she felt she had to overcome. At any rate she wrote it all up in her book *The Adventures of a Perambulator*, for Mrs Adams-Acton was an early example of the sentimental lady journalist specializing in sweetly condescending pieces about the life of children; she wrote for a publication called *Little Wide-Awake*.[15]

McLellan says that Jeanie demonstrated that she was a true aristocrat by ordering the youngest child's nurse to make a round trip on foot of twelve miles to pick up something she had forgotten, before the fixed starting time in the morning for the rest of the party. That nurse, Ellen, had to push the 'perambulator', laden with luggage as well as the child, nearly all the way to the

Broomielaw. I don't know whether Jeanie's lofty indifference to her servant's foot-weariness or her delegation of duties amounts to characteristic aristo-cratic behaviour or just to classic classless thoughtlessness, but the tasks do not seem to have harmed Ellen overmuch: she died in Arran at the age of ninety-six in 1958.[16]

I suppose that Jeanie Adams-Acton was a 'local girl made good', a native of Brodick who went out into the world beyond Arran and attained social and pro-fessional status. She seems to have had a good family life. Three of her six children, Harold, Lionel and Murray, served in the First World War and survived.[17]

Another nineteenth-century native of Arran is also noted for going out into the world and making good: Daniel Macmillan, the founder of the great pub-lishing house Macmillans, was born at the runrig farm at Achag (Corrie North) in 1813. He should probably be counted an Arran native only techni-cally, since his family moved to the mainland in 1816 following the 1814 Clearances. A descendant of Daniel was Harold Macmillan, Prime Minister of Britain after Anthony Eden's fall from grace in 1956.

Crime in a high place

One or two less savoury personalities stand out from the ruck of nineteenth-century visitors to Arran. The year 1889 saw the notorious Goatfell Murder. It took place during the great saturnalia, Glasgow Fair, when even today the whole population of the south-west of Scotland lets its collective hair down and often becomes a little boisterous. In 1889, Fair Saturday fell on 13 July, the weather was good, and the Clyde was buzzing with little paddle steamers packed with happy holiday-makers.

On Friday 12 July a young Glaswegian named John Watson Laurie was trav-elling on the excursion steamer *Ivanhoe*. For reasons known only to himself he was travelling under a false name – 'John Annandale'. A pattern-maker at a Glasgow engineering works, Laurie was a social climber.

Travelling on the same boat was a young Londoner called Edwin Robert Rose, a hail-fellow-well-met character, happy, elegantly turned out, sociable and guile-less. He had been staying at the Glenburn Hydropathic, one of Rothesay's more superior hotels, with two acquaintances from Linlithgow – Mickel and Thom – and a friend from London, the Reverend Gustavus Goodwin. Rose introduced himself spontaneously to Laurie/Annandale. Laurie responded to this approach with alacrity, perhaps because of Rose's English accent and natty costume. The *Ivanhoe* steamed its cheerful way round the beauty spots of the Upper Clyde – Tighnabruaich, the Kyles of Bute, Ardlamont – and Arran.

While building their acquaintance, Laurie and Rose noticed the sharp peak of Goatfell above Brodick, and both were taken with the adventurous notion of climbing it. Rose asked Laurie whether he would accompany him as a guide up the mountain. Laurie agreed readily (although he had never climbed it), and they both disembarked from the *Ivanhoe* at Brodick. While Rose went off to explore Invercloy and Brodick, Laurie looked for and found inferior accommodation for the following nights for them both. It was little more than an outhouse with a single bed, but Laurie took it. He agreed with Rose to climb Goatfell on Fair Monday.

The two other young men, Mickel and Thom, were to join them, but Laurie had made a poor impression on them, with his ingratiating manner and affectation of an English accent. One of them caught a hint of a darker side to Laurie's character, and warned Rose against climbing the mountain with him. Rose seems to have taken the warning seriously, but was clearly changeable and gullible. Mickel and Thom left Arran on Monday morning, but Rose stayed behind, waving them off from the Brodick quayside, arrayed in mountaineering garb and accompanied by Laurie/Annandale.

The two of them climbed Goatfell, meeting various acquaintances and other parties, and reached the top. However, after that achievement, no-one ever saw Edwin Robert Rose alive again.

That evening there were various sightings of Laurie/Annandale in the Corrie area, but the next morning he had simply vanished from the Invercloy lodging without paying his bill. No-one took this too seriously, for Arran and Bute landladies were well accustomed to being bilked, and though the police came to know of the case, the minor dishonesty was not grave enough to warrant close investigation.

Rose's brother Benjamin was worried when Rose did not meet him off the Glasgow train in London on Thursday 18 July as previously arranged. The family became alarmed and later telegraphed the Reverend Gustavus Goodwin, who was still in the Rothesay hotel which the four friends had made their base before the *Ivanhoe* expedition.

Rose had failed to turn up to pick up luggage on Wednesday 17 July as arranged in a letter written to Goodwin at Rothesay. Goodwin had not been unduly alarmed but, on receiving the family's telegram on Monday 22 July, he took the first boat to Brodick, found the Invercloy landlady, a Mrs Walker, and discovered that two young guests of hers had left to climb Goatfell on Fair Monday and had vanished; Goodwin went immediately to the Brodick police and told his story.

Laurie, still masquerading as 'Annandale', was continuing his Clyde holiday as if nothing had happened. In Rothesay on the same day, 22 July, as Goodwin's journey, he met an acquaintance, James G. Aitken, a grain merchant. Aiken, who had seen Laurie and Rose together previously, remembered that Rose had been wearing a yachting cap resembling the one now sported by Laurie.

On the morning of Friday 26 July, after requesting his Rothesay landlady to prepare a bill for him by 1 p.m., Laurie walked out of the boarding house, again vanishing without paying. He took boat and train back to Glasgow, and during the journey it was noted by a fellow-passenger that he had with him two leather cases, one black and smart, the other brown and shabby; previously Laurie had had only one case, brown and shabby. The Rothesay landlady, a Mrs Currie, sent the bill to the address given by 'Annandale', North Frederick Street in Glasgow, where no such person was known.

On Saturday 27 July, Rose's brother Benjamin arrived in Brodick, and a hue-and-cry was raised. On Sunday 28th a search party climbed Goatfell but could find no trace of either Rose or 'Annandale'. The story got into the newspapers. On 29 July James Aitken read the story and by happenstance met Laurie in the centre of Glasgow. Aitken asked him, 'What do you know about this Arran mystery?' He remembered the name Rose. Laurie blustered that it could not be the same man, since Rose had come back to Glasgow with him before going south. Aitken taxed Laurie with the cap mysteriously similar to that worn by Rose. Laurie, probably blanching, gabbled, 'Surely you don't think that I am a . . . ?' Aiken thought he was going to say 'thief', but later realized that the word 'murderer' was more likely. Laurie promised to meet him to give a fuller explanation in a pub in Glasgow that evening but did not turn up. Aitken went to the police and told them that he thought John Laurie was 'Annandale'.

Meanwhile Laurie went to where he was employed as a pattern-maker in an engineering works in Springburn near Glasgow, resigned his position there, said that he was going to become a traveller in grain (!), and, after selling his pattern-making tools, vanished completely from the locality. Then, back in Arran, on 4 August, a very large search party from Corrie and Brodick, two hundred searchers divided into four groups of fifty, set out to comb the whole of Goatfell more thoroughly than on 28 July. On the ridge between the 'Saddle' and Goatfell itself, a searcher named Francis Logan discovered, carefully concealed beneath a large boulder, the body of Edwin Robert Rose with his head smashed in, apparently by repeated blows with a heavy object like a stone. A hat was discovered in a nearby stream, carefully folded and hidden under another stone.

Immediately there ensued a nationwide manhunt for Laurie, who dodged from place to place, using various ploys to evade capture. He faked a suicide, leaving a note incriminating himself, but this failed to throw the pursuers off the scent. At the same time he gave way to his vanity in a fashion beloved of writers of detective fiction but perhaps not so common in real life – he wrote two letters to the newspapers, effectually boasting of his exploits although ostensibly denying his guilt. One of these letters was sent from Liverpool, and one from Aberdeen, but the wily police chief in charge of the investigation guessed that Laurie would not in the end move far from his home: sure enough, an off-duty policeman waiting at a rural railway station just outside the Glasgow area spotted Laurie lurking in the vicinity, gave chase, and, after enlisting the support of the coalminers at the nearby Larkhall colliery, ran him to earth in a small copse; he had tried to commit suicide with a pen-knife, but all he had done was to make his throat bleed.

At his trial in November 1889, John Watson Laurie was unsurprisingly found guilty. The defence had tried to prove that Rose's death was accidental, and in fact a small doubt lingers to this day, but Laurie's behaviour following the event tipped the balance against him. He was sentenced to be hanged in Greenock, to the consternation of the citizens of that douce burgh; no-one had been hanged there since 1834. The Town Council paid for the erection of a gallows and for the services of the famous hangman Berry, but in the end Laurie was reprieved on the eve of the execution: a slight doubt had arisen about his sanity. Everybody was relieved, including Laurie, who went on to be the longest serving prisoner in Scottish legal history. He died in 1934, after being let out on 'day release'; the governor of Perth prison was content to see him ambling around the streets, a rosy-cheeked, completely harmless old man unsuspected by other pedestrians. He also succeeded in having a quasi-romance with one of the prison visitors, and wrote her a secret letter incorporated in sheets of musical notation; his handwriting and syntax show him to have been a well-educated man.

Greenock Town Council never recovered their expenses. Edwin Robert Rose lies buried in the old churchyard south of Corrie.[18]

OS references

Arran's owners
Whitefarland NR 864 423
Imachar NR 865 405
All-t-gobhlach NR 874 435
Kilmichael NS 002 350
Balliekine NR 870 396
Dougarie NR 882 374
Corriegills NS 035 350–037 345
Kildonan NS 036 213
Clachlands NS 045 332

A tale of passion

Lagg Hotel NR 955 216

17. The 'Modern' Age

The demise of landowner control

From the late nineteenth century onward, control exercised by the landowner in Scotland and his representatives was and continued to be eroded very significantly. This was due to three factors: first, the transfer of administrative powers to County Councils brought about by the Local Government (Scotland) Acts of 1889, 1894 and 1929; the various Acts relating to crofters, including, most importantly, the Crofters' Holdings (Scotland) Act 1886; and, in Sir William Harcourt's Budget of 1894, the introduction of death duties, which inhibited the accumulation of wealth and property by influential families. Increasingly severe taxation and Land Court rent control radically affected the landowner's ability to invest capital in new developments or even in maintenance of landed estates.

The succession of local government acts absorbed Arran into a national structure of elected authorities. In 1889 the establishment of County Councils, each with a County Convener as chairman, in itself eroded the power of local landowning magnates such as the Duke of Hamilton. Many civic functions were transferred from the landholder to County Council committees.

Thus, Arran became a District of Bute County. The provision of roads in Arran had ceased, in 1881, to be a matter of old-fashioned 'statutory labour' organized on a 'corvée' basis by the factor; it now became the responsibility of the District Committee under the elected Bute County Council: this Committee built stone bridges in Arran. Similarly, responsibility for the pro-

192

vision of a police service passed from the commissioners of supply, who were creatures of the Duke, to the police committee of the elected County Council. Justices of the Peace were now to be chosen by County Council committees, and to these committees and sub-committees passed a raft of civic duties, from weights and measures inspection to administration of the Explosives Act. Already, modern local government was taking characteristic shape in Scotland.

The Crofters' Holdings Act of 1886 had conferred security of tenure upon crofters besides setting up a Land Court. Even though the Duke of Hamilton had successfully lobbied in Parliament to have the Isle of Arran excluded from the provisions of the 1886 Act, his power, or at least that of his successors, would ultimately be curtailed by this measure.

Following the seminal 1889 Local Government (Scotland) Act, there was a succession of consolidating and reorganizing measures: in particular the Local Government (Scotland) Act 1929 abolished parish councils and redistributed their functions; it set up a variety of council authorities – large, small and united burgh, city and district councils – and it reorganized the original county councils. It abolished the traditional Commissioner of Supply mechanism and transferred Poor Law (now 'Public Assistance') and education functions to the counties and counties of cities. This was a powerful piece of legislation, and in the transfer and redefinition of important functions the influence of the secular landowners was correspondingly further restricted, as was that of the many churches which, following the catastrophic decline in religious belief following the First World War, circled their wagons under the protective authority of a reunited Church of Scotland, also in 1929. Hence the large numbers of abandoned temples in Arran and elsewhere throughout the kingdom.

The transforming twentieth century: technology and wars

Even before 1900, technological advances began to have influence upon island life. In 1872 Lord Kelvin, as mentioned earlier, arranged Arran's first telegraph connection, operating from Ernest Ribbeck's post office in Brodick. The telegraph network gradually spread across the whole of Arran, so that a permanent linesman, Donald Smith, had to be appointed in 1886; he lived in Invercloy.[1] The first telephone in the island, in 1891, connected Brodick Castle and Dougarie Lodge: the control room together with the original apparatus was recently revealed by a National Trust for Scotland archaeologist in the Castle. The first motor-car ran in the island in 1897. It was owned by a Mr Fulton, a visitor to Arran staying at West Mayish farm.[2] It astonished the locals by covering the seven miles between Brodick and Sannox in thirty-five minutes. In 1913 there appeared the first 'motor charabanc', a chain-driven Albion vehicle, owned by Colin Currie of Balmichael and later commandeered for service in the First World War.

Bus services in Arran started to operate after the roadways had been improved and enlarged by the District Committee. At the end of the nineteenth century, with the improvements in land communications, there was increasing pressure from the various needs already mentioned – haulage, mobile shops, postal collections and deliveries, the tourist trade itself, and hotel transport to and from the ferry ports (Whiting Bay, Lamlash, Brodick and Lochranza, where there were piers; King's Cross, Corrie, Machrie and Pirnmill, where there were 'rowing boat connections').Tours right round the island or to the northern or southern half began to be co-ordinated with hotels and times of ferry sailings. Services covering established routes at pre-arranged times began to be offered to fare-paying passengers from about 1890 and multiplied greatly with the general conversion to motorized transport after the First World War. The last company to use horse-drawn vehicles, Currie's, ceased the practice in 1928. (Hotels continued to use horse-drawn wagonettes to pick up and set down guests until the 1930s.)

The early history of sailings to and from Arran has been gone into above (chapter 15). Post-1900 cruising and ferry services in Clyde waters deserve, and have received, chapters and whole books to themselves, but here can receive only as much attention as space will permit. The modern development of these services began when steam propulsion for the first time facilitated mass transportation of holiday-makers and others – and since the birth of the steam boat took place on the spectacularly beautiful Clyde estuary, adjacent to the hard-working but grimy megalopolis of Glasgow, ideal conditions existed for the creation of a dense network of local shipping lines carrying everything from bulk cargoes and perishable foodstuffs to crowds of scenery-hungry day trippers.

The expansion of these shipping lines in the nineteenth century of course went hand in hand with that of the various railway lines, which engaged in fierce competition, mainly for the Glasgow holiday traffic. Until well after mid-century, cruising and ferrying in Clyde waters often remained in the hands of individual private entrepreneurs, sometimes a single captain or owner of one ship – unlike the railways which, by the nature of land transport, swiftly agglomerated into heavily organized businesses with a tentacular reach and multiple employees.

In the later nineteenth century, two of these railways were the Glasgow and South-Western Railway ('GSWR') and the Caledonian Railway Company; the latter set up a front company, the Caledonian Steam Packet Company, to get round a law prohibiting railways from operating passenger shipping companies, and from 1889 this company ran a service out of the newly pur-chased port of Gourock: the GSWR evened up the situation by obtaining permission in 1891 to operate passenger shipping on their own account, and they were based in Greenock. This dual regime introduced into the Clyde many elegant paddlers and turbine-ships running to destinations all over the region, including the Arran ports. Their names have passed into legend: *Duchess of Hamilton, Marchioness of Lorne, Duchess of Argyll, Marchioness of Graham, Caledonia, Jupiter, Glen Rosa, Glen Sannox(es)* (I and II) and others.

Several of these fine ships played a gallant part in the two great wars of the twentieth century. The predecessor of the present *Waverley* was sunk during the Dunkirk evacuation in 1940. In the First and Second World Wars the Admiralty seems to have found these ships particularly suited to mine-sweep-ing. The original (1890) *Duchess of Hamilton*, built for the summer Arran service, plied faithfully on the route till the outbreak of war in 1914, when she was commandeered by the Admiralty and sunk by a mine in late 1915. Other paddle and turbine steamers on the Arran routes which swept mines or served as troop-transports and survived the first war were (Paddle Steamer) PS *Marchioness of Lorne* (1891), PS *Glen Rosa* (1893), PS *Duchess of Rothesay* (1895), and (Turbine ship) TS *Duchess of Argyll* (1906); the *Duchess of Rothesay* survived not only that war but also sinking at her moorings in Glasgow in 1919 – and the 1940 Dunkirk disaster, where she was luckier than her sister ship *Waverley*. Other vessels which emerged triumphant from the second spasm of global warfare were the *Duchess of Argyll*, PS *Caledonia* (1934) (as a minesweeper renamed HMS *Goatfell*), and PS *Jupiter* (1937) (renamed

HMS *Scawfell*, as a convoy escort, a Thames anti-aircraft vessel and minesweeper attending the 1944 Normandy landings).

The two great wars

Lamlash Bay has been recognized since the earliest days as a very suitable rendezvous for large battle fleets – including King Håkon IV's galleys at the time of the Battle of Largs and English fleets during the Tudor period. In the twentieth century the roadstead was used repeatedly for warlike purposes: even before the First World War, Winston Churchill as First Lord of the Admiralty ordered the fleet to Lamlash in 1914 in order to threaten Belfast when Ulster seemed likely to rebel against the Liberal Government's intention to grant Home Rule to Ireland; what prevented a British civil war on that occasion was the outbreak of the even more cataclysmic European civil war – Germany and Austria versus the rest.

In that war Lamlash was used again as a rendezvous or gathering point for convoys. James Inglis, the local historian of those times, often saw 'a long line of steamers leaving Lamlash ... with an escort'.[3]

A strict look-out was kept for submarines and their torpedoes – a relatively new kind of warfare then used for the first time in a major war. Many scares were reported, involving mines laid by the submarines rather than torpedoes, and once, after Thomas Kelso, the Corrie night watchman, reported suspicious sounds at sea, he received an Admiralty cheque for £25 for vigilance: a destroyer had apparently caught and sunk a mine-laying submarine. On another occasion, a noise like chain rattling was heard at night from the direction of the Corriegills peninsula: this was reported by William Davidson, the Brodick watchman, and a few hours later, at 10 a.m. a loud explosion was heard. Mines had been laid, detected and exploded.[4] The passage between Arran and the mainland was considered dangerous and sailings were frequently interrupted or cancelled.

The tourist trade, still carried on at the height of the war, suffered badly, especially towards the end of the war in 1917, when submarines were again in the neighbourhood and food supplies for the whole nation were endangered for some time. At one stage in the war Britain had food for less than a fortnight. Prices rose steeply, rationing came into force throughout the kingdom, and the Arran farmers, who had previously been rather in decline, found that they had to bring into production several hundred acres – not that this remedied the decline: the shipping difficulties meant that it was almost impossible to 'export' produce from the island.

It was at this period and afterwards that Donald 'Tattie' McKelvie, a Lamlash accountant, shopkeeper and horticulturalist, came into prominence with his several improved varieties of potato, famed throughout Britain and beyond.

> Health to McKelvie!
> Long shall we praise his name,
> While Arran men delve ye.
> 'Arran Chief', 'Arran Rose',
> 'Comrade' and 'Ally',
> Yea, where the 'Consul' grows,
> Health to McKelvie!
> ('Testimonial' Dinner, November 1925)

McKelvie 'Arran' varieties of potato are still obtainable, though not, I think, in Arran.

The Arran nobility played their traditional role in the Great War. The Marchioness of Graham set up a Red Cross branch on Arran, and, as a Red Cross nurse herself, was responsible for establishing an auxiliary Red Cross hospital for convalescent naval casualties at Lamlash, which she ran as Commandant. After the war, as Duchess of Montrose, she again took the initiative in setting up the Isle of Arran War Memorial Hospital. Her husband, the Marquis of Graham, was mobilized in August 1914 as Commander RNVR (Royal Naval Volunteer Reserve) and as such became the chief recruiting officer for the Navy in Scotland as well as other functions, none of them front line. (He was profoundly deaf.) Her mother Mary, Duchess of Hamilton (the relict of that Duke whose death without a male heir ended the Hamilton line), was Commandant of the Easton Park Red Cross Hospital throughout the war. She opened the War Memorial Hospital in 1923. This hospital is still in existence. An earlier 'fever' hospital was opened in the 1890s and at one time occupied a kind of tin shed on the road between Lamlash and Brodick; this was reconstituted after the 1929 Act and resited to a former private house in Whiting Bay. It provided supplementary services until the nationalization of 1947–48, when it was amalgamated with the War Memorial Hospital and the Whiting Bay premises closed.

In the Second World War Lamlash Bay was used again as a part of the structure of defence for the Western Approaches, and many capital ships (including HMS *Hood*) lay at anchor in the shelter of Holy Island protected by boom defences at either entrance; some concrete footings on either shore may yet survive (at Clauchlands and at King's Cross on Arran and at the north and south extremities of Holy Island). There is a tradition that centuries ago there was an actual tower, a fort at Clauchlands, but the remnants, if there are any, have yet to be identified with certainty. There are very few remains of Duchess Anne's seventeenth century quay, but some stones are still visible at low water below the shore at the Lamlash green. The naval station at Lamlash was known as HMS *Fortitude II* (formerly HMS *Orlando*), and the corresponding station at Ardrossan was called HMS *Fortitude I*. Naval Headquarters was in the requisitioned Marine Hotel and the Boom Defence Headquarters occupied the nearby Harport House. There was a 'Wrennery' at Altachorvie and Craigard (now Hightrees) was the Sick Bay. Besides protecting warships from submarine and air attack, Lamlash Bay was host to a number of training activities, including the use of landing craft and a gunnery school.

I still remember the great solemn rolling thunder of the naval guns echoing right across the Firth of Clyde; on one occasion, I saw from Ayr a tiny dot on the horizon, a huge ship dwarfed by the magnificent scenery: the next instant a tiny flame flashed from the dot and a tremendous crash, a mighty clap, rumbled across the water, setting my ears vibrating.

During the war the Clyde was an intensely busy place, with every kind of warship shuttling to and from Glasgow and the associated naval stations. One of these was an American banana boat, the *Rio de Janeiro*, which had been converted at short notice under the 'Lend Lease' scheme into an aircraft carrier renamed HMS *Dasher*. The conversion in the American yard at Hoboken had been carried out at breakneck speed (in two months, with another two months 'snagging' defects), and it was suspected that much of the workmanship was shoddy and hasty. She finally entered British service and was immediately detailed to convoy duty at the end of August 1942.

The ship was subjected to appalling weather conditions in February 1943 during one of the great North Atlantic convoys, JW53, to Murmansk. She was so badly devastated by hurricane-force winds that she had been detached from the convoy and sent to Iceland, where it was discovered that the aircraft hangar below decks was completely wrecked, with all the aircraft in it smashed beyond repair; there was also a gaping split in her hull, through which other ships could be plainly seen. After rudimentary patching, *Dasher* limped back to Dundee for major welding repairs. After this, she sailed for the Clyde, and proceeded to carry out deck landing practice lasting several days.

At 09.00 on Saturday 27 March 1943, she left Lamlash Bay to carry out further training in the Clyde; after an uneventful day she prepared at about 16.30 to sail for the Tail of the Bank at Greenock. At 16.38, without warning, as the last four aircraft were circling the ship preparatory to landing on the deck, the ship blew up with two terrible explosions and sank inside eight minutes. She foundered just south of the Wee Cumbrae, near Ardrossan. Observers witnessed the aircraft lift to the flight deck from the hangar blown sixty feet up flat into the air, before falling back into the sea.

Out of 528 personnel, only 149 were rescued. Three hundred and seventy-nine perished, very many miserably because the oil which spilt into the sea caught fire and burnt the swimmers alive.

The disaster was witnessed by many people from various points around the Clyde coastline, including Arran: Alister McKelvie of Seaview Farm, Corriegills, observed 'a wall of flame about twenty feet high and colossal black smoke'.[5] Signalman Reg Summerscales at King's Cross Point actually received a message concerning time of arrival at Greenock, by Aldis lamp from *Dasher* immediately (at 16.30) before the explosions and the ship's disappearance.[6] William John McCrae, gathering wood between Corrie and Sannox, saw *Dasher's* sailors jumping overboard while the ship rose at the bows.[7] But nobody was allowed to talk about the sinking and no reports appeared in the press. The full story was buried for many years.

John Steele suspects that the reason for the complete security blanket which the Government imposed upon the press was that *Dasher's* sinking was not the result of enemy action.[8] Torpedoes and mines are virtually ruled out; the actual explosions were prolonged and had a rumbling quality characteristic of the ignition of a fuel such as oil or petrolum: they almost certainly involved a build-up of petroleum vapour from a reported but unchecked slow leak from a faulty fuel tank; the disaster may have been triggered by the crash of an aircraft trying to land on the flight deck. One thing, however, is abundantly clear: defects of construction were such that the ship was 'an accident waiting to happen', a 'floating time-bomb'.[9]

It may be of interest to note that on page 37 of the *History of the Villages of Arran* (2nd reprint, 2002),[10] in the section devoted to Shiskine and Machrie, there is a photograph of a small sailing ship in Blackwaterfoot harbour in 1905: the vessel's name is *Dasher*, clearly legible on her transom. One wonders when the ill-fated *Rio de Janeiro* was renamed *Dasher*, and by whom. Was it a native of Blackwaterfoot?

Other warlike activities centred upon Lamlash, Brodick and the whole of Arran. One that may not be generally known is that Arran was a Commando training ground. If the early history of the Commandos is recollected at all, the monument at Spean Bridge not far from Ben Nevis may come to mind. But Arran provided just as tough a training environment for these selected soldiers who were destined to run unusual risks under cover, undertake 'special operations' and display stamina and courage beyond the normal call of duty.

In August 1940 '11 Commando', one of these specialist units, under Lieutenant-Colonel Dick Pedder, was formed at Galashiels and, after a period of induction training, undertook a route march on 28 August, arriving in Ayr on 4 September for transfer by train and ferry to Lamlash. There they settled down in the prescribed commando fashion, each man finding accommodation for himself, and the leaders of the group requisitioning the Whitehouse, once the residence of the Paterson factors, as an Officers' Mess. It was possible to summon the commandos in the morning with a bugle call, since Lamlash village was tiny even in those days. One man of the group, John Herd, was a native of Arran.

In Lamlash every technique of irregular warfare was assiduously practised, from using light infantry weapons, like the notorious 'Tommy-gun', to silent killing and unarmed combat.[11] The men were toughened by arduous physical exercises including repeatedly climbing Goatfell at speed, scrambling up sheer cliffs, cross-country running and the like. They practised landing from small craft and securing beachheads at Clauchlands Point. They deliberately fired live rounds at each other while dodging from rock to bush. They used the spire of a local church for target practice. Each man was taught to regard himself as an individual fighting unit, in contrast with conventional military training,

and thereby to increase his self-reliance and initiative under stress. The training was incessant and rigorous, all day and most of the night.

A person responsible for such harsh training might not be absolutely brim-
ming with the milk of human kindness, and Dick Pedder is reputed to have
been a deeply unpleasant man.

Toughness and initiative there was aplenty, but these qualities were of no
avail against ineptitude of planning and execution: elements of 11 Commando
took part in the fiasco of the attempted capture or assassination of Erwin
Johannes Eugen Rommel on 17 November 1941 in North Africa, which ended
with the deaths, injury or capture of several of the original force that had
trained in Arran – while their quarry was miles away from the targeted
location where he was supposed to be. Dick Pedder had earlier died in Syria.[12]
The leader of the foiled raiding party, Lieutenant Commander Geoffrey
Keyes, who had trained with 11 Commando in Arran, was killed during the
assault.[13]

During the 1939–45 war, Arran suddenly presented an unfamiliar hazard.
The island lies almost immediately opposite Prestwick Airport (and, during
the war, the adjacent Heathfield Aerodrome) on the mainland fifteen miles
away. Arran is on the direct flight-path coming into Prestwick/Heathfield
from the North Atlantic: the lofty jagged mountains present an obstacle like
a 'cheval-de-frise' – like broken glass set into cement atop a stone wall – to
transatlantic traffic and to any route hugging the west coast of Scotland. (The
Mull of Kintyre, just to the west, has nearly as evil a reputation).[14] The aircraft
of the early 1940s were still relatively primitive, and found it difficult to gain
enough height, especially when laden with petrol or munitions of war and
controlled by inexperienced crew, unaccustomed to the rapidly changing
weather conditions of the Clyde area.

Liberators, Fortresses and other heavy aircraft were delivered to Britain with
great haste and urgency from America (to begin with via Canada) in a continuous ferry operation, and they normally first touched down at Prestwick, the
busiest airport in the United Kingdom. At least fifteen war-planes between
1939 and 1945 went down in the Arran mountains – Beinn Nuis, Goatfell and
elsewhere in and around the island – and in almost all cases there were no survivors: the loss is the more grievous when it is realised that those who died
were often groups of crews of experienced flyers returning in one plane to

America to ferry more Liberators to the front. One of the worst accidents in Arran occurred on 10 August 1941, when a Liberator belonging to the Atlantic Return Ferry Organisation crashed on Mullach Buidhe, a peak in the Goatfell complex. Twenty-two men died, mainly air captains and radio officers returning to Canada in order to bring more vitally needed aircraft to Britain.

Communications after 1945

When the hurly-burly of war temporarily subsided, normal life, and progress within it, started to surface again. Civilian communications began to expand and improve. A telephone link with the mainland had been inaugurated as early as 1913 with the opening of a main post office in Brodick. After 1945 the number of telephone exchanges rose to ten. McLellan tells us that twenty-five red telephone kiosks were installed throughout Arran. Electricity for lighting and other purposes was introduced during the First World War, and the Arran Light and Power Company was set up in 1933. This was taken over after the Second World War by the North of Scotland Hydro-Electric Board, and now, at the beginning of the twenty-first century, with 'denationalisation', the electricity needs of the community are being met by, among others, Scottish Power. Transport competition accelerated in peacetime. In 1962 there were no less than seven bus companies operating from principal points around the island.[15] However, the number of private cars in the whole country had a very steep increase in the post-war period, and this of course affected Arran. Now there are only two main bus operators, Stagecoach West and Royal Mail, with regular whole-island services connecting to the Brodick and Lochranza ferry ports.

After a long period of rivalry in the early part of the century the ferry-ship services had amalgamated under the existing title of the Caledonian Steam Packet Company, and in 1923 the two railway groups controlling these services came together as the London Midland and Scottish Railway (LMSR). In 1948 the railways throughout the country were nationalized and named British Railways, and the Clyde ferry fleets were brought together and renamed 'Clyde Shipping Services': this title lasted only until 1957, when the original name, Caledonian Steam Packet Company ('CSP'), was restored. After another eleven years, reorganization of the whole nationalized concern brought into being the Scottish Transport Group, which took over the management of the CSP. In

June 1969, the Group took over a northern ferry company, David MacBrayne, which had also been nationalized in 1948, and in 1973, the CSP acquired most of MacBrayne's ferry services in the north-west. They renamed the combined fleet Caledonian MacBrayne ('Calmac'), and in 1990 this whole ferry network was detached as a separate business which issued shares; the Secretary of State for Scotland was the sole shareholder; later the responsibility was transferred to the Scottish Executive.

The development of ferry-services can be seen as falling into three phases: the era of regular (mainly paddle-steamer) service lines and cruising designed for day-trippers and other foot-passengers; the period, coinciding with the introduction of the individual motor-car, of foot-passenger services with some space for cars; and the period, starting about 1969, of the complete abandonment of foot-passenger-only ferries and cruising-ships, to be replaced throughout the Clyde area exclusively by passenger-carrying car-ferries of increasing sophistication and capacity.

At first Brodick and Lamlash were grudgingly furnished with piers – in the case of Lamlash only after 'shore boats' from the steamers had repeatedly been swamped and several tourists drowned. Brodick had no proper pier until 1872 and Whiting Bay not until 1901. But neither the dangers of landing nor the hostility of the landowners could resist the invasion of enthusiasts and others, especially as they brought a substantial income to the locals, whose accommodation and catering were soon in demand.

At Corrie, the old system of ferrying visitors ashore (to the 'Ferry Rock') was in operation for many years.[16] Before 1901 the same system of ferrying in small boats from steamships was in operation at Whiting Bay, and also at King's Cross, where there was a ferry landing. At Lamlash the pier originally built at the instance of the Good Duchess in the seventeenth century had fallen into disuse and its stonework was pillaged for building materials when the first houses were built in Lamlash village. A replacement pier was demolished in 1956, and now no large ships, ferries or otherwise, call at Lamlash, although there is a jetty for pleasure craft and for a small open boat transporting tourists and others to Holy Island, which has been owned for some years by a Buddhist community.

The sea devalued

Since the Second World War the Clyde waterway has seen a drastic decline in commercial sailings of all kinds, and has been swept bare of the once-familiar steamships that used to fuss up and down the coasts from small port to small port – Wemyss Bay, Largs, Millport, Fairlie, Irvine, Troon, Ayr, Brodick, Lamlash, Whiting Bay, Lochranza – even as far as Campbeltown and Stranraer. After the war the demand for pleasure cruises on water shrank rapidly, because of the dominance of both public and private motorized land transport on an improved and expanded road network. One celebrated relic, the *Waverley*, 'the last ocean-going paddle-steamer in the world' (can that be true?), is still (2006) gamely plying up and down the firth in the summer, calling at all the beauty spots including the Kyles of Bute, Tigh-na-bruaich and Brodick, and taking a turn round Ailsa Craig. Unnaturally neat and bright with freshly painted colours, *Waverley* is a part of Theme-Park Scotland.

There is also a complete absence of the small ships they used to call 'puffers' – tiny coasting vessels, with a primitive steam engine that 'puffed', carrying tramp cargoes between destinations which larger concerns and ships would often shun on economic grounds. Puffers were immortalised in the 'Para Handy' tales written originally as newspaper pieces a century ago by Neil Munro and given to a wider audience in an unforgettable television series: many of these little dramas were filmed in and around Arran and Brodick. Puffers developed out of pre-steam 'gabberts', small sailing barges that did the same kind of business. The original puffers were adapted from canal boats in the 1850s, hence the characteristic stubbiness of their appearance (to fit the locks of the Forth and Clyde Canal). The Hamilton family, who ran the *Brodick* paddler in the 1830s, started the Cloy Line of small steamers – owners George and Gavin Hamilton.[17] In 1895 they launched the first steamboat built in Arran, the *Glencloy*, a wooden puffer made of Brodick timber.

Even Arran's fishing fleet has long gone. The fishing industry began to decline after 1900, due to an improvement in fishing-boat design which put the purchase of new vessels beyond the means of the island fishermen; other factors were the centralization of markets and perhaps a general decline in fishing stock. The last vestiges of Arran-based commercial fishing disappeared about 1928, earlier than the other West of Scotland fleets, but no less finally.

Without the essentially workaday small craft something of the dignity of labour has departed from the Clyde, a loss for which the proliferation of pleasure-craft 'marinas' in once-industrious harbours cannot compensate. (At the moment there are captive fish farms around the Arran coast and scallop dredgers operating in Lamlash Bay: neither of these activities resembles traditional fishing, and both are alleged to give grave environmental concerns for different reasons.)

However, three witnesses to Arran's continuing importance to seafarers still function: the lighthouses. In fact, none of these interesting buildings stands on Arran's mainland – one rises from the barren rock of Pladda, the alleged retreat of the fourth-century St Blaise of Armenia off the south coast; the other two are on Holy Island (which also has a 'saintly' connection): the inner light guides shipping into Lamlash Bay from the south, and the outer light, at Pillar Rock Point on the east coast of Holy Island, faces across the wide Firth of Clyde, one of a chain of lights (Pladda is another) showing the way into the estuary. None of these lights now have keepers in situ, and all three are fully automatic, but on Holy Island the site manager is the Samye Ling Buddhist Community.

These graceful buildings are well and sturdily constructed, as are all stone lighthouses belonging to the Northern Lighthouse Board. The 95-foot tower at High Pladda[18] was built as early as 1790, by Thomas Smith. The Holy Island pair were built in 1877 (Inner), and 1905 (Outer); both are Stevenson buildings. All are still performing the function they were designed for so many years ago. At night they signal far across the estuary, three white flashes from Pladda, two from Holy Island. (The inner light, for Lamlash Bay, is not so visible from a distance.) The winking lights form one of the more romantically beautiful features of the Clyde, even if now they are pathfinders mainly for bulk carriers and NATO warships.

Nothing will ever be the same as the beautiful Clyde Steam Packets of days gone by, of the 'Marchioness' or 'Duchess' paddlers or turbine-ships. But the disappearance of the traditional cruise and ferry ships from the 'trans-Clyde' routes does not signify the demise of holiday traffic to Arran. In fact the traffic has been enhanced by the introduction of the very large and efficient ferry the *Caledonian Isles* (*Eileanan Chaledonia*) with accommodation for more than 1000 passengers and 120 cars: in summer this graceful monster receives and disgorges a flood of visitors after a double run (fifty-five minutes each way) between Ardrossan and Brodick, six times a day during the week and four times on Sundays.

More than any of her predecessors, the *Caledonian Isles* has brought the motor age comfortably to Arran and thus ensured that more people than ever before are able to spend longer periods staying over in one of the island's hotels or other holiday accommodation. We have come a long way since the days when each motor car had to balance across two rough planks laid parallel to each other from the ship-side to the quay – or to rely upon a crane lifting it overside, or even to reverse awkwardly out of a hold. Indeed the third *Glen Sannox* (built 1957) gave an improved ('drive through') service for cars, but maximum efficiency (so far) was not attained until the introduction of the *Caledonian Isles*, with full 'Ro-Ro' (roll-on roll-off) facilities and a truly cavernous car-deck in the hold. This is the only regular passenger service between Ardrossan and Brodick. The other Arran ports have fallen into disuse (except for Lochranza in the north-west, from which a small car-ferry runs to Claonaig in Kintyre and back).

In 2006, under the rules of the European Union, all Scottish ferry routes were put out to tender, and as a result the familiar red-and-black funnels with the yellow and red 'Calmac' circular logo could have disappeared from the Clyde estuary and other waterways. In 2007, however, this danger seems to have receded.

Administration and local government

After the war, Arran was included in two major local government reorganizations. Originally, following the 1947 Act, Arran was still a part (a 'landward' District) of the County of Bute. This arrangement depended in part on the historical fact that Rothesay, the capital of Bute, used to be the main channel of communication between Arran and the rest of Scotland. In fact, in more recent times, Ardrossan in Ayrshire has been the only really convenient point of contact with the mainland. Nineteenth-century railways and roads as well as steam-powered shipping had expanded Arran's horizons and cut Rothesay completely out of the loop. The increase in tourism alone created a need for streamlining. For this and other reasons, radical administrative reorganization at a local government level was highly desirable.

Before the post-war 'Beveridge' reforms of state education, only a limited number of Arran children had required secondary schooling, and they were catered for at Ardrossan Academy, crossing the firth twice a week. But then came the raising of the school leaving age, the post-war 'baby boom', and a much greater demand for places at Ardrossan Academy. Initially Bute County Council was quite willing to contemplate that such Arran children as required secondary education could be sent to Bute, where they would attend Rothesay Academy while living in lodgings during term time, it being obviously impossible for them to return home every day: the journey involved at least three stages – two ferry crossings and a rail link. Of course, that was a totally unsatisfactory solution and in the end the High School in Lamlash acquired full secondary status.

This, and other awkward anomalies spelt the end of the Rothesay connection for Arran, and in the 1973 Local Government (Scotland) Act, Bute County disappeared: the island of Bute itself became a part of the newly designated Argyll District (later to be renamed 'Argyll and Bute District') under the aegis of Strathclyde Regional Council, and Arran and the Cumbraes went to Cuninghame District, the northern segment of the former Ayrshire. Cuninghame had its headquarters in Irvine, south of Ardrossan, and from this centre spread local government functions, to give uniform coverage to the entire District, including roads, lighting, education, social services, and the administration of justice. (The District Court[19] sits in Irvine.) Burgh Councils were abolished. Medical services were gathered under a wider grouping – the Ayrshire and Arran Health Board; the fire, police and rail services kept the designation 'Strathclyde' in their titles, since they operated from a regional centre. By and large these arrangements have survived the further shake-up brought in by the Local Government (Scotland) Act 1994, which came into force in 1996: under this Act the Regions set up under the 1973 Act have disappeared, and the Districts are, as it were, autonomous, with supposedly independent control of finances. (In truth, Central Government makes major decisions relating to income and expenditure.) The new North Ayrshire District is still centred on Irvine and retains control over Arran, where local Council offices are housed in charmingly converted sea-front premises with a splendid view over Lamlash Bay.

Land ownership and use

Legislative measures continued to have a nutmeg-grater effect on the powers and status of the landowners. One symbolic event which brought this effect directly home to Arran was the 1958 transfer of Brodick Castle and its policies in lieu of estate duty to the Treasury and subsequently to the National Trust for Scotland, following the death of the Duchess of Montrose. But this was only the tip of the iceberg. Long before 1958 the grip of the Hamilton-Montrose owners[20] of Arran had slackened. Parcels of Arran land were passed on in one way or another to individual members of the previously ruling clan, but many of these sold their property on to non-Hamilton people or gifted it to bodies like the Forestry Commission, which is now the largest landowner on the island in terms of hectares.

The subdivision of Hamilton/Montrose landed property in Arran, amounting to a change in the island's political geography, initially had a knock-on effect on agriculture and general land management. The drying-up of capital investment by the big landowners was not immediately followed by government action in support of tenant farmers and others formerly dependent on the now weakened landlord. Before the outbreak of war in 1914, Imperial Preference operated at home to the detriment of local farmers, by flooding the market with cheap produce. When war erupted, as mentioned above, there were critical shortages of food, leading to a renewed demand for home-grown food, but this was only a temporary rise, a blip in the general decline. After the war, which all but destroyed the younger generation of the landed classes, the increasingly urbanized electorate, embittered by the forced proletarianization of their ancestors, were alienated from the land and ostentatiously neglected it.

In Arran these factors resulted in widespread deterioration of farmland, some of which was taken permanently out of production. This reduction in productive capacity continues – if creepingly – to this day (2006–07), and may increase if the European Union's agricultural subsidies are further withdrawn, and markets in Europe are opened to a flood of foreign produce such as rice – almost 'Globalised Imperial Preference' (not that this will benefit the unfortunate Third World producers, most of whom are at the mercy of powerful and rapacious middlemen). These developments are to be taken with repeated assertions by government to the effect that British farming in general is no longer of central importance to the economy of the country, or at least not of as great importance as the holiday industry, which has now apparently surpassed agriculture by a wide margin in contributing to the Gross National Product.

In the post-war years we have mentioned the great and constant 'reshuffling' and reshaping of local authorities that ended or at least transformed the power of the County Councils. The most important recent reforms of local government as such in Scotland were contained in the Westminster Acts of 1973 and 1994. Affecting Arran and the crofting counties were the Crofters (Scotland) Acts of 1955, 1961 and 1993, and the recently proposed Crofting Reform etc Bill now (2006) in front of the Scottish Parliament.

The Crofting Acts of the nineteenth and early twentieth centuries stabilized the contemporary tenancy situation in that it became more difficult to evict tenants from crofts, exorbitant rents were restrained and restrictions were placed upon the sale of crofting land. Arran, however, had been excluded in the nineteenth century from the list of crofting counties at the instance of the Duke of Hamilton and smallholdings in that island continued to be at risk.

In the eighteenth and early nineteenth centuries, as mentioned in chapter 13, in the later times of runrig, of enclosure and clearance, and of Burrel and the Patersons, improvement of individual farm units was discouraged by rack-renting, which exposed farmers who improved property to the risk of being outbid for the tenancy of the farm because the increased value of the farm at the next 'setting' put it beyond the purse of the improver himself. A richer farmer could acquire the farm over the head of the original tenant, who would be turned out of the home and the land which he had laboured to make more productive. The mediaeval principle of the 'kindly tenancy', facilitating the retention of farms within the same family over generations, had been lost. Now, in the twentieth and twenty-first centuries, the same problem could arise in a different context.

In 2006 a Crofting Reform Bill was introduced into the new Scottish Parliament, and alarm bells immediately started to be rung. One of the provisions would indeed have had the effect of extending the term 'croft' to cover smallholdings in Arran, correcting a long-standing anomaly caused in the first place by the influence of the landholder. But the same Bill apparently proposed to deregulate the sale of crofts and to place crofting land on the free market, open to 'community buy-outs' and bids from non-crofting interests. This proposal, well-meaning though it may have been, created dismay among those concerned with the future of crofting nationwide: it looked as if not only smallholdings but agriculture itself in the north-west and elsewhere could vanish 'like snow off a dyke' under the fierce radiance of the market for holiday homes, 'second homes' and luxury accommodation. As Brian Wilson, former MP for Cuninghame North, said in 2006:

If the law says that crofting tenancies can be sold to the highest bidder then it is absolutely certain that they WILL be sold to the highest bidder, to the steady exclusion of those who cannot compete financially. The great system of crofting tenure, more successful than any other in Western Europe in retaining population in remote areas, will thus be fatally undermined. A single generation of crofting tenants will . . . be able to cash in their assets. And then the whole thing will be gone. The property market will have been 'normalised' and the crofting nuisance will enter terminal decline . . . Arran used to be in my constituency and I know the story very well of how it was kept out of the crofting counties in the first place only through the Parliamentary lobbying of the landowner, the Duke of Hamilton. So it would be nice to see a bit of that history reversed. But that prospect also confirms the complete irrelevance of extending crofting tenure to Arran or anywhere else if the central purpose of the Bill [. . .] is to legitimise a free market in crofting tenancies. Land for building on Arran is like gold dust. The new crofts would no sooner be created than they were being decrofted and/or the tenancies sold at exorbitant prices. The whole point of crofting tenure is to keep the market out. As soon as you invite it in, the shell of a system that remains is most certainly not crofting tenure – so it's hardly worth extending it in name in order to destroy it in practice.[21]

In this way, history could repeat itself. The tenants would be priced out of the market, even though the pressure to sell out would not come from other agriculturists and eighteenth-century reforming landlords. However, the objections of Mr Wilson and others seem (October 2006) to have carried the day, and certain key proposals were withdrawn, pending a 'wide-ranging inquiry into crofting issues including the market for crofts and the status, role, functioning, and powers of the Crofters' Commission'.[22]

We shall have to wait for the results of the inquiry. One cannot help fearing that we are already beyond the point of no return in the process of reducing not merely Arran but the whole kingdom to the status of Theme-Park Scotland. As earlier mentioned, the building of retirement homes, visitor accommodation and hotel businesses in Arran has accelerated in recent years, and the island is more than halfway to becoming another Minorca, divided between the wealthy elderly and tourists: there have long been complaints, in Arran as elsewhere, that native first-time buyers find houses well beyond their purses, that local inhabitants are being priced out of their own homes.

Under such conditions, opinions about the state of health of the actual practice of agriculture in Arran vary widely – perhaps depending upon the geographical location of the informant: especially in the east, which has long been dependent on income from tourism and tourist accommodation, one finds long faces and statements that farms as features of the landscape are becoming increasingly difficult to find, with house-building taking up every available square metre of land. However, on the traditionally rural west and south (Kilmory Parish), farming is still very much a presence. According to the Scottish Executive's Environment and Rural Affairs Department (SEERAD) there are no less than 184 holdings in Arran as of June 2006, and this is actually fifty up on the 1973 figure quoted by McLennan in his second (1976) edition. Of course neither of these figures may be absolutely accurate, as there is a downward limit on the reportable areas. Also, the figures do not reveal the ownership of each holding: a single farmer or company may own several units in different parts of the island. For instance, we have seen that there are only three dairy farms surviving from a total of more than eighty which operated in the immediate post-war period: however this has not had a catastrophic effect upon milk production in the island: the three farms are relatively enormous, obviously the result of amalgamations, and they use modern techniques and improved stock to maintain production levels. SEERAD's statistics show that the total area under cultivation or used for grazing stock in Arran is 28,927.33 hectares.[23]

Many of the holdings are pastoral and arable combined – often using the open moorland to graze sheep. In June 2006 there were 30,713 sheep on the island as opposed to 33,427 quoted by McLellan for 1973. There were 4,806 cattle including dairy cattle (McLellan 1973: 4,854 beef, 3,161 dairy cattle).

The 2006 figure for poultry was 1,827 including 70 ducks and 129 turkeys and other birds; McLellan's figure for 1973 was 2,178 poultry including 74 turkeys. In Arran in 2006 crops recorded (some figures withheld for reasons of commercial secrecy) are barley (83.04 ha.), other crops for stockfeeding (44.01 ha.) and other crops for human consumption (47.793 ha.). There is some production of root crops (including potatoes), green vegetables and soft fruit, as well as nursery and glasshouse production.

There is undoubtedly a falling off in the 2006 figures, but this does not spell the end of farming in Arran – unless Mr Wilson's fears are justified. The organization known as the Farming and Wildlife Advisory Group (Ayrshire and Arran division) now advises farmers on how to 'balance nature with productivity' as a consequence of the downturn of demand for agricultural products following alleged over-production on the European scale; whether the reining back of some European agricultural subsidies will prove to have been either wise or necessary is perhaps an open question, but the FWAG provides a very useful service in helping the farming community to cope with the changed priorities in land use as well as advising on new techniques and technology, soil and waste management, water, manure, nutrients and energy. This initiative operates in conjunction with the Scottish Executive's Rural Stewardship Scheme, which helps to ensure environmental protection and enhancement i.e. development of rural practices complementary and additional to traditional farming practice. Farmers are encouraged to look beyond simple food production to conservation of the countryside. Payments are made to compensate to some extent for loss of income incurred in taking land out of production, wildlife protection, enhancement of woodlands and similar preservation practices.

Forestry

As mentioned in an earlier chapter, the geology of the Isle of Arran consists mainly of Permian and Ordovician mudstone and sandstone, with igneous dykes. Since the soil exhaustion in the Bronze and Iron Ages (see chapter 1), the island has been almost totally covered with deep peat, peaty gleys and podzols, with brown earths on the slopes of the mountains and high hills. In recent times much of the hill land in the interior may have been severely damaged under sheep: some people argue that the only way to revive it is to plant trees. Whatever the arguments, tree-planting in Arran has now been undertaken by the Forestry Commission for more than half a century. Since the initial purchase of 1,500 acres in 1952 in the Kilmichael region above Brodick to the south-east, the Commission has expanded its operations to cover a full quarter of the total area of the island, more than 11,000 hectares, of which 8,000 are under plantation, and another 3,000 open space. It is by no means a very profitable operation, since the current price of timber has fallen substantially and the difficulties of transport from Arran are great, but in terms of environmental benefit the Arran forests are of high value. Besides this, world forest denudation has reached such a critical point that enterprises such as the Arran plantations, which not only harvest but renew stock, may well in the future be seen as invaluable global assets.

The time structure of the Arran plantations has been organized into two rotations, one starting in the 1960s and 70s, and another in 1996. Within these rotations, areas are divided into five-year felling plans, with (say) five divisions between 2007 and 2031. In addition areas are marked out for long-term retention and nature reserves as well as open spaces. In the whole island the immediate (2006) harvesting programmes (subject to national and governmental approval) are for a 'coupe' of 60,000 cubic metres (150 hectares) with 150 hectares gross for restocking, 70 hectares net. A new strategy has been adopted since 1996, substantially increasing the proportion of broadleaf trees and Scots pines to other conifers (Sitka spruce), and thereby reducing the sameness of the appearance of the plantations as well as diversifying production.[24]

At one time in Arran there were twenty-eight Forestry Commission workers. With improvements in technology the number of full-time employees has dwindled to four. Besides the new machines, a difficulty, felt throughout the country, has resided in attracting workers on a long-term basis to fairly remote areas. Two people in addition are employed as part-time contractors in connection with harvesting. Yet, in spite of this reduction in staff the island's forests are thriving. The Commission adopts a very responsible attitude to wildlife and biodiversity in the areas under its control.

Tourism and other industries

In Arran tourism is now the principal source of income. The underpinning factor is of course adequate accommodation, without which prolonged holidays on the island would be severely restricted. Catering and accommodation facilities in Arran were well established by the end of the nineteenth century. We have seen how private houses offered rooms to visitors from an early date – and how in the second half of the century the steamer revolution brought in hordes of trippers. Already in Victorian times there existed a range of accommodation to cope with this influx. The charming hotel at Lagg in the south dates from 1791. Other long-established inns/hotels include the Douglas (now McAlpine) Hotel (1850s) on the seafront at Brodick, a hotel at Shedog, the Kildonan and Kinloch Hotels and, in the same district, the Breadalbane Hotel. Frequent hotel building has continued in the twentieth century. One or two hotel complexes have expanded on the lines of 'health spas' or even American Country Clubs, with swimming-pools, water-polo, gymnasia, keep-fit classes, cardiac rehabilitation groups – and luxurious restaurants. There is a proliferation of restaurants throughout the island, some of them very good.

Today (2007) there are forty-three hotels, guest-houses and boarding-houses in Arran, at least 104 sites offering self-catering accommodation (including converted farmhouses and sites with several detached houses), and three caravan/camping sites. These figures are actually down on the 1974 numbers recorded by McLellan[25] but the island's tourist prosperity does not seem to be overly affected. The flood of tourists in the high summer coming off the MacBrayne ferry at Brodick bears witness to Arran's continued attraction: family parties with children and pets; backpackers and campers; mountaineers and hillwalkers; sportsmen and sportswomen; daytrippers and people in search of longer holidays (from weekend breaks to month-long vacations); older souls returning year after year to find peace and seclusion in a holiday home or a favoured country hotel – and those who are simply in love with beautiful landscapes and seascapes; foreign tourists, transatlantic, Commonwealth, European, Japanese, Chinese; as well as organized parties of geologists, archaeologists and conservationists – and descendants of emigrants coming to the Heritage Museum at Rosaburn in search of genealogical records.

The greatest single attraction, of course, is Brodick Castle, with its gardens and country park. The building itself is magnificently shaped and landscaped, visible from far out at sea on its platform amid the trees of the estate. The interior contains many of the original Hamilton and Montrose treasures, including the silver already mentioned, and portraits of some of the principal characters from the long history of Arran – including the Good Duchess Anne and the long-suffering Princess Marie of Baden, together with her errant husband the eleventh Duke. A special bus conveys people from the ferry terminal in Brodick to the Castle, and during the season they come in crowds.

One of the indexes of prosperity in any tourist location is the number of golf courses. At the present moment, there are seven golf courses on Arran, all founded before or on the turn of the nineteenth century.[26] Five more have fallen by the wayside. As a non-golfer, I should refrain from expressing any opinion, but I cannot help admiring the scenic glories of the Brodick course, of the Lamlash course with its spectacular view of Lamlash Bay and Holy Island, and of the Shiskine course near Blackwaterfoot, with its backdrop of the great volcanic cliff of Drumadoon, at the side of the stunningly beautiful panorama of Kilbrannan Sound and the Kintyre peninsula. The other courses are, naturally, equally splendid, but I have not had the pleasure of inspecting them at close quarters.

Lamlash, with its naval associations, boasts a golf course Visitors' Book in which the names of King Edward VIII (then Prince of Wales) and King George VI (then Duke of York) are inscribed, together with that of Lord Louis Mountbatten. Winston Churchill is said to have visited Lamlash at some time during his career, but as far as I am aware he was no golfer.

Besides golf and conventional sports such as tennis or pastimes like yacht-ing, there are pony trekking, paragliding, rock-climbing and abseiling, power-boating, angling, scuba diving, water polo, 'paint-balling' and 'quad-biking'. Temptations to buy abound, especially in the field of arts and crafts, with various specialisms including locally-made candles, porcelain and mirrors besides leather products, jewellery, wood-carving, and numerous art-galleries. This category shades into the field of alternative medicine, with exotic techniques such as gemstone therapy, reflexology and aromatherapy. There are demonstration farms for tourists, and even (opening in 2007) a butterfly farm, taking advantage of rough vegetation, bushes and shrubs in one area of the island.

This survey might give the impression that Arran is totally given over to 'candy-floss' industries, catering exclusively for tourists. Of course, enterprises like the Lochranza whisky distillery or the brewery at the former 'Cladach' building near Brodick Castle have an obvious input to the tourist trade, but their products have an appeal far beyond the boundaries of the island. Arran Aromatics might be classified disparagingly as 'just another local craft': but Arran Aromatics is a very considerable perfumier concern, with global connections (their products can be bought in Singapore), making a notable contribution to the national export trade. The Torrylinn Creamery at Kilmory is part of a large concern selling cheese and other dairy products all over the south-west of Scotland and beyond. Torrylinn has successfully overcome the drastic reduction in numbers of Arran dairy farms from about eighty at the end of the Second World War to only three at present: the survival of the creamery has been due at least in part to the enormous expansion of those three farms, and the inevitable change from leaving milk in churns to be picked up at the end of farm-tracks to a proper deployment of equipment including massive tanker lorries – to say nothing of modern methods of production, and improved milk-yielding stock.[27]

Other non-tourist industries on Arran include haulage contractors, building and civil engineering firms, and a local abbatoir (leading to a ready availability of local meat products). And of course there are numerous efficient small businesses catering for local people – plumbers, bakers, laundries, garden centres, a newspaper (the *Arran Banner*), shops and stores (including a 'Co-op' supermarket: one is somehow relieved that the giant rival corner-shop-devouring supermarkets of the mainland have not yet landed at Brodick pier). There exists a fair sprinkling of professional people, lawyers, accountants, estate agents, doctors and dentists, as well as coastguards, police and firemen.

The church buildings have inevitably suffered the consequences of contraction and amalgamation of congregations. (On a recent visit to Arran I passed one on the south coast that had been converted into a desirable residence, painted in tasteful but noticeable pastel colours.) There are, however, at least fifteen active religious bodies of different kinds in Arran at the moment including the mainstream Church of Scotland and Free Church of Scotland, as well as Episcopalians, Roman Catholics, Baptists, Quakers and Pentecontalists ('Open Gate' Church). A sign of the times is that several of the congregations are led by women, both ordained and non-ordained. Many of these bodies still occupy their traditional buildings.

Conservation

In Britain generally, agriculture, extractive and manufacturing industries have declined in importance, and a new preoccupation, almost a new industry, has appeared, driven in some cases by extreme anxiety for the fate of the planet itself. Mining, manufacturing and agriculture pursued their particular interests with such single-minded energy that until very recently they have been blind to the effects of pollution and resource exhaustion upon the environment. This includes the extermination of species which in a conventional human perspective either are a nuisance or are subject to limitless exploitation – such as fish. The tendency is not unrelated to the aggressive, even triumphalist dismissal of the importance of history and historical artefacts and monuments. But the days of this attitude may be numbered. Government has at last begun to appreciate the threats under which we all continue to lead our daily lives – an understanding symbolised by the 'global warming' crisis caused by excess CO^2 and methane emissions – and the (limited) response to these problems represented by the Kyoto protocols.

The small area with which we are concerned, the Isle of Arran in the United Kingdom, has been identified as of great importance in almost every field of conservation – from aquatic and terrestrial zoology to geology and the preservation of historical buildings. The government of Scotland has recognized that simple public awareness of the problem is a vital part of the solution, and the strong publicity required is assigned to the tourist authorities. In this case the Ayrshire and Arran Tourist Board have taken a leading part in organizing and funding various initiatives aimed at heightening public awareness. In addition there is a whole network of national and local bodies which have come together to support conservation in Arran, including the Farming and Wildlife Advisory Group already mentioned, the Scottish Forestry Commission, the Royal Society for the Protection of Birds, the Scottish National Trust (with a leading role for the Brodick Castle Rangers and other staff), the Community of Arran Seabed Trust (COAST), Scottish Natural Heritage, the Arran Natural History Society – and, indeed, the European Union. In practical terms there are two main kinds of task to be undertaken by such organizations: actively promoting conservation by safeguarding special natural features and creatures, or resisting encroachment where a conflict of interest occurs; and displaying and interpreting their achievements to the public – those for whom they labour either in triumph or in hope.

Following the Wildlife and Countryside Act 1981, Scottish Natural Heritage designates various Sites of Special Scientific Interest ('triple-SI sites'), of which there are several on Arran and Ailsa Craig. Many of these sites are a bird-watcher's delight: the Scottish Forestry Commission has a large SSSI within its boundaries round the big southern mountain Tighvein, which is a habitat and nesting area for the very rare bird of prey, the hen harrier – as well as merlin (our smallest bird of prey) and the little black, red and white stonechat. Other SSSIs include the northern high mountain area: here nest two pairs of Golden Eagles, huge birds of prey, also very rare (to be seen in the vicinity of the Boguille, a high point on the Sannox – Lochranza road). The White-tailed (Sea-) Eagle, the greatest of all British birds of prey, does not live in Arran but is occasionally sighted over cliffs and coastal mountains on the island. Ospreys, a very rare species not living in Arran, are sighted 'passing through' on migration in spring and autumn. Other birds which do inhabit Arran include peregrine falcons and ptarmigans, and red kites, recently saved from extinction, may occasionally be seen. Gannets, guillemots and fulmars sit on off-shore rocks in groups of three or more waiting to dive after passing fish.

Ailsa Craig (SSSI) was once the nesting-ground of one of the largest puffin colonies in Scotland; after declining nearly to extinction because of human over-fishing, this colony is beginning to re-establish itself on the high sheer cliffs of this huge volcanic plug.

The Boguille is not far from Loch a' Mhuilinn , overlooking Catacol and Lochranza) where research has been carried out on pollen grains of two very rare varieties of *Sorbus* endemic trees (*Sorbus arranensis*, Arran Whitebeam, and *Sorbus pseudofennica*, Arran Service-tree), which established themselves more than six thousand years ago in Arran. This again is not far from the Gleann Diomhan Nature Reserve on the Catacol River, where actual specimens of the trees survive; these two kinds of trees are considered to be the most endangered in Scotland, found only in Arran.[28] In fact the whole of the island is peppered with more than a hundred officially designated Ancient Woodland Sites, from Lochranza to Dippin Wood. Arran is recognized as a unique museum of early post-glacial forest.

Besides birds and trees, Arran is home to many species of land animals, some of which are endangered species. The red squirrel, nearly succumbing in other parts of Britain to the grey squirrel, may be encountered in the policies of Brodick Castle. About two thousand wild red deer inhabit the uplands of the island. Otters are to be seen at dawn and in the evening on the beaches on the west coast. Badgers are reported also on the west coast near Imachar. Both common and grey seals are found on the shores and on off-shore rocks all around the island. Bottlenose dolphins, porpoises and even Minke whales (lesser rorquals) can be observed in Arran waters, as can basking sharks, the largest species of shark in the world.

The Community of Arran Seabed Trust (COAST) is a very active conservation organization, and they engage in the second task referred to above, vigorous defence of endangered natural habitats. In Lamlash Bay a kind of seaweed called 'maerl' resembling coral is found: it provides a vital breeding ground for fish. This seabed growth has been seriously damaged by systematic dredging by scallop fishermen, and the fish population in Lamlash Bay has been drastically reduced as a consequence. COAST now pursues a determined campaign to make the bay into a Marine Protected Area, which would revive the maerl by prohibiting scallop dredging, and thereby make possible the regeneration not only of the fin-fish population but also of shellfish beds including scallops. So far they have not succeeded in convincing SEERAD (2006) but they are working on it. In the meantime they have successfully averted another danger to Lamlash Bay – the construction of a sewage outfall pipe into the centre of the bay right on top of the maerl beds. By such means, conservationists patiently and doggedly achieve their ends.

COAST also assist conservation ends by conducting boat tours around Arran and scuba diving, showing off the multiplicity of underwater life in all its variety, shapes and colours. In May 2006 they participated in the first Arran Wildlife Festival along with the other organizations mentioned above, and the festival was held again in 2007.

OS references

Conservation
Tighvein NR 998 273
Boguille NR 971 482
Loch a'Mhuilinn NR 913 477
Gleann Diomhan Nature Reserve NR 923 468

In the following two appendices I have reproduced some of the songs and oral tales collected by William Mackenzie for his *Book of Arran*. It is regretted that we can provide only a selection because of the limitations of space. The pieces here are of high value because of the inherent sense of historic Gaelic culture expressed in the distinctive but now vanished Arran dialect. Readers who wish to acquaint themseves with more songs and tales, as well as Mackenzie's considered opinions, are referred to *The Book of Arran* (Volume 2). I have gathered Mackenzie's numbered notes at the end of each Appendix. Other notes will be found at the end of each individual or translation.

Appendix I

Songs in the Gaelic of Arran

from The Book of Arran
by William Mackenzie

Arainn Bheag Bhòidheach[1]

O Arainn bheag bhòidheach!
'S grinn do chleòca 's an t-samhradh,
Tha do bhruthain làn neoinein
'S do mhòinteach làn ceann-dubh.[2]

Tha do bhric bhallach dhùbh-ghorm
Ri cùrsachd troimh d' aibhne'an
'Sa chuthag rìomhach, cuir smùid dith
A' tigh'nn an dlùths air a' bhealtuinn.

Do fhraoch badanach cùbhraidh,
'S mil 'na driùchd air gach ceann dheth,
Cnothan abuich, 's iad dùbailt
A' lùbadh do challtuinn.

Bonnie Little Arran

O! Bonnie little Arran,
Grand is thy mantle in summer,
Thy braes full of daisies
And thy moorlands of canach.

Thy trout spotted and dark blue
Sporting briskly in thy waters,
And the bonnie cuckoo letting off its steam
As the summer approached.

Thy heather so bunchy and fragrant
With honey in drops on each head,
Ripe nuts and in clusters
Bending the hazel branches.

Marbh-Rann[3]

Chaidh an Comunn, chaidh an Comunn, chaidh an Comunn air chùl,
'S gur coma gach comunn ach an comunn bhios fìor,
Chaidh an comunn o chéile, dh'fhàg sud deurach mo shùil,
'S gu 'm b'e luinnsearachd Sheumais bu neo-aoibhneach dhuinn.

B'e do thurus gu Ile 's a' mhìos roimh 'n a' Mhàirt
Dh'fhàg muladach m'inntinn o nach till thu gu bràth,
O 'n a thug iad thu thairis gu eilean Da-bhàrr,
Is d' fhàgail air cladach mar bhradan air tràigh.

'Se Seumas MacDhaidhidh a chreach sinn gu bràth,
O 'n a thug e thu thairis gu eilean Da-bhàrr,
'S o nach tilleadh e dhachaidh agus aithris mar bha,
Bhiodh na ciadan gun mhailis[4] mach mu do bhàs.

Bha thu foinnidh, deas, dìreach, 's bu rìoghail do chainnt,
Bha do thlachd anns an fhìrinn, 's do mhi-thlachd 's a' cheilg,
D' fhalt buidhe 's e amlagach, bachlagach, clann,
Sùil bu ghuirme bha daite glé mheallach 'n ad cheann.

'S iomadh ban-tighearn rìomhach le sìod agus sròl,
Eadar Arainn 'us Ile 'us Cinntìre nam bó,
A bheireadh an saoghal 's d' fhaotainn-sa beo,
'S iad uile glé thùrsach o 'n a chaochail thu òg.

Tha d'athair 's do mhàthair gach là 's iad fo ghruaim,
Gun nì air an t-saoghal a ni' challdach so suas,
Gus an ruig iad an t-àite 's am fògrar gach gruaim,
Far nach inntir deur sàrach gu bràth air an gruaidh,

O! 's mairg nach ròghnaicheadh companaich fhìor,
Air am biodh eagal an Tighearn ar muir 'us air tìr,
Bhiodh 'aran dha deimhinn agus 'uisge dha fior,
'S air deireadh a làithean bhiodh aige deagh chrìoch.

Elegy

The company, the company, the company is dissolved,
Unworthy the company, but the company that's true,
The company has parted – that left my eye in tears,
'Twas the heartlessness of James that left us in sorrow.

'Twas thy journey to Islay the month prior to March
That left me so sad, since thou wilt never return,
And since they took thee away to Island Davaar
And left thee stranded like a salmon on the shore.

'Twas James Davidson that for ever deprived us,
Since he took thee away to Island Davaar,
And returned not home to relate how it was,
Hundreds, without delay, would be out about thy death.

Handsome and shapely thy form, and royal thy speech,
In truth was thy pleasure, thy displeasure in deceit,
Thy yellow hair so curly, wavy, and bunchy,
Thy bright blue eye so winning in thy head.

Many a lady dressed in silk and grandeur,
'Twixt Arran and Islay, and Kintyre of the kine,
Would give the world to have thee as their own,
And they all in sorrow, since young thou didst die.

Thy father and mother are each day under grief,
With nought in the world to compensate the loss,
Until they reach the place whence all the sorrow is dispelled,
Where no bitter tear will ever moisten their cheek.

O! the pity on those who true companions don't choose,
Who would fear the Lord on sea or on land,
To him his bread would be sure and his water be pure,
And at the end of his days he happy would be.

Oran Gaoil

Rinneadh an t-òran so le Domhnull MacMhuirich air dha bhi air a ghlacadh
le Maraichean a' Chrùin ri àm Cogadh na Frainge.

Nuair thàinig mi thairis bha mi 'm barail 's an dùil
Gu 'n deanainn mór bheairteas mur tachradh droch chùis,
Ach mu 'n d' fhuair mi air astar no mach as an dùthaich,
Chuir iad mi fo ghlasaibh mar ghaduich' no cù.

Chuir iad mi du 'n *press-room*, agus ghlais iad mi ann,
Far an robh sinn mór chuideachd air ar cumail gu teann,
Le sùil[5] cur thairis do 'n armailt 's an Fhraing,
'S gun chridh' againn feuchainn am fàgail gun taing.

Thoir mo shoraidh uam thairis gu Arainn nam beann,
Agus innis do m' leannan mar thachair 's an àm,
Gu 'n deachaidh mo ghlacadh le gaisreadh[6] ro theann
Nach éisdeadh uam facal 's gun stàth dhomh bhi cainnt.

Ach o n' tha mi gu iosal 's nach leig iad mi 'n àird,
Ni mi litir a sgriobhadh a dh'innseas mar tha,
'S nuair ruigeas i dachaidh cha 'n 'eil ag' nach bi iad
Cho tùrsach 's a dh'fhaodas iad 's daoine aca slàn.

Ma tha 'n dàn domh 'dhol dachaidh gu Arainn nam beann,
Gus an dean mi, ghaoil, d' fhaicinn cha chaidil mi ann,
Cha chaidil mi uair 's cha tig suain air mo cheann
Gus am bi mi ri d' thaobh-sa gu sìobhalt' a' cainnt.

Ach ma bhios thusa cordte 'us pòsda fo 'n chléir
Mu 'n ruig mise dhachaidh 's gu 'm faighinn air sgeul,
Cha 'n fhaiccar mi 'n Arainn no 'm fagus do m' dhaoin'
'S a chaoidh fhad 's is beò mi cha phòs mi aon té.

Làn mulaid 'us tiamhachd ni mi triall feadh an t-saoghail,
Gus an caith mi mo bhliadhnan am fiabhrus do ghaoil,
'S nuair theid iad uil' thairis bi'dh na rannan so fhéin
Aig daoine 'g an gabhail 's a' gal as mo dhéidh.

Tha do ghruaidh mar an caorann 's do mhala chaol mar it' eòin,
Sùil mheallach 's bòidhch' sealladh rinn mo mhealladh 'n am òig,
O'n' fhuair mi ort sealladh 'n àm gearradh na mòin'
Cha deach thu as m' aire 's gu'm b' aighearach sud dhomhs'.

Tha mi 'm barail nach bi thu fo mhi-ghean no tàir,
Ged a thu'irt mi ruit leannan 's nach gabh thu dheth nàir',
Nach gabh thu dheth doilgheas 's nach tog thu mi ceàrr
Oir aig laigse na feòla bu bhòsd leam a ràdh.

Na bi thusa fo shraonais, a ghaoil, ged tha mi
Air ro bheagan de 'n t-saoghal gun chaoraich gun mhaoin,
Oir chualas mar fhìrinn mu ar sinnsir o thùs
Nach d' fhuair iad mar thrusgan ach duilleach 's iad rùisgt'.

Ach ged ni iad mo chumail, 's mo chur thun nam blàr,
'S ged 's éiginn domh fulang 'us m' fhuil thoirt gu làr,
Cha dean mi ort dì-chuimhn', 's cha sìolaidh mo ghràdh,
'S a chaoidh fhad 's is beò mi gu'r math leam thu slàn.

Love Song
By D. Currie
Literal translation by J. Craig

When first I came over I hoped and expected
To gather great riches should no evil thing happen,
But before I had travelled or had got out of the country,
They put me in ward like a thief or a dog.

They put me into the press-room, and locked me there,
Where we were a great company held by force,
Intending to draft us into the army in France,
And we durst not try to escape in spite of them.

Carry my compliments over to Arran of the bens,
And tell my sweetheart how it all happened,
That I have been captured and closely held by a crew
Who would not listen to a word, my speech unavailing.

Since I am laid low and they won't let me rise,
I shall write a letter to tell how I fare,
When it reaches home no doubt they will be
Sorrowful enough, and their own folk in health.

If it be my fate to go home to Arran of the bens,
Until I see thee, my love, no sleep shall I take;
I shall not sleep for an hour, nor my eyes close in slumber
Until I am beside thee, sweetly conversing.

But if thou be betrothed and lawfully married
Before I reach home, and I come to hear of it,
I shall not be seen in Arran, nor near my people,
And while I live I shall never marry another.

Full of sorrow and melancholy I shall wander through the world,
Till I spend my years in the fever of thy love,
And when all is over, these verses of mine
Will be sung by the people who will mourn for me.

Thy cheek like the rowan, thine eyebrows so slender,
Winning, lovely eyes which beguiled me when young;
Since I first saw thee at peat-cutting time
I have never forgotten thee, and glad was the vision to me.

I believe thou shall neither be displeased nor disdainful
Although I have called thee sweetheart, nor think it a shame,
That thou shalt neither repent it nor take me up wrong,
For thro' the weakness of the flesh I 'd be proud to say it.

Do not be offended, my love, though my possessions are few,
Though I have neither sheep nor herds;
For we have heard as a truth of our ancestors of old,
That no garment they had but a covering of leaves.

Although I be detained and sent to the war,
And though I must suffer and shed my blood on the ground,
I shall never forget thee nor my love get cold,
And while life remains, I shall wish thee well.

Am Bas[8]
Le Iain Macfhionghuin

Tha mise air mo bhuaireadh 'us truas orm fhéin,
Tha am bàs mu ar bruachan a' bualadh gu treun;
An sean 'us an t-òg 'us gach seòrsa fo 'n ghréin,
An t-ìosal 's an t-uasal cha truagh leis an aog.

Cha toir e aon urram do fhear a chinn léith,
Ach bheir e dha turrag a chuireas e thaobh;
A' mhaighdeann as brionnaiche 's as iolapaich' ceum,
Grad sàthaidh e gath innte, 's cha 'n amhairc 'n a dhéidh.

An t-òganach uallach a ghluaiseas gu réidh
Le siubhal deas, socrach nach dochainn am feur;
Grad cuiridh e acaid an aisnein a chléibh,
'Us tilgidh e thairis e à sealladh na gréine.

Tha àm agus àit aig gach cùise fo 'n ghréin,
Ach ullachadh bàis tha so ghnàth chum ar feum;
Tha sud air a ràitinn ri càch 'us ruim fhéin,
'Bhi daonnan ri faire mu'n glac sinn an t-aog.

Death
By John Mackinnon

I am troubled and full of compassion,
For death is around our borders striking heavily;
Old and young of every rank under the sun,
The low and high, for them no pity has death.

No respect does he show to him of the hoary head,
But gives him a blow which knocks him aside;
The comeliest maiden of lightsome step
He suddenly pierces with his arrow and looks not behind.

The cheerful youth who gently treads,
With quiet, easy step that injures not the grass,
Quickly he wounds through the chest,
And throws him over out of sight,

There is a time and place for everything under the sun,
But preparation for death is always needful;
It is told to others and to me
To be always watchful ere death overtakes us.

Fuadach a' Ghobha Bhig

Rinneadh an t'òran so leis a' Ghobha Bheag (Iain MacMhuirich, Tormór) air
dha bhi air a chur s an Eilean airson meirle-shithinn (poaching).

Air maduinn chiùin shamhraidh mu'n eireadh a' ghrian,
'S mu'n nochdadh i blàths air aon àite no fiamh,
Bhiodh mise tigh'nn dachaidh le m' bhàta 's le m' liòn,
Gu dùbhradh a' Chaisteil, gun airsneal, le m' iasg.

Nuair ruiginn an còmhnard as bòidhche fo 'n ghréin,
Bhiodh m' inntinn aig sòlas leis na h-eòin air gach géig,
An druideag 's an smeòrach gu ceòlmhor a' seinn,
'S an uiseag 'g am freagairt thar leacainn na beinn.'

'S sud a' bheinn bhiòidheach 's mi 'chòmhnuidh r' a sàil,
Far an d'fhuair mise m' àrach 's mo thogail le bàigh,
'S tric a bha mi air m'uilinn m'a mullach 's m'a tràigh,
A' feitheamh nan tunnag 's mo ghunna 'n am làimh.

'S boidheach, badanach, dualach am fraoch uaine a' fàs,
Air aodann na guallainn far an gluaiseadh an t-àl,
'S mo mhàthair tigh'nn o'n bhuaile 's gach cuach aice làn,
Bu mhilis an fhuarag[9] dheanta suas leis a' bhlàth.

Cha 'n 'eil aite air thalamh mar Bhealach-nam-Meann,
Far an robh mi ré tamuill – mi-fhéin 'us mo chlann,
Ach b'fheudar dhomh gluasad 's an uair sin gun taing,
O'n a thuit do 'n a' chùis mi bhi dlùth do na *Laing*.

Chuir am Bàillidh mach paipeir 's gach ceàrna mu'n cuairt,
Gun iad thabhairt dhomh àite no fardach car uair,
'S na 'n toireadh, gu 'n iòchdadh iad cìs a bhiodh cruaidh,
'S gu 'n rachadh da-rìreadh am piòsan[10] thoirt uap.'

'N sin thog mi mo bhat-a fo m' ascaill 's an àm,
'Us thug mi mo chùl ris gach lùchairt a bh' ann,
'Us leag mi mo chùrsa gu dùthaich nan Gall,
'S bha soitheach na smùide 'g am ghiùlan a nall.

'Dol seachad air a' Choire – bu chorrach a cóm,
Caòir gheal fo a toiseach 's i sgoltadh nan tonn.
Bha mise 'n am laighe gu h-airsnealach sgìth,
'S gu 'm b'fhearr leam na m'fharadh bhi 'n Arainn air tìr.

Bha gaoth agus gaillionn 'n ar déidh a bha trom,
Bha 'n fhairg' ag éirigh 's a' leum thar na croinn,
Ach dh'fhalbh i gu h-uallach nuair fhuair i muir lom,
'Us thug i sinn sàbhailt gu caladh nan long.

Nuair ràinig mi Grianaig bha fiamh air mo ghnùis,
'Dhol a steach do'n each-iarruinn 's na ciadan ann dùint',
Bu sgalanta 'shéideadh e air a *Railway* glan ùr,
'S cha b'e gearran na sréin' chumadh ceum ri a chùl.

'Us thug e mi 'Ghlascho – gu baile nan Gall –
'Us thuiginn an cànain ged nach b'i Ghàidhlig a bh' ann
Bha mise cho teòm' ruitha féin air a cainnt,
'S gu 'n tuiginn 'g a leughadh an sgeul a bhiodh ann.

Tha mise an dràsd ann an dùthaich nan Gall,
'S cha mhór nach do sgoilt iad le 'n obair mo cheann,
Tha gach aon diubh cho lùghmhor le òrd anns gach làimh,
'S gur cosmhuil a' chùis ri *Waterloo* anns an Fhraing.

Ach bi'dh 'mhuinntir a dh'fhògair mi 'n aghaidh mo mhiann
Gun chaora, gun ghobhar, gun bhó air an t-sliabh,
Nuair bhios mis' anns an Todhar[11] gu foghainteach, fial,
Ag òl as mo chopan, 's a' gabhail mo bhiadh.

The Poacher
By James Craig, Kilpatrick, Arran
Song composed by John Currie, Tormore, on his being expelled from Arran for poaching

In the calm summer morn ere the sun with its rays
Would awaken in beauty our valleys and braes,
With my take in my skiff I so gaily would come
To the shade of the castle where nestled my home.

On reaching my refuge my heart would rebound
With joy to the chorus which echoed around,
To the merle's thrilling love-notes the lark would reply
From the lift o'er the hilltop far hid from the eye.

Oh, fair were the braes by the cabin I loved,
Where early I played, where in manhood I roved,
Where often I crouched with my gun on my knee,
Awaiting the mallard that seldom got free.

And green was the heather which covered yon hill
Where cows in the summer would wander at will,
When the maids brought their pails reaming full from the fold,
Our drink was then sweeter than nectar of old.

Dear *Beallach nam Meann* how my heartstrings were torn,
When banished the spot where my darlings were born.
'Tis my fate in the lowlands to nourish my wrongs,
Since fortune once placed me too near to the Longs.[12]

The factor ordained in the pride of his power
My kin should disown me, if e'en for an hour
They'd shelter or aid me, his ire they would feel,
Be stripped of their farms and crushed by his heel.

With my stick in my hand – it was all I possessed –
I steered for the lowlands with grief in my breast,
My back to my home and the Isle of my birth,
While the swift steamer bore me soon over the Firth.

'Twas out from the Corrie she knelt to the breeze,
With foam 'neath her prow as she ploughed o'er the seas,
While I in her lee, lying sorry and sore,
Would forfeit my fare to be safely ashore.

The gale on our quarter hard after us roared,
The waves in their anger came dashing on board,
But swiftly she sailed when the Garroch she passed,
And brought us all safe to our haven at last.

At Greenock the iron horse filled me with fear,
As it sped o'er the rails in its rapid career,
Far heard was its neigh and unrivalled its pace,
The fleetest of steeds were soon left in the race.

It brought me to Glasgow 'mid strangers to dwell,
Where the language was strange and their manners as well;
But I soon grew expert in that alien tongue,
Though dearer the Gaelic I lisped when young.

I now live with strangers and far from my kin,
With my head nearly split with the tumult and din,
So quickly his hammer each riveter plies,
Waterloo never equalled the clanging and noise.

But those who expelled me from Arran shall be
Without sheep on the moorland or cow on the lea,
While I open-handed shall live in Tormore,
To drink from my cup yet and eat of my store.

Oran Na Dibhe
A rinneadh leis a' Ghobha Bheag, Iain MacMhuirich.

Air maduinn Di-luain 'nuair ghluais mi do'n Abhainn[13]
'Us mise gun chuarain, 's am fuachd 'ga mo dhàthadh,
Bha caraid dhomh shìos, 's e gu sìobhalt le *Brathar*,
Bha gloin' ac' air bòrd, 'us an còmhradh mu mhnathan.
   Mo ghille donn òg.

'N sin tharruing mi suas gu luath chum mo gharaidh,
'O'n thachair 's an uair gu 'n do ghluais mi nan rathad,
'Us fhuair mise cuach o 'n duin'-uasal 's o m' charaid,
A dh' fhògair gach smuairean 's am fuachd as mo chasan.
   Mo ghille donn òg.

'N sìn labhair an t-Òsdair's[14] cha b'e chòmhradh mo roghainn,
Cha dean thu dhomh dìoladh 's cha 'n lochd thu dhomh peighinn,
Bha mo chreideas cho suarach, 's nach cualas a leithid,
'S rinn Iain an uair sin gluasad gu Seideag.
   Mo ghille donn òg.

'N sin ruithinn 'us leumainn gu h-aotrom 's gu beathail,
Cha 'n fhaicteadh mo chùl leis an stùr 'bha o m' chasan,
Ged robh agam-sa triùir, cha bhiodh cùram 's an rathad
Nach ruiginn an t-àite far am b' àbhaist dhomh fanachd.
   Mo ghille donn òg.

'Nuair a rainig mi Flòiridh[15] – 'bhean chòir 'us a h-ìghnean
Ghlac i 'm botull air sgòrnan 'us dhòl i air Iain,
Thu'irt i 'théid thu do 'n chlòsaid 'us òlaidh thu rithist'
'Oir 's e do luchd-seòrsa 'chuir sòrd air an t-snidhe.
   Mo ghille donn òg.

Shuidh mise sìos cho sìobhalt 's a b'aithne,
'Us tharruing mi 'n sìoman 'bha sìnt 'ris a' bhalla,
'S nuair tharruing mi 'n sìoman thàinig nigh'nag le cabhaig,
Is fhuair mi mo dhìol de fhìor Uisg'-na-bracha.
   O'n chailin donn òg.

'S a mhaduinn 'nuair dhùisg mi, bu shiùbhlach mo chridhe,
Mo mhuineal air rùsgadh, 'us mo shùilean a' sileadh,
Mo bhrù mar an fhùirneis le ùbraid na dibhe
'S mo bhilean a' taomadh 'mach faoileachd mo chridhe.
   Mo ghille donn òg.

Och! mo mhollachd le dùrachd air ùghdar na dibhe,
'S tric a dhùin e mo shùilean 's a dhùblaich e'n t-slìghe,
'S a dh'fhàg e mo sheòrsa a' pògadh na dìge,
'Nan laighe 'nan òrraisg 's an còmhradh ri spioraid.
    Mo ghille donn òg.

Song on Drinking

Composed by John Currie, an Gobha Beag; translated by James Craig

Last Monday in footgear tattered and old,
I steered for the village half singed by the cold,
Where talking of women with their glass by the fire,
I met with a friend and a fellow Macbriar.
    Hard drinking, my boy.

So to warm me I sat then with little delay,
Since fortune had sent me for once in their way,
Each gave me a flagon which banished and beat
The care from my heart and the cold from my feet.
    My fair-haired boy.

But the landlord began then to talk of the way
My kind drank his liquor but never would pay,
How my credit was lower than credit e'er stood,
So I sheered off for Shedag as hard as I could.
    My fair-haired boy.

I could leap then so lightly and race on the green,
With such dust from my heels that my back was not seen.
Had I but three glasses I'd manage my way
To the snug little shelter where often I lay.
    My fair-haired boy.

When I got to Big Flora, good woman, she quaffed
My health in a bumper, and gave me a draught,
Said, 'In to the taproom and drink once again,
'Tis your sort made my roof so long proof to the rain.'
    My fair-haired boy.

So I gladly sat down in the room I loved well,
Caught the cord by the wall, softly tinkled the bell,
Then the girl at my call quickly came to the door,
And I got of good liquor what filled me – and more.
    From the fair maid, my boy.

In the morning I woke to my heart's fast career,
With raw-feeling throat and eyes dropping the tear,
My breast like a furnace all glowing with fire,
And my lips fast ejecting my 'bosom's desire.'
    My fair-haired boy.

Och ! My curse on the drink that has darkened my way,
And blinded mine eyes till I've oft gone astray,
Often laid in the ditch those who shared in my revels,
To wallow in vomit and talk with blue devils.
    My fair-haired boy.

Màiri Òg

Oirinn o na ho i u,
Oirinn o na ho i u,
Oirinn o na ho i u,
'S e mo rùn a rinn m' aicheadh.

Fhir nan ciabhagan donna,
Is nan gorm-shùilean soilleir,
'S tric a chum mi riut coinneamh
Ann am bothan glinn àirigh.
   Oirinn o na ho i u, etc.

'S nuair a chithinn thu tighinn
As a' bheinn le d' chuid sithinn,
Riut gu 'n éireadh mo chridhe
Gun fhios do mo màthair.
   Oirinn o na ho i u, etc.

Ach ma chuir thu nis cùl rium,
'S gu 'n d' rinn thu mo dhiùltadh,
'S i mo ghuidhe 's mo dhùrachd
Nigh 'n an Diùc a bhi 'm àite.
   Oirinn o na ho i u, etc.

'S mur an leannan dhuit mise
Cuireadh am fortan bean ghlic ort
Is cha mhisde do phiseach
Gu 'm bheil mis' ann 'n gràdh leat.
   Oirinn o na ho i u, etc.

Tha mo chiabhan air glasadh
'S le mo shùilean cha 'n fhaic mi
O na dh'fhàg mise 'n caisteal
'S an Aich[16] a tha laimh ris.
   Oirinn o na ho i u, etc.

O cha 'n iarrainn de dh' athchuing
Ach trocair do m' anam,
'Sa bhi 'n àite do mhnatha
'S mi 'g altrum do phàisdean.
   Oirinn o na ho i u, etc.

Young Mary

Oirinn o na ho i u,
Oirinn o na ho i u,
Oirinn o na ho i u,
It is my love who has rejected me.

O! thou of the auburn locks
And bright blue eyes,
Oft have I met thee
In the shieling of the glen.
     Oirinn o na ho i u . . .

And when with thy venison
I would see thee coming from the ben,
My heart would arise to thee
Unknown to my mother.
     Oirinn o na ho i u . . .

But if thou didst reject me,
And my suit hast denied,
My wish and prayer are
That the Duke's daughter be in my place.[17]
     Oirinn o na ho i u . . .

And if thou be not my lover
Let fortune a wise wife give you,
And thy good-luck be none the worse
That I have given you my love.
     Oirinn o na ho i u . . .

My locks are getting grey
And my eyes growing dim,
Since I left the castle
And the wee burnie by it.
     Oirinn o na ho i u . . .

No other wish would I ask
But mercy to my soul,
And to be thy lawful wife
Nursing thy children.
     Oirinn o na ho l u . . .

Oran a Rinneadh le Domhnull Macmhuirich[18]
Turus do Irbhinn le Uisge-Beatha

An dùl a chaidh mi thun na marachd
Le Alasdair an Dròbhair,
Shéid a' ghaoth 'n iar 'na srannaibh,
'S chuir i car 's an t-seòl oirnn;
'S nuair thug i *heel* do 'n bhàta,
Cha robh *cutter* 'dh'fhaodadh feuchainn
Teachd a nìos ruinn air an t-snàmh ud,
'S i mar eun 's na neòil ogainn.

Bu lurach i a' gearradh uisg',
'Us sruth 'dol o a bòrdaibh,
Cha robh lóng mhór 's na h-uisgeachan
A chumadh rithe seòladh;
Laigh i nunn fo làn a h-aodaich –
Cùrsa dìreach 's 'n oidhche reubach,
Gaoth 'n iar-thuath teachd fuar thar Gaoid-bheinn[19]
'S cha do ghéill i òirleach.

'S ann mar so thu'irt Raonall an sgiobair,
'S mithich dhuinne deòrum[20]
A ghabhail as a' bhuideal bhiorach
A mhisneachadh ar dòchais;
'S nuair a fhuair sinn sud 'nar buadhan
Cha robh de luchd-rìgh mu'n cuairt dhuinn
'Chuireadh eagal oirnn no cluadan,
'Us cuaillean ann ar dòrnaibh.

Bhuailemaid gach neach a thigeadh,
'S mhilleamaid an dòchas,
Bhiodh gach ceann dhiubh aca briste,
'Us silteach fal' o 'n srònaibh;
Ach dh'éirich suas a nis MacGrabhan,
'Us air an ailm thug e tarruing,
Stiùiridh mis' 'ars esan,' a' chailinn
Thun na gaineimh chòmhnaird.

'S o na fhuair sinn e fo 'n ghaineimh,
Falaicht' mar bu chòir dha,
Ghluais sinn le cheil' gu baile,
'S cadal trom 'g ar leònadh;
'S mo thruaigh nach do rinn mi faire,
Ged robh mì gun chadal fhathast
Mu 'n do leig sinn leis a' ghaisreadh
E roimh 1à Di-dòmhnuich.

Bu lurach iad a' slaodadh bhuideal,
'S Luidein ag an seòladh,
Clootie 'togail orra 'n ultaich,
'S e 'g an cur an òrdugh ;
'S dh'innseadh esan dhaibh gu beurra
Gu 'n robh iad 'n an daoine feumail,
'S ged a ghoideadh iad dheth taoman
Nach biodh h-aon an tòir orra.

Gu'm b' e fhéin àrd-righ a' pheacaidh,
'Us nach b'eagal d 'an luchd-seòrsa
'S nach biodh cùram dhaibh no gealtachd
Fhad 's bhiodh esan leòtha;
Ach 's cinnteach leam gu'm faigh iad fhathast
Ladhran loisgte anns an teallaich,
Mur an sguir, 's mur toir iad thairis
Leantuinn air an spòrs 'ud.

The Smugglers
Translation by J. Craig

The trip I went a-sailoring
With Alister the Drover,
The squally west wind caught our sails,
Our boat went nearly over.
Then heeling to the breeze that blew,
'Twas vain for cutters to pursue
As faster than a bird e'er flew
Through smoking drift we drove her.

'Twas rare to see her snowy wake
As snarling billows maul'd her,
The fastest frigate on the seas
Could ne'er have overhaul'd her;
Unreefed, unyielding on she passed
Through darkening night and strengthening blast,
While nor-west showers came scourging fast
From Goatfell's craggy shoulder.

Our skipper Ronald then arose
And said, My jolly quorum,
To raise our hopes we'll broach a cask
And drink a hearty jorum.
When through our veins we felt the heat
King's men would ne'er make us retreat,
But stick in hand, would boldly meet
And well with cudgels claur 'em.

We'd dash the hopes of all who came
Intending to oppose us,
And pack them off with bleeding crests,
And torn and bloody noses.
Long-leggèd Crawford then got up
And caught the tiller in his grip,
Quoth he, I'll steer our trusty ship
To land e'er morning shows us.

We hid our stuff beneath the sand,
Though little that avail'd us,
Then went our weary way to town
While sorely sleep assail'd us.
Would that a better watch we set,
Though we should ne'er have slumbered yet,
Ere we allowed such rogues to get
Our store ere morning hail'd us,

Oh, rare to see the rascals run
With kegs that ne'er paid duty,
'Twas Luidein laid their burdens on,
The orders came from Clootie.
His lies he glibly would relate,
How useful they were to the State,
And though they stole, 'twas to abate
Their thirst with lawful booty.

That he was aye the sinner's friend,
Their kind need never fear him,
Nor need they care what might befall
So long as he was near them;
But much I fear they need not boast,
Some later day they'll count the cost
When at his hearth their toes he'll toast,
And for their labour jeer them.

Notes

[1] Said to have been composed by Donald Currie 'at the fishing.'

[2] 'Ceann-dubh' would seem to be misapplied here, as the 'Canach' is pure white; but it is the black head, before the white down grows on it.

[3] The above verses were composed on the death of a young Arran gentleman who was drowned in Campbeltown loch about the beginning of the nineteenth century. It was suspected that he was thrown overboard by the captain of a cutter in which he happened to be at the time, in order to obtain possession of the unfortunate man's sister, who was also on board.

[4] Delay.

[5] With a view.

[6] Troops, meaning here the press-gang.

[7] Doubt.

[8] This hymn is incomplete.

[9] Meal and milk mixed together, crowdie.

[10] Pieces of land.

[11] Tor-mór called also in Arran *An Todhar*.

[12] The informers.

[13] Also known as Bun na dubh-abhainn = Blackwaterfoot.

[14] The late Ebenezer Bannatyne: he had the honour of entertaining such distinguished guests as the late Duke of Hamilton and Louis Napoleon.

[15] Big Flora; the innkeeper's wife.

[16] Aich, the burn by Loch Ranza Castle.

[17] As a rejected lover.

[18] In Arran the M of the Mac is not pronounced (i.e. 'acMhuirich), and the final *ch* also is silent.

[19] *Gaoid-bheinn*, Goatfell

[20] *Deòrum* (jorum) is always associated with a big drink of whisky. The etymology is uncertain, unless it be from *deur*, a drop of drink, *deuran*, a small drop, and *deorum*, a big drink; or it may be a corruption of *deagh dhram*, a good drink.

Appendix 2

Traditional Tales in the Gaelic of Arran

from *The Book of Arran*
by William Mackenzie

Am Figheadair Crotach

Bho chionn fada nan cian bha figheadair beag, crotach a' còmhnuidh an Loch-Raonasa. Latha 's e 'dol do'n bheinn a bhuain rainich, thainig e gu h-obann air buidheann shithichean 'us iad mu theinn 'a damhsadh ann an lagan uaine, grianach, uaigneach. Làn neònachais laigh e sìos aig cùl gàraidh-balla a chum 's gu'm faiceadh e iad ri'n cleasachd. Bu lùghmor 's bu sgiobalt iad air an damsadh, agus b' e am port-a-beul a bh' aca 'Di-Luain, 's Di-Màirt; Di-Luain 's Di-Màirt.' Cha b' fhada gus an d' fhàs e sgìth de 'n phort ghoirìd so agus leum e gu 'chasan 'us ghlaod e mach ' 's Di-ciadain'.

Air faicinn duine an dlùths dhaibh, chlisg na daoine beaga, ach cha do chuir sin stad air an àbhacas; lean iad air damsadh ris a' phort, 'Di-Luain, Di-Màirt, 's Di-ciadain,' agus chunnaic iad gu'm b'fheairrd am port an car a chuir am figheadair ann. Chum an taingealachd a nochdadh dha, thug iad a' chroit bharr a dhroma 's chuir iad air mullach a' gharaidh-balla i. Chaidh am figheadair dhachaidh gu suigeartach cho aotrom ri iteig 's cho direach ri ràite. Thuit gu'n robh figheadair crotach eile a' còmhnuidh an Loch-Raonasa aig a' cheart àm so, agus air dha chluinntinn mar fhuair a choimhearsnach rèidh de 'chroit, chuir a roimhe gu'm feuchadh esan an seòl ceudna chum faotainn rèidh de 'chroit fhéin. Suas gabhar e thun na beinne far an robh na sithichean, agus fhuair e iad an sin a' damhsadh cho lùghmor 's a bha iad riamh. Dh' éisd e riu car tiotan, agus an sin ghlaodh e mach 'Di-Luain, Di-Màirt, Di-ciadain, Di-'r-daoin, Di-h-aoine, Di-Sathuirne'; ach an àite gleus a b'fhearr chur air a' phort, 's ann a mhill e'muigh 's a mach e. Bha na daoine beaga cho diombach dheth airson a' phuirt a mhilleadh, 's gu'n do thog iad croit an fhir eile bhàrr a' ghàraidh, agus spàrr iad an darna croit air muin na croit' eile 's chuir iad dhachaidh e da uair na bu chrotaiche na bha e roimhe.

The Hunchbacked Weaver

Ages long ago there was a hunchbacked weaver dwelling in Loch Ranza. One day as he was going to the hill to cut brackens, he suddenly came upon a band of fairies as they were actively engaged at dancing in a green, sunny, secluded hollow. Full of curiosity he lay down at the back of a turf dyke in order to observe their antics. Active and nimble were they at the dancing, and the tune they had was 'Monday, Tuesday; Monday, Tuesday.' He soon got tired of this short tune, and he jumped to his feet, and shouted out 'and Wednesday'.

On seeing a man near them, the little folk started, but that did not put a stop to their diversion; they continued dancing to the tune 'Monday, Tuesday, and Wednesday,' and conceived that the tune was the better of the turn the weaver put in it. In order to show him their gratitude, they took the hump off his back and placed it on the top of the turf dyke. The weaver went home rejoicing, light as a feather and straight as a ramrod. It happened that another diminutive hunchbacked weaver resided at Loch Ranza at the very same time, and on hearing how his neighbour got rid of his hump, he determined that he would try the same plan in order to get rid of his own hump. Up he goes to the hill where the fairies were, and he found them there dancing as lively as ever. He listened for a short time, and then shouted out, 'Monday, Tuesday, Wednesday, Thursday, Friday, Saturday'; but instead of improving on the tune, he spoiled it out and out. The little folk were so displeased at him for spoiling the tune, that they lifted the other man's hump off the dyke and placed a second hump on the top of the other, and sent him home twice as hunched as he was before.

[Told of fairies in Scotland and Ireland, of pixies in Cornwall, of corrigans in Brittany. In a Japanese version the affliction is not a hump but a wen on the forehead. In all cases the essential idea is the same.]

Na Sithichean – Claoinead

Bha tuathanach d'am b'ainm MacCùca aon uair a' còmhnuidh ann an Claoinead. Thug a bhean leanabh thun an t-saoghail, agus bha na h-ingheanan 's a' choimhearsnachd, mar bu ghnàth, a' faire ré na h-oidhche a' frithealadh do'n leanabh 's d'a mhàthair. Aon oidhche chualas ùpraid uamhasach anns a' bhàthaich, mar gu 'm biodh an crodh 'gan gaorradh gu bàs. Leum an luchd-faire gu'n casan agus chaidh iad do'n bhàthaich a dh'fhaicinn dé b'aobhar de'n t-straighlich. Cha robh nì cearr ri fhaicinn, bha an crodh gu sàmhach, foisneach 'nan laighe a' cnàmh an cìr. Nuair a thill iad air an ais cha robh sealladh de bhean-an-taighe ri fhaicinn – chaidh i as an t-sealladh gu buileach, agus a réir coslais, air a toirt air falbh le na daoine beaga. Bha am fear aice gu tùrsach a' caoidh call a mhnatha, agus air dha aon latha a bhi 'g obair aig beul abhainn na Slaodraich, chunnaic e sgaoth de na daoine beaga a' dol thar a chinn, agus thilg e an corran-buana 'bha 'na laimh 'nam measg. Cha luaithe rinn e sin na co bha 'na seasamh 'na làthair ach a bhean fhéin. Gàirdeach 's mar bha iad a' chéile choinneachadh a rithist, thuirt i ris: 'Fhir mo ghràidh, cha 'n 'eil e 'n comas dhomh a dhol leat, ach ma dh'fhàgas thu dorus beulaobh agus dorus cùil au taighe fosgailte air oidhche àraidh, theid mi-fhéin agus cuideachd de na daoine beaga a steach eadar an da dhorus. Bi thusa 'nad shuidhe a' feitheamh, agus nuair a chi thu 'n cothrom tilgidh tu mo chleòca-pòsda tharam, agus aisigear mise dhuit.

Bha gach nì mar a thubhairteadh, ach nuair a thàinig a bhean 'na shealladh cha robh de mhisnich aig an duine bhochd na thilgeadh an cleòca thairte. Bha i 'smèideadh gu teann, dùrachdach ris, ach air do na daoine beaga thuigsinn ciod a bu rùn di, spiol iad a' bhean bhochd air falbh, a dh'aindeoin gach oidheirp a rinn i a saorsa' fhaotainn, agus cha 'n fhacas riamh tuilleadh i. Anns a' chòmhradh a bh' aice r' a fear dh'innis i dhà gu'n robh na Sithichean math dhi, agus nuair a bhiodh e 'sguabadh na h-àtha, gun a sguabadh tur glan, ach beagan ghràinean fhagail a bhiodh aca gu itheadh.

The Fairies of Claoinead

A farmer of the name of Cook resided at one time at Claoinead. His wife gave birth to a child, and the neighbouring maidens, as was the custom, sat up at night and attended to the child and its mother. One night a terrible uproar was heard in the byre, as if the cattle were being gored to death. The attendants jumped to their feet and went to the byre to see what was the cause of the noise. There was nothing wrong to be seen, the cattle were quietly and peacefully lying chewing their cud. When they went back, the housewife was nowhere to be seen – she had totally disappeared, and to all appearance was taken away by the little folk.

Her husband was sorely lamenting the loss of his wife, and one day as he was working at the mouth of Sliddery burn, he saw a multitude of the little folk going over his head, and he threw the reaping-hook, which he had in his hand, in their midst. No sooner had he done so than who was standing in his presence but his own wife. Glad as they were to have met each other again she said to him: 'My dear husband, it is not in my power to go with you, but if you leave the front door and back door of the house open on a certain night, I and a company of the little folk will enter between the two doors. Be you sitting waiting, and when you see an opportunity you will throw my wedding-cloak over me, and I shall be restored to you.'

Everything happened as was said, but when his wife had come in sight, the poor man had not so much courage as to throw the cloak over her. She earnestly made signs to him, but the little folk, perceiving her intention, snatched the poor woman away in spite of her efforts to get her freedom, and she was never seen more. In the conversation she had with her husband, she told him that the fairies were good to her, and when he would be sweeping the kiln not to sweep it altogether clean, but to leave some grains that they would have to eat.

[The power of the reaping-hook is in its metal. Cold iron is the master of these beings. In the ballad of the *Young Tamlane* the lady secures her changing lover, after many transformations, by casting her green mantle over him. Women in childbed were particularly open to fairy interference.]

Sithichean Dhruim-a-Ghineir

Bho chionn fada bha buidheann shithichean a' còmhnuidh ann an Cnoc 'ic Eòghain an Druim-a-ghìneir. Bha iad fhéin agus tuathanach àraidh do'm b'ainm Macmhurchaidh anabarrach càirdeil mu chéile. Bhiodh esan a' dol gu tric air chéilidh leò, ach bha e daonnan a' deanamh brath-ghabhail gu'n sàthadh e sgian, no snàthad-mhór, no crioman iaruinn de'n t-seòrsa sin, am bràigh an doruis aca a chum an rathaid a bhi réidh dha gu teachd a mach. Oidhche de na h-oidhchean a chaidh e' choimhead orra, fhuair e iad uile cruinn air mullach a' chnocain mu theinn ag ullachadh airson turuis éiginn. Spìon gach aon diùbh geodhasdan, agus air dhaibh facail dhìomhair aithris, chaidh iad casan-gòbhlach air a' gheodhasdan, agus an àird gabhar iad anns an adhar cho aotrom ri iteig. Rinn Macmhurchaidh an nì ceudna, spìon esan geodhasdan, chaidh e casan-gòbhlach air, agus ag aithris nam briathran-sìthe suas gabhar e as an déidh cho luath 's cho aotrom ri h-aon diubh fhéin. Stiùir iad an cùrsa nunn thar Maol Chinntìre, an rathad a bu ghiorra gu Eirinn. Ann an ùine ghoirid fhuair Macmhurchaidh e fhéin ann an cidsin tuathanaich an Eirinn far an robh bean-an-taighe 'na laighe ri uchd a' bhàis, agus gach sean chailleach 's an àite a' frithealadh dhi. Ann am priobadh na sùla spiol na sithichean a' bhean bhochd air falbh, agus dh'fhàg iad 'na h-àite ploc fiodha an cruth na mnatha. An sin thog iad orra thun an dachaidh air a' cheart dòigh anns an d' fhàg iad, 'us Macmhurchaidh agus bean an tuathanaich 'nan cuideachd. Nuair a ràinig iad an cnocan-sìthe an Druim-a-ghineir, thug iàd a' bhean do Macmhurchaidh airson gu'n deachaidh e leotha do dh' Eirinn, 'us dh'fhan i leis mar a bhean-phòsda.

Seachd blìadhna an déidh so, air feasgar blàth samhraidh thàinig déirceach bochd Eirionnach an rathad agus air dha bhi sgith, shuidh e air a' chloich-chnotaidh' ri taobh dorus Mhicmhurchaidh. Bha bean-an-taighe a' bleoghan nam bó agus gach uair a rachadh i seachad eadar a' bhàthaich 's an taigh-bainne, theireadh an déirceach: 'Ma tà, mur bitheadh gu'n do chuir mi mo bhean le mo dhà làimh fhéin anns a' chiste-mhairbh mhionnaichinn gu 'm bu tusa i.' B'e deireadh an sgeòil gu'n d'fhalbh a' bhean leis an déirceach Eirionnach – a fear-pòsda dligheach.

The Fairies of Druimaghineir

A long time ago a band of fairies had their abode in Cnoc 'ic Eoghain in Druimaghineir. They and a certain farmer named MacMurchie were very friendly with each other. He would often be going to visit them, but always took the precaution to thrust a knife, a darning-needle or a piece of iron of that kind above the door so as to keep the way clear for him to come out. One of the nights on which he went to visit them, he found them all assembled on the top of the hillock, busily preparing for some journey. Each one of them pulled a ragwort, and having repeated some mystic words they went astride the ragwort, and up they went into the air as light as a feather. MacMurchie did the same thing, he pulled a ragwort, went astride on it, and having repeated the fairy words up he goes after them as swiftly and lightly as any of themselves. They directed their course over beyond the Mull of Kintyre by the shortest route to Ireland. In a short time MacMurchie found himself in the kitchen of a farmer in Ireland, where the housewife was bedfast and at the bosom of death, and every old woman in the place attending her. In the twinkling of an eye the fairies snatched the poor woman away, and left in her place a log of wood of the appearance of the woman. They then betook themselves home in the same manner as they left, with MacMurchie and the farmer's wife in their company. When they reached the fairy mound in Drumaghineir, they bestowed the woman on MacMurchie because he accompanied them to Ireland, and she remained with him as his wife.

Seven years after this, on a warm summer evening, an Irish beggar came the way, and being tired, he sat down on the husking-stone[2] at the side of MacMurchie's door. The housewife was milking the cows, and every time she passed between the byre and milkhouse the beggar would say: 'Well, if I had not placed my wife with my own two hands in the coffin, I would swear that thou art she.' The end of the story was that the woman departed with the Irish beggar – her lawful husband.

A' Bhean-Ghluin Agus na Sibhrich[3]

Bho chionn fada roimhe so, bha seana chailleach a' còmhnuidh ann am Baile-mhìcheil a bhiodh ri banachas-ghlùin. Air latha àraidh 's i' buain le h-aon de na coimhearsnaich, dé thàinig trasd uirre ach losgann mòr, grannda 's i trom le losgainn òga. 'Tha mi 'guidhe 's ag aslachadh ort,' ars a' chailleach, 's i 'cur an losgainn a thaobh le bàrr a' chorrain ghobhlaich, 'nach dealaich thu ri do luchd gus am bi mo dhà làimh-se timcheall' ort.' Cha robh tuilleadh air aig an àm, ach oidhche no dhà an déidh sin, có thàinig thun an doruis aice ach gille air muin eich 'na dheannaibh, agus e 'glaodhaich uirre i 'dh' éirigh gu luath, luath, a' dheanadh cuideachaidh 'us cobhair air mnaoi a bha 's a' ghlaodhaich.[5] Ghreas i uirre, 'us chaidh i air muin an eich aig cùlthaobh a' ghille, ach an àite crùn an rathaid a ghleidheadh 's ann a ghabh e a muigh 's a mach rathad cùil Aird bheinn. 'C'àite fo chromadh nan speur' ars' a' chailleach, 'am, bheil an aire dhuit dol, no cia fhada tha romhad?' 'Se luaths do theangaidh,' ars an gille, 'a ghluais do chasan an nochd, chuir thu Ban-rìgh nan Sibhreach beaga fo gheasaibh 's i an riochd losgann, 's cha 'n fhaigh i fòir no fuasgladh gus am bi do dhà làimh timcheall uirre, ach air an anam a tha 'nn do chorp feuch nach gabh thu biadh no deoch no tuarasdal, air neo bithidh thu mar tha mise, fo shileadh nan lòchran, gun chomas tillidh gu taigh no teaghlach.'

Ràinig iad uamh Aird-bheinn, agus chaidh iad a steach do sheòmar cho breagh, 's nach fhaichte a leithid 's an domhan. Bha Ban-righ nan Sibhreach air leabaidh, 'us mòran de na sibhrich bheaga a' feitheamh 's a' freasdal uirre. Rinn a' chailleach gach nì a bha feumail, 's cha robh fada gus an do rugadh mac mòr, meamnach. Nuair a bha 'n leanabh glan, sgeadaichte, thug iad sàbh do'n bhean-ghlùin a dhungadh a shùilean, chum 's gu faigheadh e sealladh an dà shaoghail. Ach thuit gu'n do thachais a' chailleach a mala 's an sàbh air a meuran, 's cha luaithe a thachais na fhuair i sealladh an dà shaoghail 'n a leth-shuil; agus a nis an seòmar a chitheadh i cho breagh leis an darna sùil, chitheadh i leis an t-sùil eile e 'na tholl dorcha làn neadoch an damhan-alluidh. O'n a bha a h-uile nì deas, cha robh ach biadh 'us deoch a chur air a beulaobh, ach dhiùlt i muigh 's a mach e. B'eiginn leotha 'n sin gu'n gabhadh i pàigheadh airson a saothrach, agus thairig iad dhi làn an dùirn de'n òr; ach an t-òr a bha cho buidhe, bòidheach do'n darna sùil, cha robh air ach coslas innearach do 'n t-sùil eile, agus cha ghabhadh i dubh no dath[6] dheth. O'n a chunnaic[7] na sibhrich nach robh math dhaibh a bhi rithe chuir iad i air druim an eich, agus an sin dh'aithnich i an gille gu'm b'e mac coimhearsnaich a bh'ann a ghoideadh le na sibhrich, agus dùil aig a mhuinntir gu'n do shiubhail e. Ràinig a' chailleach a bothan fhéin mu ghoir a' choilich, 's cha luaithe a ghlaodh e na chaidh an gille 's an t-each as an t-sealladh, agus cha 'n fhaca i iad gu bràth tuilleadh.

The Midwife and the Fairies

Long before now an old woman dwelt in Balmichael who practised midwifery. On a certain day as she was reaping with one of the neighbours, what came across her but a big, ugly frog, heavy with young. 'I pray and beseech you,' said the old wife, as she put the frog aside with the point of the sickle, ' that you will not part with your burden until my two hands be about you.' There was nothing further at the time, but a night or two thereafter who should come to her door but a youth on the back of a horse in hot haste, and calling to her to arise quickly to give assistance and succour to a woman in childbed. She hastened and mounted the horse at the back of the youth, but instead of keeping to the crown of the road, he kept out and out by way of Aird-bheinn. 'Where, under the bend of the sky,' said the old wife, 'do you mean to go or what distance is before you ?' 'It is the quickness of your tongue that moved your feet to-night; you put the queen of the fairies under a spell and she was in the form of a frog, and she will get neither help nor deliverance until your two hands be about her, but on the soul in your body see that you take neither food nor drink nor hire, or else you will be as I am, under the dripping of the torches, without the power to return to house or family.'

They reached the cave of Aird-bheinn, and they entered a room so grand that the like could not be seen on earth. The queen of the fairies was in bed, and many of the little fairies waiting and serving her. The old wife did all that was necessary, and it was not long until a big, strong son was born. When the infant was washed and clothed they gave an ointment to the midwife to anoint his eyes so that he would get the view of the two worlds. But it happened that the old wife scratched her eyebrow, with the ointment on her fingers, and no sooner had she done so than she got a sight of the two worlds with her one eye; and now, the room which she would see so grand with the one eye, she would see it with the other eye a dark hole full of cobwebs. Since everything was in readiness, food and drink were set before her, but she refused it out and out. They must needs, then, that she would accept a hire for her labour, and they offered her a handful of gold; but the gold that was so yellow and beautiful to the one eye, it was but like dung to the other, and she would not take it at all. When the fairies saw they could not prevail on her, they set her on the horse's back, and it was then she knew the youth – that he was the son of a neighbour who was stolen by the fairies, and his people thinking he had died. The old wife reached her own home about the cock-crowing, and no sooner had the cock crowed than the youth and horse disappeared, and she saw them no more.

[A widespread story common in Wales, Ireland, Man, Cornwall, and Brittany. Usually the eye anointed with the salve is blinded afterwards by a fairy, who by this means has been recognised. In such a case it is the fairy midwife who attends a mortal, when the husband thus accidentally acquires the fairy vision and suffers blinding.]

APPENDIX 2

An Tuathanach Agus Na Sibhrich[8]

Air do thuathanach àiridh aig an robh gabhail-fearainn anns an eilean so anns na làithean a tha seachad, a bhi aon latha an toiseach an Earraich anns an achadh a leantuinn nan each anns a' chrann-treabhaidh,[9] bhuail mar bu tric an t-acras e. Ars esan ris fhéin, 'Na 'n robh agam ach greim arain, chumadh e suas mi gu àm an trathnòin.' Air dha teachd gu ceann-iomaire an achaidh, mhothaich e fàile taitneach a chuir barrachd geurachaidh air a chàil – fàile bonnaich air ùr dheasachadh.[10] Ars esan, 'Bu mhath leam crioman de'n bhonnach sin itheadh,' agus lean e air aghaidh aig cùl nan each anns a' chrann gus an do thill e rithist gu ceann an iomaire; agus de chunnaic e ach bonnach air ùr dheasachadh na laighe air an làr fa chomhair. Chuir so ìoghnadh air, ach thog e 'us dh'ith e am bonnach, agus bonnach a bu mhilse cha d'ith e riamh. 'Gu dearbh,' ars esan. 'Bu mhath leam bolla de 'n mhin o'n d'rinneadh am bonnach sin fhaotainn.' Thug e car eile le na h-eich, agus air dha teachd a rithist gus an àite cheudna, faicear bolla mine 'na shuidhe air an làr. Dh' fhuasgail e na h-eich as a' chrann, agus thug e am bolla mine dhach-aidh, agus a leithid de mhin cha d'ith e riamh – bha i cho milis, blasda.

Thòisich e air breithneachadh mu'n chùis, agus thàinig e gus a' chomh-dhunaidh gu'm be so obair nan sibhreach, agus gu'm b' e a dhleasdanas an caoimhneas a dhioladh. Nuair a thàinig a' mhin fhéin as a' mhuileann, dh'fhàg e bolla dhi aig ceann an iomaire far an d'fhuair e roimhe so bonnach agus min nan sibhreach; agus thug iad-san leo min an tuathanaich. Uine ghoirid an déidh so thachair na sibhrich air anns an achadh, agus bha an caoimhneas air tionndadh gu feirg; chionn ghlac iad e, agus ghabh iad air le buailteanan gu math agus gu ro mhath.

Dh'fheòraich iad deth, 'Carson a thug thu dhuinn min de'n t-seors' ud?' 'Thug mi dhuibh,' ars an tuathanach, 'min cho math 's a bha agam'; ach ars iadsan, 'a' mhin a thug sinne dhuit b' ann de'n ghraine-mullaich a rinneadh i.' 'Ma tha sin mar sin,' ars esan,' bheir mise dhuibh min cho math ris a' mhin a thug sibhse dhomhsa.'

Leis a' ghealladh so leig iad an tuathanach mu sgaoil, agus dachaidh ghabh e cho luath 's a bheireadh a chasan e, agus bhuail e an grainemullaich de'n arbhar, chuir e do'n mhuileann e, agus dh'fhàg e bolla de'n mhin far am faigheadh na sibhrich i. Bho sin gus an do shuibhail e bha e-fhéin agus na sibhrich 'nan deagh chàirdean.

The Farmer and the Fairies

The following little tale is told of a certain farmer that had a lease of land in this island in the days gone by. One day in the beginning of spring, as he was in the field following the horses in the plough, he was struck, as often happened, with hunger. Said he to himself, 'If I had but a bit of bread it would keep me up until noontide.' As he came to the head-rig he felt a pleasant smell which gave an additional sharpening to his appetite – the smell of a newly baked bannock. Said he, 'I would like to eat a piece of that bread,' and followed on behind the horses in the plough until he again returned to the head-rig, and what did he see but a bannock newly baked lying on the ground before him. This astonished him, but he lifted up and ate the bannock, and a sweeter

251

bannock he never ate. 'Truly,' he said, I would like to get a boil of the meal from which that bannock was made.' He gave another turn with the horses, and having again come to the same place, he sees a boll of meal sitting on the ground. He loosened the horses out of the plough and brought the boll of meal home, and such meal he never ate – it was so sweet and well-tasted.

He commenced to think about the matter, and came to the conclusion that this was the work of the fairies, and that it was his duty to reward their kindness. When his own meal came from the mill he left a boll of it at the head-rig where he got, before this, the bannock and meal of the fairies, and they brought with them the meal of the farmer.

A short time after this the fairies met him in the field and their kindness was turned into anger, for they seized him and thrashed him severely with flails. They asked him, 'Why did you give us meal of that kind ?' 'I gave you,' said the farmer, ' as good meal as I had.' 'But,' said they, 'the meal which we gave you, it was from the top-grain that it was made.' 'If that is so,' said he, ' I will give you meal as good as the meal you gave me.'

With this promise they released the farmer, and home he went as fast as his legs would take him, and he threshed the top-grain of the corn, sent it to the mill, and left a boll of the meal where the fairies would get it. From then until he died, he and the fairies were good friends.

An Tuathanach Agus A' Chailleach

Air là àraidh bho chionn fada chaidh tuathanach de mhuinntir Chille-Phàdair do'n Leaca-bhreac a bhuain rainich. Ann-an teis-meadhon na buana thàinig dùbhradh air an speur, agus air dha amharc suas, de chunnaic e ach mar gu'm biodh sgaoth tiugh bheachann eadar e 's a' ghrian. Thilg e an corran a bh'aige 'na làimh suas anns an adhar, agus có a thainig a nuas mu na cluasan aige ach a bhean fhéin a dh'fhàg e aig an taigh, mar shaoil e, gu tinn 'n a leabaidh. Rug e uirre, cheangail e i agus chuir e tarsuinn air druim na làire ceanainn[11] duibh' i, 'us dh'fhalbh e dhachaidh leatha. Air dha an taigh a ruigheachd thilg e a bhean ann an cùil mhosain 's an t-sabhull, agus chaidh e a dh'fhaicinn ciamar bha cùisean a' dol anns an taigh. Sheall e mu 'n cuairt, agus de chunnaic e ach seana chailleach dhubh, ghrànda, 'n a laighe anns an leabaidh, agus i air chrith leis an fhuachd. 'Tha thu fuar a chailleach,' ars an tuathanach, 'Och ! 's ann fuar a tha mi,' ars ise – 'tha na crithean-nam-beo[12] a dol tromham.' 'Mata,' ars esan, 'feumaidh sinn gealbhan a chur air a gharas thu.' Chaidh e gu cùil na moine agus chuir e targan[13] math gealbhain air a ròstadh damh. Nuair a bhris an gealbhan a mach ann an grìosaich theth, rug e air a' chaillich 'us thilg e i an teis-meadhon na grìosaiche. Cha bu luaithe a mhothaich a' chailleach an teas 'na làdhran na thug i sgread na dunaich aisde, agus suas an luidhear gabhar i, 's cha'n fhacas sealladh tuilleadh dhi.

An sin ghabh an tuathanach ceann ròpa, us ghabh e air a bhean gu min[14] 's gu garbh, gus an do gheall 's an do bhòidich i nach rachadh i air an turus cheudna tuilleadh, agus o sin suas rinn i bean mhath umhal dha.

The Farmer and the Old Woman

On a certain day long ago a Kilpatrick farmer went out to Leaca-bhreac to cut brackens. In the very middle of his cutting a darkening came over the sky, and as he looked up, what did he see but something like a thick swarm of bees between him and the sun. He threw the reaping-hook which he had in his hand up into the air, and who came down about his ears but his own wife whom he left at home, as he thought, ill in bed. He laid hold of her, tied her, and put her across the back of the black, white-faced mare and went home with her. When he reached the house he threw his wife into a chaff corner in the barn, and went to see how matters were going in the house. He looked around, and what did he see but a black, ugly old woman lying in bed, shivering with the cold. 'You are cold, old woman,' said the farmer. 'Och! it is cold that I am,' said she, 'the living shiverings are going through me.' 'Well,' said he, 'we must put on a fire that will heat you.' He went to the peat corner and put on a good lump of a fire that would roast an ox.

When the fire broke out into a heat, he caught the old woman and threw her into the very middle of the hot fire. No sooner had the old woman felt the heat about her toes, than she let out a terrible yell, and up the chimney she went, and never more was seen. Then the farmer took a rope and thrashed his wife thoroughly and roughly until she promised and vowed that she would never again go on a like journey, and from then on she made a good obedient wife to him.

[Bees, both in England and Scotland, are closely connected with the soul or spirit, which may issue from the mouth of a sleeper in this form. In the Highlands a death must be told to the bees. A case of throwing a supposed changeling into the fire occurred in Ireland some years ago.]

The Lost Piper

There is an old story of a piper called Currie, who, accompanied with his dog, went into a cave playing the pipes. The tune he played was 'Currie will not return; the calves will be cows before Currie returns,' etc., etc. I never heard the rest of it. He never returned but the dog came out at some place in Cantyre, without its hair.

There is a legend about the King's Caves to the effect that there is a subterranean passage from the caves to somewhere else in Arran. An adventurous piper undertook to explore this passage, armed only with his bagpipe and accompanied by his dog. After he had proceeded some distance he met with enemies, because the following wailing words were played loudly upon his pipe, which clearly indicated that he could proceed no farther.

Mo dhìth! Mo dhìth! 's gun tri laimh agam.
Bhiodh dà laimh 'sa phiob 'us lamh 'sa chlaidheamh;

which might be literally rendered in English –

Woe's me, woe is me not having three hands,
Two for the pipe and one for the sword.

He, the piper, never returned; his dog, however, made his way out, but bereft of his hair.

[This is a familiar piece of lore, of which perhaps the best-known example is connected with an alleged subterranean passage between Edinburgh Castle and Holyrood. But it has numerous other localities. Descending below the earth, the piper wanders into Fairyland, the Hades or underworld, and cannot return.]

Na Mèileachain[15]

Ann an Arainn fada roimh so bha ri fhaotainn seòrsa de chreutairean glé neònach ris an abradh iad 'Na Mèileachain' – cha bu daoine iad 's cha bu bheathaichean iad. Thigeadh iad an sealladh gun iárraidh 's gun fhios cia as a thainig iad, agus nuair a dh'fhalbhadh iad cha mhotha bha fios c'àit' an deachaidh iad.

Bha aon de'n t-seòrsa so ré ùine fhada aig teaghlach a bha chòmhnuidh aig ceann mu dheas an eilein. Bhiodh e dol a mach 's a steach leis an eallaidh, agus a' laighe ann am baidheal fhalaimh aig ceann na bàthaiche. Fad na h-ùine a bha e aca cha'n fhacas riamh e ag itheadh, ach a h-uile oidhche an déidh do bhean-an-taighe an gealbhan a smàladh, thilgeadh i cràglach mine air an t-slabhraidh, agus nuair a dh'éireadh iad 's a' mhaduinn bhiodh i glan imlichte. Chaidh cùisean air an aghaidh mar so ré uine fhada gus an do phòs mac an taighe, Aon latha 's e anabarrach fuar, thilg a' bhean òg seana chòta air a' mhèileachan g' a dhìon o'n fhuachd, ach 's ann a ghabh an creutair bochd a leithid de thàmailt 's gu'n do thog e air, is dh'fhàg e an taigh a' caoineadh gu dubhach, agus cha 'n fhacas riamh tuilleadh e. 'Tha mi coma co dhiù,' arsa seana-bhean-an-taighe, 'mur innis e dà rud – dé an éifeachd a tha 'nn am bun a' chlàdain, agus brìgh fallus an uibhe.'

The Bleaters

In Arran a long time ago was to be found a kind of curious creatures called 'the Bleaters' – they were neither man nor beast. They would come unbidden – whence, no one knew; and when they would take their departure, it was unknown where they went.

A family in the south end of the island had one of this kind for a long time. He would be going out and in with the cattle, and lying in a cow-stall at the head of the byre. During the whole time he was with them he was never seen eating; but every night, after the goodwife would smoor the fire, she would throw a handful of meal on the pot-hanger, and when they arose in the morning it would be licked clean. Things went on in this way for a long time until the son of the house married. One day, and it was very cold, the young wife threw an old coat over the 'Mèileachan' to protect him from the cold, but the poor creature took such offence that he made off, and left the house weeping sadly, and he was never seen more. 'I care not whatever,' said the old wife of the house, 'if he does not tell two things – what virtue is in the root of the burr, and what substance in the sweat of an egg.'

[The *Mèileachan* or 'bleater' is really the young one of the *Glaistig*, a thin grey woman dressed in green, a mortal endowed with the fairy nature, who is attached to a house. Here it acts as a sort of brownie, and is got rid of by a means familiar in many brownie stories, as in the English one 'The Cauld Lad of Hilton':

Here's a cloak and here's a hood!
The Cauld Lad of Hilton will do no more good.

A rhyme to the same effect is known of a brownie in the Shetland Isles, of brownies in the Scottish Lowlands, and of the *Gunna* in Tiree:

Triuthas air Gunna
'S Gunna ris bhuachailleachd,
'S na mheal Gunna 'n triuthas
Ma ni e tuille cuallaich.

Trews upon Gunna
Because Gunna does the herding,
But may Gunna never enjoy his trews
If he herds cattle any more.

(Gregorson Campbell's *Superstitions of the Scottish Highlands*, p. 189).]

A' Bhean Chrodhanach

Aig an àm de'n bhliadhna anns am biodh na bà air an cur gu àirigh chaidh dà nighean òg a bhuineadh do cheann mu thuath Arainn le an cuid cruidh air àirigh am bràigh Loch Iorsa. Nuair a bhiodh cuibhrionn ìme agus càise deas aca rachadh té dhiubh dhachaidh leis, a' tilleadh thun na h-àirigh an ath latha, agus an té eile air a fàgail leatha fhéin. Aon oidhche nuair a bha aon diubh a' gabhail mu thàmh, thainig bean choimheach gu dorus a' bhothain àirigh ag iarraidh fàrdaich car na h-oidhche, is i air call a rathaid. Gu mòr an aghaidh a toile dh'fhosgail an nighean an dorus, agus a steach ghabh a' bhan-choigreach. Bha i 'na boìrionnach anabarrach àrd, agus cha bu luaithe 'chaidh i steach na theich madadh-chaorach na h-inghinn le greann gus an oisinn a b'fhaide air falbh de 'n bhothan. Cha b' fhada gus an deachaidh a' bhean choimheach a laighe, agus bha an nighean òg a' cumail a sùla gu geur uirre, chionn cha robh ach beagan earbsa aice ann am bana-chompanach na h-oidhche. Sùil d'an d'thug a' chailin faicear i le uamhas, crodhan dubh sìnte mach fo 'n aodach leapa. Ghabh i leithsgeul eiginn gu dol a mach, agus air dhi taobh a mach a' bhothain a dheanamh, anns na buinn gabhar i sios le beinn, cho luath 's a bheireadh a casan i, agus am madadh 'na cuideachd.

Ach cha b'fhada ruith dhi nuair a chuala i farum 'na déidh, agus thuig i àn sin gu'n robh a' bhean-chrodhanach air a luirg. Stuig i am madadh innte, agus thug e aghaidh dhanarra uirre ach stad cha do chuir e air a siubhal. Bha 'bhean-chrodhanach a sìor dheanamh suas ris a' chailin, agus nuair a ràinig i taigh a h-athar, a h-anail as an uchd agus a cridhe 'na sluigean, bha 'chailleach mhór cho dlùth dhi 's nach robh ùine aice ach an dorus a chrannadh air sròin na caillich, gun urrad 's am madadh fhaotainn a steach. Fhuaradh am beathach bochd anns a' mhaduinn 'na mhirean as a' chéile, 's gun aon ribeag fionnaidh air fhagail air.

The Hoofed Woman

At the time of year when the cows were being put to the hill-pastures, two young maidens belonging to the northern part of Arran went with their cattle to a shieling on the upper part of Loch Iorsa. When they had a quantity of butter and cheese ready, one of the girls would go home with it, returning to the shieling the following day, and the other was left alone. One night, as one of them was retiring to rest, a strange woman came to the door of the hut seeking shelter for the night, as she had lost her way. Much against her will the maiden opened the door, and in walked the stranger. She was a very tall woman, and no sooner had she entered than the girl's sheep-dog, with an angry look, betook himself to the farthest corner of the hut. It was not long until the strange woman went to bed, and the young girl was keeping a watchful eye on her, for she had but little faith in her companion of the night. As she glanced round, the girl sees with horror a black hoof stretched out from under the bed-clothes. She made some excuse to go out, and on reaching the outside of the hut, she took to her heels and down the hill she went as fast as her feet would take her, and the dog in her company.

But she did not run far when she heard a sound behind her, and then she understood that the hoofed-woman was on her track. She spurred the dog at her and he made a bold attack, but her progress he did not stop. The hoofed-woman was constantly making up on the girl, and when she reached her father's house, breathless and her heart in her throat, the big woman was so near to her that she had but time to bar the door in her face, without as much as getting the dog inside. The poor beast was found next morning mangled to pieces, and not a hair left on him.

An Tuathanach Agus an Uamh-Bheist

Bha tuathanach aon oidhche a' marcachd dhachaidh gu Clachaig o Loch-an-Eilein, agus ann an lagan uaigneach de'n rathad ghrad leum rudeigin air druim an eich air a chùlaobh, agus cho grad leum e rithist gu làr. Thug an t-each clisgeadh as, agus air falbh ghabh e 'na dheann ruith; ach cha b'fhada gus an robh an rud a bh'ann a rithist air druim an eich, agus air ais gus an làr mu'm b'urrainn do'n mharcaiche greim a dheanamh air. Chaidh an seorsa cleasachd so air aghaidh car tacan, ach mu dheireadh rug an tuathanach air rud-na-cleasachd, agus cheangail e gu diongmhalta e le bann leathraich a bh'aige. Nuair a ràinig e a dhachaidh dé bha 'na chuideachd ach òg-bheist, aon de shliochd nan uamh-bheistean a bha tuineachadh an sud 's an so am measg frògan an eilein, agus a bha 'nan culaidhuamhais do'n choimhearsnachd. Cheangail e suas an t-òg-bheist ri posta gòbhlach a bha 'cumail a suas spàrran an fharaidh, ach cha b'fhada gus an do lorgaich an t-seana-bheist a mach h-àl, agus gu borb 's le bagradh dh'iarr i a shaorsa 'thoirt dha, ag radh:–

> 'Fliuch, fuar m' fheusag,
> Cuir a mach mo mhinnseag,[16]
> No 's i 'chlach as àird' ad thaigh
> Gu grad a' chlach ìsle.'

Bha an tuathanach toilichte a bhi cuidhte dhiubh araon, agus nuair a fhuair an t-seana-bheist a h-àl 'na gairdeanan, thubhairt i ris, 'Tha mi an dòchas nach do leig thu ris dhaibh éifeachd uisge uibhe no bun na feanndaig.'

The Farmer and the Monster

A farmer was one night riding home to Clachaig from Lamlash, and in a lonely hollow of the road something suddenly leaped on the horse's back behind him, and as quickly leaped again to the ground. The horse was startled, and off he went at full speed; but it was not long until the thing again was on the back of the horse, and then on the ground before the rider could lay hold of it. This sort of caper went on for a while, but at last the farmer seized the intruder and tied it securely with a leather belt which he had. When he reached his home, what had he in his company but a young monster, one of the offspring of the monsters which had their abode here and there amongst the recesses of the island, and which were a source of terror to the neighbourhood. He tied up the young monster to a forked post which was supporting the rafters of the loft, but it was not long until the old monster tracked out her offspring, and fiercely and threateningly demanded its release, saying:

> 'Wet and cold my beard,
> Put my darling outside,
> Or the highest stone in thy house
> Will soon be the lowest.'

The farmer was glad to be rid of them both, and when the old monster got her young in her arms she said to it, 'I hope you have not revealed to them the virtue of egg-water or of the root of the nettle.'

[This is apparently the Glaistig and her Mèileachan, for which see note on p. 270]

An Leannan Crodhanach

Bha cailin òg ann aon uair aig an robh gille dreachail mar leannan. Bhiodh e gu tric a' dol g'a faicinn an uaigneas, ach cha'n innseadh e 'ainm, no far an robh e chòmhnuidh. Gach uair a rachadh e 'choimhead uirre gheibheadh e i daonnan ri snìomh. Bha e ro dheònach gu'n ruitheadh i air falbh leis, agus a sìor ghuidhe uirre i dhol leis; ach dhiùlt i sin a dheanadh. Uair de na h-uairean a chaidh e g' a faicinn bha i air tì toiseachadh air sac mòr rolag olainn a shnìomh. Thairig e dhi gu'n snìomhadh esan an sac rolaig na'n gealladh i dhà a dhol leis. Bha i sgìth de'n obair, agus thug i gealladh dhà gu'n rachadh i leis air chùmhnant gu'm biodh i saor o'n ghealladh na 'm faigheadh i a mach 'ainm mu'm biodh an sac rolaig snìomhte. 'S e bh'ann gu'n do thog e 'n sac air a dhruim is ghabh e'n rathad. Air oidhch' àraidh na dhéidh sin, air dhi a bhi dol gu taigh caraid, agus a' dol thairis air àllt domhain ann an àit' uaigneach, chual' i fuaim cuibhle-shnìomhaich agus duanag òrain ag éirigh a ìochdair an ùillt. Chuir so iongantas air a' chailin agus theann i dlùth do'n àite as an d'thàinig an fhuaim. Dé chunnaic 's a chual' i ach sean duine crìon, crìopach, dubh-neulach, 'na shuidhe aig cuibhil mhòir a' snìomh gu dian, agus a' seinn gu h-aighearach:

    ' 'S beag fhios a th'aig mo leannan-sa
    Gur "Crodhanach" is ainm dhomh.'

Thuig a' chailin a nis an seòrsa leannain a bh' aice, agus gu'm b'ann am frògan an ùillt a bha' àite-còmhnuidh. Nuair a chuir e crìoch air an obair chaidh e a rithist a dh'fhaicinn na cailin, agus a dh'iarraidh duais a shaothrach. Cho luath 's a chunnaic ì e dh'aithris i na briathran a chual' i:

    ''S beag fhios a th'aig mo leannan-sa
    Gur "Crodhanach" is anm dhomh.'

Cha luaithe chuala 'Crodhanach' na facail sin, na as an t-sealladh gabbar e 'na shradan dearga suas an luidhear, agus tuilleadh dragh cha do chuir e air a' chailin.

The Secret Name

There was once a young girl who had a handsome sweetheart. He would be often going to see her in secret, but would not tell his name, nor where he dwelt. Every time he went to visit her he would always find her spinning. He was very desirous that she should elope with him and always beseeching her to go with him; but this she refused to do. One of the times that he went to see her she was about to begin to spin a sack of wool. He offered that he would spin the sack of wool if she would promise to go with him. She was tired of the work, and gave him a promise that she would go with him on condition that she would be free from her promise if she found out his name before the sack of wool was spun. With this he put the sack on his back and went on his journey. On a certain night after that, as she was going to a friend's house, and crossing a deep stream in a lonely place, she heard the sound of a spinning-wheel and a lilt of a song coming from the bottom of the stream. This astonished the girl, and she drew near the place whence the sound came. What did she see and hear but an old, dark, wizened man sitting at a large wheel, spinning hard and singing cheerfully:

'Oh! little does my sweetheart know
That "Crodhanach" is my name.'

The girl now understood what kind of a sweetheart she had, and that his dwelling was in the deep recesses of the stream. When he had finished his work he went again to see the girl, and to request the reward of his labour. As soon as she saw him she repeated the words she had heard:

'Oh! little does my sweetheart know
That "Crodhanach" is my name.'

No sooner had 'Crodhanach' heard those words than out of sight he goes in red sparks up the chimney, and no more did he trouble the girl.

[On this type of story a book has been written called from the English version 'Tom, Tit, Tot.' The story is known as of the 'Rumpelstiltskin' class, that being the German name. The Banffshire variant is 'Whuppity Stoorie.']

Uruisg Allt-Uilligridh

Ann an Allt-Uilligridh tha linne ris an canar gus an là an duigh, 'Linne-na-Béist.' Tha e air a ràdh gu'n d'fhuair an linne an t-ainm so chionn gu'n robh, a réir an t-sean sgeòil, Uruisg uamhasach aon uair a gabhail còmhnuidh ann an còsan na linne. Thuit gu'n robh fear òg aig an Uruisg so – Mèileachan a b'ainm dha – agus air uairean dh'fhàgadh e bruachan an ùillt agus ghabhadh e cuairt troimh na h-achaidhean.

The Uruisg[17] of Allt-Uilligridh

In Allt-Uilligridh there is a pool which is called to this day 'The Monster's Pool.' It is said that the pool got this name because that, according to tradition, a terrible Uruisg at one time dwelt in the caverns of the pool. It happened that this Uruisg had a young male one – called Mèileachan – and at times he would leave the banks of the stream and would take a turn through the fields.

Innis Eabhra

Tha An Innis Eabhracha, reir beul-aithris, 'na eilean a tha fo dhruidheachd, agus 'na laighe fo 'n fhairge dlùth do dh' Eilean-an-iaruinn a mach o thraigh Choire-chraoibhidh. Air uairean bhitheadh e an sealladh cho soilleir 's gu'm faicteadh na h-adagan arbhair aìr na h-achaidhean, agus na mnathan a' cur an luideagan a mach air thiormachadh. Tha e nis mu leth-chiad bliadhna bho 'n chunnacas mu dheireadh e. Aon latha air do thuathanach a bhi mach ag amharc as déidh a spréidh, de chunnaic e ach an t-eilean ag éirigh as an fhairge dlùth do'n chladach, agus a chum 's gu'm faigheadh e sealladh a b'fhearr dheth ruith e thun a' chladaich. Car tiotan chaill e sealladh air an fhairge ann an lagan troimh 'm b'eiginn da siubhal, agus air dha an àirde ruigheachd bho 'm faiceadh e 'mhuir cha robh an t-eilean r' a fhaicinn – chaidh e as an t-sealladh gu buileach.

Air do bhata Arannach aon uair a bhi fàgail ceadha Ionaràir, agus dìreach mu'n do sheòl i, tha e air a ràdh gu'n d'thainig duine àraidh – coigreach – le lothag ghlas air taod, ag iarraidh turus-mara. Thug an sgiobair air bòrd iad, 's chuireadh am bàta mach gu fairge. Nuair a thainig iad dlùth do dh' Eilean-an-iaruinn thòisich an lothag ri sitrich, agus chualas sitreach eile 'ga freagairt o dhoimhne na fairge. An sin dh'iarr an coigreach air an sgiobadh a tilgeil thar an taobh, agus air dhaibh sin a dheanadh thug e cruinn-leum as a déidh agus chaidh iad, araon, as an t-sealladh. Bliadhna 'na dhéidh so, có a thachair air an sgiobair aig margadh Ionaràir ach an duine ceudna do'n d' thug e turus-mara. 'Chunnaic mi thusa roimhe so,' ars' an sgiobair. 'Ma chunnaic,' ars' an duine, 'cha 'n fhaic thu fear eile gu brath,' agus am priobadh na sùla, thugar sgailc le bhois do'n sgiobair 's an aodann, 'ga fhagail dubh dall.

Tha e air a ràdh gu'n cluinneadh na h-iasgairèan, 's iad a' feitheamh a' lìontan a thogail, air oidhchean ciùin, sàmhach, crònan tiamhaidh ciùil agus ranntachd òran ag éirigh suas a Innis Eabhrach, mar so:

'Càit an d'fhàg sibh na fir gheala, Ho ro 's golaidh u lé?
Dh'fhàg sinn iad 'san eilean mhara, Ho ro 's golaidh u lé.
Cùl ri cùl 'us iad gun anail, Ho ro 's golaidh u lé.'

Ma 's fìor an sgeul, thainig tuathanach a bha an Cillephàdair aon latha air maighdean-mhara a Innis Eabhrach agus ì 'na suaìn chadail aìr an tràigh, 's a cochull-druidheachd ri 'taobh. Rìnn e greim air a' chochull agus ghabh e a rathad thun a thaighe, 's cha robh aic' air ach gu'm b'éiginn dhi dhol leis. Thainig iad a réir a' chéile cho math 's gu'n do phòs iad, agus bha mac 'us nighean aice dha. Seachd blìadhna 'na dheidh sin air dha bhi anns an eaglais air là sabaid àraidh, agus air tilleadh dhachaidh cha robh à bhean air thoiseach air. 'Se bh' ann gu'n robh na pàisdean ri cleasachd anns an t-sabhull, agus thainig iad tarsuinn air rud a chuir ioghnadh orra. 'Nan deann-ruith chaidh iad thun am mathar a' glaodhaich 'A Mhathair! A Mhathair! thigibh agus faicibh an rud bòidheach a tha aig m'athair falaichte anns a' chùil-mhosain.' Is math a thuig am mathair dé an 'rud boidheach,' a bh' ann, agus thuirt i ris a' chloinn, 'thoiribh a steach an so e agus bheir mise ceapaire math òrdaig dhuibh.' Rìnn na pàisdean mar dh'iarradh orra, agus mar bha dùil aice, 'se an cochull druidheachd a bh' ann da rìreadh. Rinn i greim air a' chochull, 's cha luaithe fhuair i 'na làmhan e na thugar aisde gus a seann dachaidh anns a' mhuir. Air uairean thigeadh i gu Rudha'n-lòin a' gairm air a pàisdean, agus chunnacas iad 'na cuideachd 'us i 'cìreadh am fuilt agus a' seinn dhuanagan daibh. Aon latha lean am balachan a mhathair air a' mhuir, agus cha 'n fhacas sealladh tuilleadh dheth, ach thill a' chaileag dachaidh. Dh'fhàs i suas 'na h-inghinn eireachdail, phòs i, agus a réir an sgeòil, tha cuid d' a sliochd a lathair gus an là an diùgh.

Island Eabhra

Innis Eabhra, according to tradition, is an enchanted island, lying under the sea, near to the Iron Rock off the Corriecravie shore. At times it would he seen so distinctly that the corn stooks were visible in the fields, and the women putting out their clothes to dry. It is now about fifty years since it was last seen. One day as a farmer was out looking after his flock, what did he see but the island rising out of the sea close to the shore, and in order to get a better sight of it he ran towards the shore. For a short time he lost sight of the sea in a hollow through which he had to pass, and on reaching the height from which he could view the sea, the island was nowhere to be seen – it had entirely disappeared.

An Arran boat at one time was about to leave Ayr quay, and just before sailing, it is said that a certain man – a stranger – with a grey filly by the halter came and asked to be taken on board. The skipper took them on board, and the boat was put off to sea. When they approached the Iron Rock, the filly began to neigh, and other neighing was heard in response from the depths of the sea. Then the stranger asked the crew to throw her over the side, and this being done, he gave a sudden leap after her and both disappeared. A year after this, who met the skipper at Ayr market but the same man to whom he gave the passage on his boat. 'I saw you before now,' said the skipper. 'If you did,' said the man, 'you will not see another for ever,' and in the twinkling of an eye struck the skipper with his palm a blow on the face, leaving him black blind.

It is said that the fishermen, as they waited to lift their nets would hear, on calm, still nights, a weird sound of music and snatches of songs coming up from Innis Eabhra, thus:

Where have you left the fair men, Ho ro golaidh u lé ?
We left them on the sea-girt isle, Ho ro golaidh u lé.
Back to back with no breath in them. Ho ro golaidh u lé.

If true the tale, a Kilpatrick farmer one day came upon a mermaiden from Innis Eabhra while she was sound asleep on the shore, and her magic cloak by her side. He snatched the cloak and went on his way, to his house, and she had no alternative but to go with him. They agreed so well together that they got married and she bore him a son and daughter. Seven years after that he was at church on a certain Sabbath day, and on returning home his wife was not before him. It happened that the bairns were diverting themselves in the barn, and they came across a thing which astonished them. In hot haste they ran to their mother, shouting, 'Mother! Mother! Come and see the beautiful thing my father has hidden in the chaff-comer.' Well did their mother understand what the 'beautiful thing' was, and she said to the children, 'Bring it in here and I will give you a good thumb-piece.' The children did as they were told, and as she expected, it was the magic cloak indeed.

She laid hold of the cloak, and no sooner did she get it into her hands, than off she went to her old home in the sea. At times she would come to Rudha 'n-lòin to her children, and they would be seen in her company, and she combing their hair and singing songs to them. One day the little boy followed his mother to the sea, and never was seen again, but the girl returned home. She grew up to be a handsome lass. She married, and according to the tale, some of her offspring are alive to the present day.

[One of the innumerable variants of the 'Swan Maiden' type – so called because the magic dress is the feathers of that bird – in which the possession of the garment gives power over the supernatural maiden.]

Notes

[1] Also called *clach-chnocaidh* locally.
[2] Hollowed stone into which grain was put and beaten until freed from the husks.
[3] Locally pronounced '*sibhridh*,' the *ch* being silent after *i*.
[4] Pronounced *tiomall* locally.
[5] *na laidhe-shiùbhla*, in childbed ('*s a*' *ghlaodhaich*, literally in the crying).
[6] *dubh no dath*; meaning, in any form or colour = an absolute refusal.
[7] Locally the final *c* is not pronounced.
[8] *Sithichean*.
[9] *Crann treabhaidh*, or *beairt-threabhaidh*, or simply *beairt*; hence (*leantuinn nan each anns a' chrann treabhaidh* is rendered very briefly locally as: *leantuinn na beairt*.
[10] *fhùinneadh*.
[11] From *ceann*, head and *fionn*, white; *ceann-fhionn*, white faced; *ceanann* or *ceann-fhioun dubh*, a black animal with white face.
[12] Equivalent to an intensity of trembling.
[13] A good heap.
[14] *Min*, minute, thorough; *gu min*, thoroughly. Similarly *garbh*, rough; *gu garbh*, roughly.
[15] Supposed to be so called from the bleating sound which they uttered.
[16] Literally, my little kid, but here used as term of endearment.
[17] The Uruisg was supposed to be a huge being of solitary habits that haunted lonely and mountainous places. In it the qualities of man and spirit were curiously commingled. There were male and female Uruisgs, and the race was said to be the offspring of unions between mortals and fairies.

References

Abbreviations

PSAS Proceedings of the Society of Antiquaries of Scotland
DES Discovery and Excavation in Scotland
OUGS Open University Geological Survey
PPS Proceedings of the Prehistoric Society
GUARD Glasgow University Archaeological Research Division
SAJ Scottish Archaeological Journal
SHS Scottish History Society
SWRI Scottish Women's Rural Institute

Chapter 1

1. Ballantyne, C. K. and Dawson, A.G. 'Geomorphology and Landscape Change' in Edwards and Ralston 26
2. *MacGregor's Excursion Guide to the Geology of Arran*, revised & edited MacDonald, J.G. and Herriot, A. (contrib. King B.C.), Geological Society of Glasgow 1983, 14
3. *MacGregor's* 22–23, following Gunn and Anderson
4. *MacGregor's* 23–4
5. Rolfe, W.D. Ian, 'The Giant Fossil "Centipede" Trail of North Arran', *The Arran Naturalist*, Summer 1973 4–9
6. Clark, N.D.L., Aspen, P. and Corrance, H., 'Chirotherium barthii Kaup 1835 from the Triassic of the Isle of Arran, Scotland', *OUGS Journal* 2001
7. Van Wessel, Cornelis T., letter in Arran Heritage Museum Archives, 9 October 1995
8. Firsoff, V.A., 'The Gemstones of Arran', *Gems* September–October 1970 9–13
9. cf. Ballantyne and Dawson, loc. cit. 27
10. Drumlins are oval-shaped mounds such as are to be found in the neighbourhood of Blackwaterfoot in the south-west; moraines, piled-up heaps of earth and rock, are everywhere to be found in the neighbourhood of the mouths and lower courses of streams; eskers are ridges of gravel and sand laid down by vanished glacial streams, and kames are also composed of gravel and sand piled up into steep ridges often resembling a cock's comb

Chapter 2

1. Boyd, W.E. and Dickson, J.H., 'A post-glacial pollen sequence from Loch

a'Mhuilinn, North Arran: a record of vegetation history with special reference to the history of endemic Sorbus species', *New Phytologist* 1987, 107, 232. cf Robinson, D.E. and Dickson, J.H. 'Vegetational history and land use: a radiocarbon-dated pollen diagram from Machrie Moor, Arran, Scotland', *New Phytologist* 1988, 109–230

2. cf. Noble, G., 'Islands and the Neolithic farming tradition', *British Archaeology* 71, July 2003

3. Gorman, F., Lambie and Bowd, C. (1) 'Machrie, Arran (Kilmory Parish): knapping site'; (2) 'Machrie, Arran (Kilmory Parish): fieldwalking'; *DES* 1993, 79, 80. Gorman, Murray and Lambie, F.B. and E., 'Machrie, Arran (Kilmory Parish), Mesolithic site', *DES* 1995, 72

4. Inglis, J.C., *Brodick Old and New* (Ardrossan 1930) 92

5. Lacaille, A.D., *The Stone Age in Scotland* (London 1954) 154–5; 'Donations to and purchases for the Museum and Library', *PSAS* 91 1957–8 200

6. Gorman, Murray and Lambie, F.B. and E., 'Kildonan, Arran (Kilmory Parish), Mesolithic site', DES 1995, 72

7. Gorman, Lambie and Bowd, F.E. and C., 'Porta Leacach, Dippin, Arran (Kilmory Parish): knapping site' *DES* 1993 79

8. Charred hazelnut shell from pit 6110 +/ - 90bc OxA - 1601; Oak charcoal from west quarry 5920 + / - 90bc OxA - 1600; and charred hazelnut shell from firespot 5350+/- 90bc OxA - 1599. Affleck, Charles and Hughes, T.L., A. and I., 'Arran, Auchareoch (Kilmory p) mesolithic settlement', *DES* 1985, 41

9. Harry, R., 'The King's Caves, Blackwaterfoot (Kilmory Parish): natural sea caves' *DES* 1994 63 and 1995 72

10. McArthur, J., *The Antiquities of Arran with a historical sketch ...* (Edinburgh) 1873 85-6 (2nd ed.)

11. Balfour J.A., 'The ecclesiastical remains on the Holy Island, Arran', *PSAS* 43, 1908–9, 151-6

12. MacSween, A. and Parker Pearson, M., quoted in Barclay, G.J., 'The Neolithic' in Edwards and Ralston 134

13. Robinson and Dickson 230

14. Lynch 1981, quoted Robinson and Dickson 230

15. Robinson and Dickson 230

Chapter 3

1. Mackie, E.W., 'New Excavations on the Monamore Neolithic chambered cairn, Lamlash, Isle of Arran, 1961' *PSAS* 97 1963–4) 12

2. Robinson and Dickson 230.

3. Barclay, G.J., 'The Neolithic', in Edwards and Ralston 147

4. Rowley-Conway, P., 'Great Sites: Balbridie' in *British Archaeology* 64, April 2002

5. Neolithic buildings have also been discovered in Ireland, notably at Ballynagilly in Tyrone in the north-west (c. 3700 ^{14}C cal BC). and indeed there seems to have been a cross-cultural connection between Northern Ireland and the south-west of Scotland. It may well be that Neolithic dwellings in Arran have simply not yet been discovered.

6. Baker, F., 'Bridge Farm, Machrie Moor, Arran ... prehistoric agriculture' *DES* 1999 65.

7. Barber, J., 'Kilpatrick, cairn hut platform and field fences', *DES* 1979 34; 'Kilpatrick, Isle of Arran, Argyll and Bute, Strathclyde Region NR 905 266, cairns, hut platform

and field fences', *PPS* 46, 1980 367–8

8. Gorman, F. and Murray, B. 'Sliddery, Arran (Kilmory Parish), cists, stone settings,? hut circle, pitchstone working sites', *DES* 1995 72

9. cf Ashmore, P. J., *Neolithic and Bronze Age Scotland*, (Historic Scotland 1996) Ill. 11, p. 99 etc

10. GUARD, 'Machrie Farm, Arran (Kilmory Parish), prehistoric ard marks', *DES* 1997 56; Taylor, T. and Hunter, T., 'Excavation of sub-peat agricultural features on Machrie Moor, Arran', *SAJ* 22 2 September 2000, 179–85

11. Barber and Lehane, J. and D., 'Arran: Machrie Moor and Glaister' in *Burnt Offerings: international contributions to burnt mound archaeology,* ed. Condit, E. Dublin 1990 79 (site 24, 101)

12. Coles, J.M., 'Scottish Early Bronze Age metalwork' *PSAS* 101 1968–9 81

13. McLellan, R., *Arran* (Newton Abbot 1970) 76

14. Coles, J.M., 'Scottish Late Bronze Age metalwork: typology, distributions and chronology' *PSAS* 93 (1959–60) 89

15. See Campbell, T., *Ayrshire: a Historical Survey* (Edinburgh 2003) 81

16. McArthur, J., *The Antiquities of Arran with a historical sketch of the island embracing an account of the Sudreyjar under the Norsemen* (Edinburgh 1873 2nd ed.) 90; cf. Mac Cana, P, Celtic Mythology (Feltham 1983) 40 and *passim*, and Harbison, P., *Pre-Christian Ireland: From the First Settlers to the Early Celts* (London 1989) 136ff

17. Gorman, F., Lambie, E. and Bowd, C., 'Kilmory, Arran (Kilmory Parish): stone axe' *DES* 1993 79

18. A corroded bronze dagger-blade, found at Collessie in Fife, with a gold fillet surrounding the (vanished) haft, has been dated to approximately 2200 BC, and is taken at present as marking the beginning of the Bronze Age in Scotland. See Ashmore 80–1

Chapter 4

1. Fraser, I.A., *The Place Names of Arran* (The Arran Society of Glasgow 1999) 143. Mr Fraser translates Sliabh nan Carraigean as 'Moor of the Standing Stones'.

2. Right in the middle of Site 1 Dr Haggerty's team discovered a nineteenth-century egg-shaped Schweppes bottle left there by a previous excavator in 1861.

3. See Haggerty, A., 'Machrie Moor, Arran: recent excavations at two stone circles', *PSAS* 121 (1991) 51–94

4. MacKie, E.W., *Science and Society in Prehistoric Britain* (London 1977) 186

5. Barclay, G.J., 'The Neolithic' in Edwards and Ralston 139

6. See Harbison, P., *Pre-Christian Ireland: From the First Settlers to the Early Celts* (London 1988) 126 and ill. 77

7. Jung, C.G., *The Secret of the Golden Flower* (London 1938) 99 and *passim*

8. Read, H., *Education Through Art* (London 1961) 185–8

9. Haggerty 61 illus. 5

10. McLellan 70

11. Perks, A., 'Stonehenge: a View from Medicine', *Journal of the Royal Society of Medicine* (February 2003) 96: 94–8

12. In connection with the Greek letter theta, it may be relevant to note that the

(ancient) Greek word for 'feminine' is θηλυζ, thelus: the stem may indicate a common root. θηττα, thetta, means a 'hired servant-girl', but this is simply a feminine form of θηζ, thes, 'serf, bondman'.

13. Perks 96: 94–8
14. Beckinsall, S., *British Prehistoric Rock Art* (Tempus 2002) 14, illus. 6 and 7
15. Beckinsall *ibid.*
16. Balfour 277–8; Marshall, D.N., 'Carved stone balls', *PSAS* 108 (1976-77) 65

Chapter 5

1. Robinson and Dickson 233
2. McArthur in 1873 mentions an 'iron sword, much oxidised' found beneath peat in Monamore Glen, but the whereabouts of this relic are unknown – if it has survived (McArthur, J., *The Antiquities of Arran with a historical sketch of the island embracing an account of the Sudreyjar under the Norsemen* (Edinburgh 1873) 2nd ed. 91). Pieces of haematite iron have been found at the King's Cross Dun and the remains of a bloomery were reported by Balfour to have been found within Glenashdale hillfort, but this has not been confirmed (Balfour 182–3, 185–6). A fragment of iron was found by Professor Bryce in 1909 in the exterior organization of the chambered tomb at Dunan Beag where it had been deposited during or after the Iron Age (Bryce, T.H., 'On the cairns of Arran, no. III ...' *PSAS* 43 [1908–9] 341–50)
3. Thomas, C., 'The animal art of the Scottish Iron Age and its origins', *Archaelogical Journal* 118 (1961) 23
4. But see McLellan 82
5. 'Echdi' can be linked with the Latin word Equus ('horse'); Latin was also a 'Q'-language although comparatively distant from Celtic
6. cf. Duncan, A.A.M., *Scotland: the Making of the Kingdom* (Mercat Press 1996) 42
7. Æla or Ailsi (Ælfsige): Johnston J.B., *Place-Names of Scotland* (London 1934: repub. 1970 S R Publishers) 79; Ealasaid: Watson, W.J. , *The Celtic Placenames of Scotland* (Edinburgh 1993), 515
8. Johnston 60
9. Cameron (1890) quoted Fraser 11
10. Fraser *ibid*
11. Byrne 1973
12. Fraser, Ian A., personal communication 2004
13. Johnston 87, Watson 120–1
14. Jackson, K.H., *English Historical Review* 78 319
15. From Bannerman, J, 'Senchus Fer nAlban' [*Celtica* 7 (1966), 8 (1968) and 9 (1971)], *Studies in the History of Dalriada* (Edinburgh 1974) 111 and *passim*. The word 'Senchus' is often translated as 'History' (Skene, Bannerman et al) but since in this example it obviously referes to a muster of rowers to be provided from houses in various locations in tribal areas, might it not be seen as a Gaelic version of the Latin Census, pidgin Latin for an enrolment (of the men of Alba)?
16. *The Venerable Bede, A History of the English Church and People*, tr. Leo Sherley-Price (Harmondsworth 1955) 40

Chapter 6

1. cf. Ziegler, M., 'Artur mac Aedan of Dalriada', *The Heroic Age I* (Belleville, Illinois 1999: http://www.mun.ca/mst/heroicage/issues/1/haaad.htm)
2. cf. Mackenzie 2–3
3. Robinson and Dickson 237
4. McLellan 33
5. 'Arran' (Irish; author unknown; twelfth century) in Jackson, K.H., *A Celtic Miscellany:* Translations from the Celtic Literatures (Harmondsworth 1975) 70–1
6. Jackson, K.H., 'The British Latin Loanwords in Irish', *Language and History in Early Britain: A Chronological Survey of the Brittonic Languages First to Twelfth Century A.D.* (Edinburgh 1953) 122 ff
7. See article on 'Kilbride' in *The Old Statistical Account* (Edinburgh) 1794; other versions have the renaming about 1830
8. Watson 306
9. Watson ibid
10. Balfour 259
11. Goodall ed., *Scotichronicon* i vi, ii x
12. Monro, D., *Description of the Western Isles of Scotland* (1549) 48
13. Harry, R., 'Holy Island, Lamlash (Kilbride Parish): early Christian and monastic site' *DES* 1994, 63
14. Fisher, I., *Early Mediaeval sculpture in the West Highlands and Islands, RCAHMS/ Society of Antiquaries of Scotland Monograph* series 1 (Edinburgh 2001) 63–5
15. Fisher 65–9
16. cf. McLellan 94
17. Ogham is vaguely reminiscent of Devanagari (Hindi/Sanskrit) script (adopted ? 300 BC), whose stem-line however is normally horizontal.
18. Mac Cana 35–6
19. Jackson, K.H., 'An Ogham inscription near Blackwaterfoot', *Antiquity* 47 (1973) 53-4
20. Mackenzie 77

Chapter 7

1. McLellan Robert 99
2. cf. Nicolaisen, W.F.H., *Scottish Placenames* (London 1986) 127; also Campbell 35 (for the Gaelic/Cymric relationship disclosed in Kyle and Carrick on the one hand and Cuninghame on the other)
3. Robinson and Dickson 233
4. Shetelig, H. et al, 'Civilisation of the Viking settlers in relation to their old and new countries', *Viking Antiquities in Great Britain and Ireland* (Oslo 1954) Part VI 75
5. Mackenzie 16
6. The link between Man and the Isles is indicated even today by the name of the Christian bishopric, Sodor and Man; the name 'Sodor' derives from the Norse word Sud(e)rejar, the Southern Islands, including Arran as well as the Kintyre Peninsula, which was counted an island for all practical purposes.
7. Corpus of Electronic Texts (CELT): Anon, *Annals of the Four Masters* (University College, Cork 1997–2005) Part 261112–3

Chapter 8

1. The foundation of Saddell Abbey is clouded in mystery which is not likely to be dispersed soon. One tradition states that Somerled himself founded the Abbey probably round about 1160. Another tradition names King Ragnvald, who may have died in 1207. It is quite possible that Somerled began the foundation and that his son enlarged it. The matter is explored at some length in Brown, A.L., 'The Cistercian Abbey of Saddell, Kintyre', *Innes Review* (1969) Vol XX.2

2. cf. Fairhurst, H., *Exploring Arran's Past* (Arran 1982–99) 85

3. Olsen, M. in Shetelig 6, 169

Chapter 9

1. Duncan, A.A.M., *Scotland: the Making of the Kingdom* (Edinburgh 1996) 544-6

2. Bain's *Calendar of Documents*, i No. 1836, quoted Mackenzie 26

3. Nat MSS.Scot., II No viii, quoted Nicholson, R., *Scotland: the later Middle Ages* (Edinburgh 1997) 59

4. Raising of the dragon flag signified 'no quarter', 'take no prisoners.'

5. A.A.M. Duncan does not give much credit to Barbour: he reckons that Rathlin would have been too exposed and that Bruce, even if he had been forced by bad weather to have landed there, would have taken the first opportunity to make for the nearest secure territory, Islay, where he may have terrified the inhabitants and come to terms with MacDonald of Islay at Dunyvaig Castle. See Barbour, J., *The Bruce*, ed. Duncan, A.A.M. (Edinburgh 1997) 148 fn.

6. Barbour 172 fn

7. *Registrum de Monasterio de Passelet* (Paisley Abbey Register) (Maitland Club, Edinburgh 1832) 129; quoted Mackenzie op. cit. 78

8. The prefix 'Sir' in the Middle Ages could be more or less equivalent to the modern 'Reverend'

9. Mackenzie 36

10. Mackenzie 79

11. Mackenzie 83–4

12. Exchequer Rolls i 57

13. Martin, M., *A Description of the Western Isles of Scotland* (London 1703) 224

Chapter 10

1. McLellan op. cit. 121

2. Nicholson 132

3. Nicholson 330; quoting Pitscottie's *Historie I* 40–6, and *Chron Bower II* 514

4. Mackenzie 51

5. Exchequer Rolls, quoted MacKenzie 38–9

6. Mackenzie 44

7. Exchequer Rolls vi 531, quoted MacKenzie 57

8. Mackenzie 64

9. Mackenzie 59: Kildonan and the Castle, the two Feorlines, Dippin, the three Largies, the two Kiscadales, Glen Easdale, and Clachan

10. McLellan 124

11. Mackenzie 65 quoting *Hist. MSS* xi vi 20, and *Registrum Magni Sigilli* s.d. No. 2741

12. *A Diurnal of Remarkable Occurrents that have passed within the Country of Scotland* (Bannatyne and Maitland Clubs) 15, quoted Donaldson, G., *Scotland: James V–James VII* (Edinburgh 1976) 62
13. Mackenzie 66
14. In particular, Cuninghame/Montgomery and Campbell/Kennedy. cf. Campbell op. cit. 84–5.
15. Mackenzie op. cit. 58
16. ibid. 59–60
17. ibid. 62–3
18. Mackenzie 92–3
19. ibid. 94
20. ibid. 95
21. ibid. 96
22. Hist. MSS 'Hamilton Papers' 224–5 quoted ibid. 98
23. Register of Privy Council ii quoted ibid. 99
24. ibid. 100

Chapter 11

1. Furgol, E.M., *A Regimental History of the Covenanting Armies* (Edinburgh 1990) 16
2. Mackenzie104
3. Hist. MSS. Commission, Earl of Eglinton, No. 155, as quoted Mackenzie 92 with corrections by McLellan 132
4. Mackenzie 103
5. Mackenzie 141
6. Mackenzie 141
7. McLellan 136; Inglis [1930] 20
8. James Hamilton was styled Earl of Arran from 1689
9. These cups were destroyed five years later, on 7 November 1710, when the manse at Kilmory may have been hit by lightning, and the house and all its contents reduced to ashes. On that occasion '[n]othing escaped but he (Mr [Dugald] Bannatyne) and his wife, and their servants, with their lifes, by leaping out at the windoues'. (Robert Wodrow, *Analecta, or History of Remarkable Providences,* i 307, quoted Mackenzie 142)
10. McLellan 136

Chapter 12

1. 'A List of Persons Concerned in the Rebellion 1745–46' Scot. Hist. Soc. viii 326, quoted Mackenzie 112
2. Mackenzie 140
3. All the examples of Kirk Session judicial activity given here are taken from Mackenzie's *Book of Arran* Vol II 148-54
4. Mackenzie 149–50
5. Mackenzie 151
6. Mackenzie 151
7. Mackenzie 294–5

8. Probably a skin rash in humans or pock-marks ('holes') in cattle, often supposed to have been caused by contact with prehistoric arrow heads taken to be missiles or weapons used by elves.
9. Mackenzie1 145–7
10. Nicholson 273 fn 90
11. McLellan 202
12. Mackenzie 161
13. Naomi Mitchinson
14. M'Millan, Reverend A. quoted Mackenzie 206-7
15. Paterson 141
16. Bonar, Reverend Andrew A. *Thirty Years of Spiritual Life in the Island of Arran* (Glasgow 1889) 6
17. 'Clapping of hands and exclamations were common in the congregation among some of the people. It was disturbing to many who went to church to worship.' Mackenzie 208
18. Quoted Mackenzie 210
19. Quoted Mackenzie 210–1

Chapter 13

1. In older Scots terminology: a but, outer room, often kitchen of a house, and a ben, the inner room, often the better accommodation; not always applicable to a long house
2. Mackenzie 176
3. See Storrie, M.C., 'Landholdings and Population in Arran &c.' Scottish Studies 11 (1967) 54-5
4. Inglis (1930) 6
5. McLellan 151
6. Pennant 176; quoted Mackenzie 172
7. Storrie 54–5
8. Factor's report of 1800 (Brodick MS G) quoted Storrie 55
9. Storrie 55
10. Storrie 55
11. McLellan 161. Forty-three holdings were of reasonable size, others varying between two and forty acres
12. Storrie 55
13. Later in the century, following a sharp reduction in the price of sheep, sheep-walks in the upland moors and mountains gave way to reservations for grouse-shooting and deer-stalking, and later still to plantations under the aegis of the Forestry Commission
14. McLellan 174
15. Quoted Mackenzie 212
16. Mackenzie 211–2
17. Macleod, Donald, 'History of the Destitution in Sutherlandshire' (twenty-one letters in Edinburgh Weekly Chronicle 1840–1) quoted Grimble Ian, *The Trial of Patrick Sellar* (London 1962; Edinburgh [Saltire Society] 1993) 58–9
18. Marryat, Frederick *The Settlers in Canada* (Leipzig 1840) 8

19. Mackenzie 223
20. 6 Brodies, 6 Campbells, 10 Cooks, 9 Crawfords, 2 Cristies, 6 Fullertons, 2 Gordons, 2 Hamiltons, 7 Henrys, 28 Kelsos, 13 Kerrs, 10 McKelvies, 15 McKenzies, 51 McKillops, 19 McKinnons, 2 Murchies, 2 Nichols, 12 Sillarses, 10 Stewarts: Mackenzie op. cit. 225
21. McLellan 164
22. Mackenzie 213
23. Mackenzie 213
24. Mackenzie 212
25. Numbers quoted McLellan 208
26. Brown, Reverend Thomas, *Annals of the Disruption* (Edinburgh ND) Part III 32
27. McLellan 171
28. Mackenzie 249
29. Quoted in Devine, T.M. , *The Great Highland Famine: Hunger, Emigration and the Scottish Highlands in the Nineteenth Century* (Edinburgh 1988) 120

Chapter 14

1. McLellan 163
2. Inglis (1930) 79
3. Mackenzie 126–7, Inglis (1930) 79
4. Mackenzie 126–7
5. Mackenzie 129
6. Mackenzie 133–4
7. Inglis (1930) 77
8. Inglis (1930) 120
9. Mackenzie 170 and 229
10. Mackenzie, quoting Paterson 152

Chapter 15

1. Mackenzie 178 fn
2. Mackenzie 180–1
3. Mackenzie 187
4. Quoted in McCrae, Morrice 'The Case for State Medical Services for the Poor' The Highlands & Islands 1850 (Royal College of Physicians) Edinburgh 2006 (website) 4, 1
5. Geo. III, ch.54. 11 June 1803
6. Mackenzie 159-60
7. Mackenzie 162
8. Inglis (1930) 161
9. Headrick, Reverend J., *A View of the Mineralogy, Agriculture, Manufactures and Fisheries of the Island of Arran* (Edinburgh 1807) 18
10. Inglis (1930) 29, 74
11. McLellan mentions only Captain Shannon of Bennecarrigan, Robert Stoddart of Sannox, Lieutenant MacKirdy of Bennan and Major MacAllister of Springbank

Chapter 16

1. *North British Advertiser*, Saturday, 29 September 1838; quoted Mackenzie 227–8
2. Mackenzie 189
3. Teignmouth, *Sketches of the Coasts and Islands of Scotland* (1836) ii 394
4. Mackenzie 213
5. Headrick 63, 106
6. McLellan 194
7. Inglis (1930) 74
8. Inglis (1930) 77
9. Inglis (1930) 65–7
10. Inglis (1930) 14
11. quoted Mackenzie 242
12. Scott, 'The Lord of the Isles', *Poetical Works* (Edinburgh 1883) 546
13. 'Cairgen Weans', discovered among papers held by the Arran Heritage Museum. James Paul Crawford is unknown even to Google. The word 'Cairgen' is said to be a name given to strangers, not natives of Arran. Without dissenting from this translation, I wonder if the word is not connected with the Gaelic *Carraigean*, which I suspect is in turn connected with the Breton *Korrigan*, a pagan nature spirit often lonely, cold and windswept: the 'cairgen' weans might be lonely, cold, windswept and possessing a desolate supernatural presence. I offer this as a perhaps wild conjecture. The poem was originally inscribed in an early Visitors' Book at the Lagg during the latter half of the nineteenth century. See chapter 4.
14. Inglis (1919) 165
15. Stirling, A.M.W., *Victorian Sidelights: from the papers of the late Mrs Adams-Acton* 194–206
16. McLellan 185
17. Inglis (1930) 14–18 109–110
18. For further detail on the Goatfell murder, see House *passim* and Roughead *passim*

Chapter 17

1. Inglis (1919) 50
2. *History of the Villages of Arran* (SWRI Arran Federation 2002) 12
3. Inglis (1919)16
4. Inglis (1919) 12-3
5. Steele, John, *The Tragedy of* HMS *Dasher* (Argyll Publishing 1995) 71
6. Steele 72
7. Steele 75
8. Steele 17
9. Steele 116
10. *History of the Villages of Arran* (SWRI 2002)
11. Asher, Michael, Lost Oasis Expeditions: Get Rommel (http://lost-oasis.org/rommel.html 2003) 10–11
12. Asher 19
13. Keyes, E., *Geoffrey Keyes VC MC Croix de Guerre of the Rommel Raid* (London 1956) 234

14. The Mull of Kintyre's sinister reputation is still sustained: in 1994 a Chinook helicopter carrying twenty-five senior intelligence officers and four crew from Northern Ireland ran full tilt on to Beinn na Lice on the western side of the Mull of Kintyre in cloud. There were no survivors. Some people blame pilot error; others do not.

15. McLellan 195 (Ribbeck, Gordon, Lennox, Stewart, Bannatyne, Weir, MacMillan, running respectively from Brodick, Lamlash, Whiting Bay, Kildonan, Blackwaterfoot, Machrie and Pirnmill)

16. See the plate section

17. Inglis (1919) 56. The three Hamilton brothers – George, Gavin and James – operated back-up services in the Merchant Navy during the First War and all survived (Inglis 1919, 32)

18. Another lighthouse is now inactive, at Low Pladda – close to the base of the active tower

19. Part 4 of the Criminal Proceedings etc (Reform) (Scotland) Bill, introduced into the Scottish Parliament in February 2006 makes provision for 'the establishment of Justice of the Peace Courts (JP Courts) eventually replacing the district courts'. If this reform passes into law, it will effectually lead to reinstatement of the traditional name of these subordinate courts; Arran had JP Courts in Brodick for many centuries.

20. Following the failure of the male Hamilton line in 1906 the heiress, Lady Mary Louise, married into the Graham family, and former Hamilton property in Arran came into the ownership of the Duke of Montrose

21. Wilson, B., 'Focus', *West Highland Free Press* local newspaper for the Isle of Skye and Western Isles ...' No. 1764, 17 February 2006

22. Brankin, R., Deputy Rural Development Minister, reported statement in the *Herald*, 22 September, 2006

23. Figures provided by the Analytical Services Division of SEERAD's Science and Analysis Group. Grassland for grazing five years and older: 3,310 ha; total crops and grass: 4,852.33 ha; rough grazings: 22,322.27; woodland 434.09; other land (roads, yards, buildings): 1,318.64

24. These details were gleaned from Mr Andy Walker of the Forestry Commission in Arran as well as from official FC publications kindly made available by Mr Walker.

25. McLellan 225–7

26. Glen, Jean, *Brodick 1897–1997: a Century of Golf* (Brodick Golf Club 1997) 48. The golf-courses referred to are as follows: Lamlash (1889), Corrie (1892), Whiting Bay (1895), Shiskine (1896), Brodick (1897), Lochranza (1899) and Machrie (1900)

27. These modern developments, however, cannot disguise an underlying trend against milk-production in general throughout the land, and it has recently been claimed (in a BBC radio programme, 'You and Yours', at the beginning of December 2006) that in less than five years it will become literally impossible to obtain fresh milk anywhere in Great Britain: in the programme the finger of accusation was levelled at the supermarkets, whose relentless downward pressure on the price of milk in favour of the consumer has forced hundreds of dairy-farmers out of the market. Arran no less than other places has suffered drastically from this bias.

28. Boyd and Dickson 236–242; see also Robertson, A. (2004), 'Status Review of the Arran endemic whitebeams Sorbus arranensis and Sorbus pseudofennica' (Scottish National Heritage Commissioned Report No. 056 (Roame No. FO3(1)4)

Bibliography

Affleck, Charles and Hughes, T L, A and I, 'Arran, Auchareoch (Kilmory p) mesolithic settlement', *DES* 1985

Annals of the Four Masters (University College, Cork 1997–2005) Corpus of Electronic Texts (CELT): Anon., Part 261112–3

Asher, Michael, *Lost Oasis Expeditions: Get Rommel* (http://lost-oasis.org/rommel.html 2003)

Ashmore, P J, *Neolithic and Bronze Age Scotland,* (Historic Scotland 1996)

Baker, F: 'Bridge Farm, Machrie Moor, Arran ... prehistoric agriculture'; *DES* 1999

Balfour J A. 'The ecclesiastical remains on the Holy Island, Arran', *PSAS* 43, 1908–9

—, *The Book of Arran* vol. I (Glasgow 1910)

Ballantyne C.K. and Dawson A.G. 'Geomorphology and Landscape Change' in Edwards and Ralston eds, *Scotland After the Ice Age: Environment, Archaeology and History 8000 BC–AD 1000* (Edinburgh University Press 2003)

Bannerman J. 'Senchus Fer nAlban' [*Celtica* 7 (1966), 8 (1968) and 9 (1971)]

—, *Studies in the History of Dalriada* (Edinburgh 1974)

Barber, J: 'Kilpatrick, cairn hut platform and field fences', *DES* 1979 34

—, 'Kilpatrick, Isle of Arran, Argyle and Bute, Strathclyde Region NR 905 266, cairns, hut platform and field fences', *PPS* 46, 1980

Barber, J. and Lehane, D. 'Arran: Machrie Moor and Glaister' in *Burnt Offerings: international contributions to burnt mound archaeology* (ed. E. Condit) Dublin 1990

Barbour, J. *The Bruce,* ed..Duncan A.A.M. (Edinburgh 1997)

Beckinsall S. *British Prehistoric Rock Art* (Tempus 2002)

Bede, *A History of the English Church and People,* tr. Leo Sherley-Price (Penguin Books 1955)

Bonar, Rev. Andrew A. *Thirty Years of Spiritual Life in the Island of Arran* (Glasgow 1889)

Boyd, W. E. and Dickson, J.H. 'A post-glacial pollen sequence from Loch a'Mhuilinn, North Arran: a record of vegetation history with special reference to the history of endemic *Sorbus* species, *New Phytologist* (1987)

Brown, A.L. 'The Cistercian Abbey of Saddell, Kintyre', *Innes Review* (1969) vol. XX

Brown, Rev. T. *Annals of the Disruption* (Edinburgh ND) Part III

Bryce, T.H. 'On the cairns of Arran, no. III ...' *PSAS* 43 (1908–9)

Bussell, G. *Arran: Behind the Scenes* (Gillean Bussell 1999)

Campbell T. *Ayrshire. A Historical Guide* (Edinburgh 2003)

Childe, V. Gordon, *Scotland before the Scots* (London 1946)

Clark, N.D.L., Aspen, P. and Corrance, H. '*Chirotherium barthii* Kaup 1835 from the Triassic of the Isle of Arran, Scotland', *OUGS Journal* (2001)

Close, R. *Ayrshire and Arran: an illustrated architectural guide* (Edinburgh 1992)

Coles J.M. 'Scottish Late Bronze Age metalwork: typology, distributions and chronology' *PSAS 93* (1959–60)

——, 'Scottish Early Bronze Age metalwork' *PSAS 101* (1968–9)

Crawford, James Paul: 'Cairgen Weans', a poem discovered among papers held by the Arran Heritage Museum

Devine, T.M. *The Great Highland Famine: Hunger, Emigration and the Scottish Highlands in the Nineteenth Century* (Edinburgh 1988)

A Diurnal of Remarkable Occurrents That Have Passed Within the Country of Scotland Since the Death of King James the Fourth Till the Year MDLXXV (Edinburgh, Bannatyne Club, 1833)

Donaldson, G. *Scotland: James V–James VII* (Edinburgh 1976)

Downie, R.A. *All About Arran* (London and Glasgow 1948)

Duncan, A.A.M. *Scotland: the Making of the Kingdom* (Edinburgh 1996)

Edwards, K.J. and Ralston, I.B.M.,eds., *Scotland after the Ice Age: Environment, Archaeology and History 8000 BC–AD 1000* (Edinburgh [2nd ed.] 2003)

Fairhurst, H. *Exploring Arran's Past* (Isle of Arran Museum Trust 1982)

Fforde, Lady Jean *Feet on the Ground: from Castles to Catastrophe* (Glasgow 2001)

Firsoff, V.A. 'The Gemstones of Arran', *Gems* September–October 1970

Fisher, I. *Early Mediaeval sculpture in the West Highlands and Islands,* RCAHMS/SocAntScot Monograph series 1 (Edinburgh 2001)

Fordun, J. and Bower, W. *Scotichronicon* (Edinburgh 1759) Goodall *ed.*

Fraser, I.A. *The Place Names of Arran* (The Arran Society of Glasgow 1999)

Furgol, E.M. *A Regimental History of the Covenanting Armies* (Edinburgh 1990)

Glen, J. *Brodick 1897–1997: A Century of Golf* (Brodick Golf Club 1997)

Gorman, F. and Murray, B. 'Sliddery, Arran (Kilmory parish), cists, stone settings,? hut circle, pitchstone working sites', *DES 1995*

Gorman, F., Lambie, E and Bowd, C. 'Machrie, Arran (Kilmory Parish): knapping site' *DES 1993*;

——, Machrie, Arran (Kilmory Parish): fieldwalking'; *DES 1993*

——, 'Kilmory, Arran (Kilmory parish): stone axe' *DES 1993*

Gorman, F., Murray, B. and Lambie, E. 'Machrie, Arran (Kilmory parish), Mesolithic site', *DES 1995*

Grimble, I. *The Trial of Patrick Sellar* (London 1962; Edinburgh [Saltire Society] 1993)

Haggerty, A. 'Machrie Moor, Arran: recent excavations at two stone circles', *PSAS 121 1991*

Hall, H.S. *Tramping in Arran* (Falkirk 1947)

Harbison, P. *Pre-Christian Ireland: From the First Settlers to the Early Celts* (London 1989)

Harry, R. 'The King's Caves, Blackwaterfoot (Kilmory Parish): natural sea caves' *DES 1994 and 1995*

——, 'Holy Island, Lamlash (Kilbride Parish): early Christian and monastic site', *DES 1994*

Headrick, Rev. J. *A View of the Mineralogy, Agriculture, Manufactures and Fisheries of the Island of Arran* (Edinburgh 1807)

Henshall, A.S. *The Chambered Tombs of Scotland* vol. 2 (Edinburgh 1972)

History of the Villages of Arran (SWRI Arran Federation 2002)

House J, 'The Goatfell Case,' *Murder Not Proven* (Glasgow 1984)

Inglis, J.C. *Brodick – Arran and the Great War 1914–1918* (Edinburgh, Oliver and Boyd 1919) [1919]

—, *Brodick – Old and New* (Ardrossan 1930)

Jackson, K.H. *English Historical Review,* 78

—, The British Latin Loanwords in Irish', *Language and History in Early Britain: A Chronological Survey of the Brittonic Languages First to Twelfth Century A.D.* (Edinburgh 1953)

—, *A Celtic Miscellany: Translations from the Celtic Literatures* (Penguin 1975)

—, An Ogham inscription near Blackwaterfoot', *Antiquity* 47 (1973)

Johnston, J.B. *Place-Names of Scotland* (London 1934)

Jung, C.G. *The Secret of the Golden Flower* (London 1938)

Keyes, E. *Geoffrey Keyes, VC MC Croix de Guerre, of the Rommel Raid* (London 1956)

Lacaille, A.D. *The Stone Age in Scotland* (London 1954) 154–5

—'Donations to and purchases for the Museum and Library', *PSAS* 91 1957–8

Lambert R A (ed.), *Species History in Scotland: Introductions and Extinctions since the Ice Age* (Edinburgh 1998)

McArthur, J, *The Antiquities of Arran with a historical sketch of the island embracing an account of the Sudreyjar under the Norsemen* (Edinburgh 1873 2nd ed)

Mac Cana, P. *Celtic Mythology* (Feltham 1983)

McCrae, M., 'The Case for State Medical Services for the Poor' *The Highlands & Islands 1850* (Royal College of Physicians) Edinburgh 2006 (**website**)

McCrorie, I, *Lochranza Pier* (Caledonian MacBrayne, Gourock 2003)

MacDonald, J.G. and Herriot, A. (contrib. King, B.C.) rev. & ed.,*MacGregor's Excursion Guide to the Geology of Arran,* Geological Society of Glasgow 1983

Mackenzie, W.M. *The Book of Arran vol. II: History and Folklore* (Glasgow 1914)

MacKie, E.W. *Science and Society in Prehistoric Britain* (London 1977)

—, New Excavations on the Monamore Neolithic chambered cairn, Lamlash, Isle of Arran, 1961' (*PSAS* 97 1963–4)

McLaughlin, B. *Molaise of Arran: a saint of the Celtic church* (W J McLaughlin, Whiting Bay, Arran 1999)

McLellan, R. *Arran* (Newton Abbot 1976)

Macleod, D. 'History of the Destitution in Sutherlandshire' (21 letters in *Edinburgh Weekly Chronicle* 1840–1)

MacSween, A. and Parker Pearson, M., in Barclay, G.J. 'The Neolithic' in *Scotland after the Ice Age (eds.* Edwards, K.J. and Ralston, I.B.M.) Edinburgh 1997 and 2003

Marryat, F. *The Settlers in Canada* (Leipzig 1840)

Marshall, D.N. 'Carved stone balls', *PSAS* 108 (1976–77)

Martin, M.*A Description of the Western Isles of Scotland* (London 1703)

Mitchell-Luker, B. *Arran Bus Book* (Brodick1983)

Monro, D. *Description of the Western Isles of Scotland, called Hybrides* (1594) (Glasgow 1818)

Morris, Ronald W.B. *The Prehistoric Rock Art of Galloway and the Isle of Man*

Nicholson, R. *Scotland: the later Middle Ages* (Edinburgh 1997)

Nicolaisen, W.F.H. *Scottish Placenames* (London 1986)

Noble, G. 'Islands and the Neolithic farming tradition', *British Archaeology* 71, July 2003

Paterson, J. 'Account of the Island of Arran', *Transactions of the Highland and Agricultural Society of Scotland* (vol. XI, 1834)

Pennant, T. *A Tour in Scotland and Voyage to the Hebrides* (Dublin 1775)

Perks, A. 'Stonehenge: a View from Medicine', *Journal of the Royal Society of Medicine* (February 2003)

Pitscottie, Robert Lindsay of *The Historie and Chronicles of Scotland, 1436–1565*, ed. Mackay, A. (Scottish Text Society 1899)

Registrum de Monasterio de Passelet (Paisley Abbey Register) (Maitland Club, Edinburgh 1832)

Ritchie, A. *Viking Scotland* (London 1996)

Roberts, J.L. *Lost Kingdoms: Celtic Scotland and the Middle Ages* (Edinburgh 1997)

Robinson, D.E. and Dickson, J.H. 'Vegetational history and land-use: a radiocarbon-dated pollen diagram from Machrie Moor, Arran, Scotland', *The New Phytologist* 109, 1988

Rolfe, W.D. Ian, 'The Giant Fossil "Centipede" Trail of North Arran', *The Arran Naturalist*

Roughead, W. *The Trial of John Watson Laurie (Notable British Trials)* (Edinburgh and London 1934)

Rowley-Conway, P. 'Great Sites: Balbridie' in *British Archaeology* 64, April 2002

Scott, Sir Walter, 'The Lord of the Isles', *Poetical Works* (Edinburgh 1883)

Shetelig H. *et al.*, 'Civilisation of the Viking settlers in relation to their old and new countries', *Viking Antiquities in Great Britain and Ireland* (Oslo 1954) Part VI

Statistical Account of Scotland, The (Glasgow 1793)

Steele, J. *The Tragedy of* HMS Dasher (Glendaruel 1995)

Stirling, A.M.W. *Victorian Sidelights: from the papers of the late Mrs Adams-Acton* (London 1954)

Storrie, M.C. 'Landholdings and Population in Arran &c.' *Scottish Studies* 11 (1967)

Stringer, K.J. 'Periphery and Core in Thirteenth-Century Scotland: Alan son of Roland, Lord of Galloway and Constable of Scotland' (in *Mediaeval Scotland: Crown, Lordship and Community* [ed. Grant, A and Stringer, K.J.], Edinburgh 1998)

Taylor, K. and Hunter, T. 'Excavation of sub-peat agricultural features on Machrie Moor, Arran', *SAJ* 22 Sept 2000

Teignmouth (John Shore, 1st Baron Teignmouth) *Sketches of the Coasts and Islands of Scotland* (London 1836)

Thomas, C. 'The animal art of the Scottish Iron Age and its origins', *Archaeological Journal* 118 (1961)

Thompson, R. and A., *The Milestones of Arran* (Lamlash 2000)

Van Wessel, C.T. Letter in Arran Heritage Museum Archives, 9 October 1995

Watson,W.J. *The History of the Celtic Place-Names of Scotland* (Edinburgh and London 1926 and 1993)

Wilson B. 'Focus', *West Highland Free Press Local Newspaper for the Isle of Skye and Western Isles ...*' no. 1764, 17 February 2006

Wodrow, R. *Analecta, or History of Remarkable Providences*, Edinburgh 1842

Ziegler, M. 'Artur mac Aedan of Dalriada', *The Heroic Age* I (Belleville, Illinois 1999: http://www.mun.ca/mst/heroicage/issues/1/haaad.htm)

Index